THE PHOTOROMANCE

THE
PHOTOROMANCE

A Feminist Reading of Popular Culture

PAOLA BONIFAZIO

The MIT Press
Cambridge, Massachusetts
London, England

This book was set in Adobe Garamond Pro by New Best-set Typesetters Ltd. Printed and bound in the United States of America.

Library of Congress Cataloging-in-Publication Data

Names: Bonifazio, Paola, 1976- author.
Title: The photoromance : a feminist reading of popular culture / Paola Bonifazio.
Description: Cambridge, Massachusetts : The MIT Press, 2020. | Includes bibliographical references and index.
Identifiers: LCCN 2019054074 | ISBN 9780262539289 (paperback)
Subjects: LCSH: Fotonovelas--Italy--History and criticism. | Romance fiction--History and criticism.
Classification: LCC PN6714 .B663 2020 | DDC 741.5/3543--dc23
LC record available at https://lccn.loc.gov/2019054074

10   9   8   7   6   5   4   3   2   1

To Mamo

Contents

Acknowledgments

I want to thank:

My parents and my sister who have never read photoromances but always trusted that I had something important to say about them.

The many archivists and librarians who patiently worked with me on this project. Without their help, this book never could have been written.

The Office of the Vice President for Research and the College of Liberal Arts at the University of Texas at Austin, respectively, for the subvention grant that allowed this publication to happen (in color!) and for a Humanities Research Award that funded research for this project.

My friends and colleagues Alessandra Montalbano and Jonathan Mullins for their thoughtful comments on drafts of this manuscript; Giovanna Faleschini for her useful advice on this project; and Silvia Carlorosi for her encouragement.

Ruth Ben-Ghiat, Giorgio Bertellini, and Nicoletta Marini-Maio for their mentorship.

My colleagues in the Department of French and Italian for their support and for allowing me to take time off from teaching when I most needed it.

Victoria Hindley, the most enthusiastic and experienced acquisition editor I could have ever wished for, Gabriela Bueno Gibbs, and everyone else at MIT Press who helped in making this book.

Samantha Gillen for proofreading my manuscript.

All the Facebook members of photoromance fan groups who participated in my study, and all the anonymous users who responded to my research survey.

My graduate students, particularly those in my seminar Media Convergence and Transmedia Storytelling in Italy, for their challenging questions.

Silvia and Valeria for their friendship.

Petre, for I can always count on him and because he's much better than me with titles.

Pinguino, because life would not be as good without a dog.

Marco, just because he is.

INTRODUCTION: HALL OF SHAME

Susanita reads photoromances—a form of graphic storytelling, including captions and balloons but using photographs instead of drawings (figure I.1).[1] Mafalda, and many people like her, considers them cheap and trite narratives of love relationships—in a word, stupidities. Demeaned and chastised in public opinion, photoromances have not received much attention in scholarship either: dismissed as accessory or derivative forms of women's literature or attacked as tools of cultural domination, especially in leftist critiques of mass culture, in Italian and Latin American Studies.[2] To counter such negative responses and lack of interest, the goal of this book is to demonstrate the relevance of Italian photoromances in a transnational market. Significantly, strategies of narrative production across media platforms (comics, cinema, pulp fiction), business synergies between cultural industries (publishing, film, television, music), and participatory culture have all defined these hybrid texts, I argue, in ways that anticipated by a few decades the dynamics of production, distribution, and reception thriving under the current digital revolution. Further, this book aims to review the role female readers have played in the making and success of the photoromance industry, and to defy the social stigma historically attached to reading photoromances. Throughout the globe, critics did not grant readers like Susanita any agency, consistently attributing the stultifying and/or corrupting effects of sentimental narratives (in either moral or political terms) to the passivity, naïveté, or blunt stupidity of their consumers, particularly women. These critics also historically constructed the image of a victimized and helpless female fan, looking to escape her daily life in the fantasy of romantic plots (as in Susanita's own response to Mafalda's comment).[3] My research demonstrates that derogative portrayals of female fans ultimately reveal not only cultural anxieties toward

Figure I.1
Comic strip. © Joaquín Salvador Lavado (QUINO), Todo Mafalda, Ediciones de la Flor

the spread of mass culture, but also political resistance to the possible appropriation of this culture by female audiences.

I am using the term *fan* here to indicate the affective as much as irrational bond that characterizes the relationship between readers and photoromances in their negative representations. It is fandom that left- and right-wing Italian and French politicians anathematized, especially in the 1950s and 1960s; fans whom films and newsreels, television hosts and journalists ridicule, until today, in Italy and abroad. When involved in the business, directors or performers (especially when they already had or wished for a film career) felt the need to justify their decision on economic needs or argued that they thought of embarking on a pedagogical mission.[4] In both cases, the effect is to create a hierarchy between producers and consumers in the name of proximity: the latter are too close to both texts and celebrities to be able to critically approach them. In this respect, the photoromance fan is inevitably feminized: women are both the privileged subjects of representation, in parodies or critique, and the main target audience; moreover, the media itself is labeled as "feminine" for it prompts shallow, emotional, and irrational behaviors. In this book, I show how female fans of photoromances embody the culture of consumption that is nurtured by this industry and that is threatening to authors (both writers and film directors) and their intellectual and political allies. Neither emancipated nor coopted by the media system, these fans, I argue, undermined the patriarchal order of Italian culture and society, particularly in the fifties and sixties, as well as the aims of radical feminist groups in the 1970s.

A CONTROVERSIAL MEDIUM

Also known as *roman-photo* (in French) and *fotonovela* (in Spanish), the so-called *fotoromanzo* was born in Italy in 1947 and then successfully exported all over the world, selling millions of copies per week.[5] The Italian neologism has different translations in English; although sometimes referred to as photonovel, I prefer to use *photoromance* in this book since the term appears in the title of *Darling* and *Kiss*, the two magazines that first introduced the genre in the United States, in the late seventies.[6] The first photoromance appeared in the Italian weekly magazine *Sogno* (Dream), published by Angelo Rizzoli and Co. (from now on, Rizzoli).[7] Arnoldo Mondadori Editore's illustrated magazine *Bolero Film*, the first to use the term, came out a few months after, while Edizioni Universo's *Grand Hotel*, already popular for its drawn romances, followed a few years later in 1950.[8] In the early fifties, *Grand Hotel*, *Bolero Film*, and *Sogno* each sold hundreds of thousands of copies, and about one and a half million altogether.[9] These numbers do not include those readers who did not buy the magazines themselves, and who either listened to the stories during communal readings or who shared the issue among friends (in this case, reaching a number above four million).[10] Several other publications with a focus on photoromances came out concurrently or a few years later, most noticeably Cino Del Duca's *Intimità* (Intimacy) and Mondadori Editore's *Confidenze* (Secrets), which also included narratives of so-called "real-life" experiences modeling the American magazine *True Story*, created by Bernarr Macfadden in 1924. By the early 1960s, 10.8 million Italians read a photoromance each week; in the 1970s, this number declined but remained high, around seven million.[11] All magazines feature various columns from relationship counseling to cooking advice, as well as romantic novels published in installments and illustrated news. Among others, *Bolero Film* defines itself on the cover page as a "weekly publication of photoromances, short stories, entertainment," while *Confidenze*'s original title is *Confidenze di Liala*, using the name of the most popular romance writer in Italy, Liala, so that the magazine's content would be immediately familiar to buyers. However, *Bolero Film* and the others eventually became known simply as *fotoromanzi*, and today are still called this. Initially, the term was used in the press to distinguish them from other women's magazines, despite the fact that the latter also included photoromances (also employed was *fumetto*, the Italian word for comics). Such distinction pertained more appropriately to the economic and cultural strata of their respective (preferred) readership. Particularly in the 1950s and 1960s, while women's magazines were directed at middle-class house-wives, photoromances targeted working-class women with little or no education.[12] In fact, data collected through the decades show that a good percentage of this audience was masculine: in the mid-1970s, 30 percent of readers of *Bolero Film* and *Grand Hotel* were men.[13] There were also considerable differences between readerships of the main series: both younger and older readers from all parts of society bought *Grand Hotel*; mostly young girls between sixteen and thirty-four years old and from the lower-middle classes read *Bolero Film* and *Sogno*. Lumping together such variety of readers under the feminine and working-class labels was indeed a marketing strategy and, at the same time, a cultural bias. Publishers sought to tap the increasing purchase power of women and established long-term partnerships with advertisers of cheap personal or household products (including soap, toothpaste, detergents) and small appliances. Critics from all sides of the political and cultural spectrum (intellectuals, journalists, Communist politicians, Catholic government officials) intersected gender and class definitions with the intention (or the effect) of demeaning the reading material. *Roba da servette* ("stuff for female servants") is the derogative (at times condescending) expression used in the copious news and journal articles that debated the cultural and moral value of photoromances, in Italy and abroad, and that became a widespread opinion still seen today in the press and used in everyday conversations. These attitudes were common throughout the fifties and sixties in other national contexts and fit into a current broader debate against popular culture, in both Europe and the United States.[14] The same treatment given to pulp romances and film melodrama in this period applies in greater scope to fotoromanzi, fotonovelas, and roman photos: all of which are con-sidered repetitive and shallow in content and, moreover, using techniques borrowed from other media (film, comics, photography) in cheap and standardized packages to indoctrinate or stultify women.[15]

Depictions of photoromance readers in Italian films ranged from pathetic or ironic perspectives that attempted to downplay the phenomenon to bitter, dramatic, or sarcastic visions of the end of civilization.[16] Among others, *Lo sceicco bianco* (The White Sheik, dir. Federico Fellini, 1952, written by Fellini and Antonioni) attacks the photoromance industry (its improvised, inefficient, unprofessional mode of produc-tion) through the story of a female fan who is, according to Jan Baetens, "brainwashed by the exotic dream world of the first photonovels."[17] In the film, the protagonist Wanda believes that her favorite photoromance hero (interpreted by comic actor

Alberto Sordi) could save her from the dull existence of a petty-bourgeois wife in provincial Southern Italy. While in Rome with her husband for their honeymoon, Wanda looks for her idol only to find out that he is, in fact, neither romantic nor heroic but rather a fake, like the whole industry. The film satirically represents a day on the set at a Roman beach, supposedly the exotic landscape of a romantic story, where actors are totally incompetent and the director a frustrated boss. Wanda even attempts to commit suicide, once her dream is shattered, although she jumps in the Tiber where the water is only up to her knees. But in the end, she goes back to her spouse and the film closes with them getting a special meeting with the pope. Wanda's agency as a fan is sporadically addressed in the story, for example, when she first goes to visit the publisher not only to meet her favorite celebrity but also to hand in the manuscript of a photoromance she had written. Ultimately, though, Wanda appears as a gullible woman mystified by the fantasy of her own emancipation, and unable to break through the conformism of her marriage. In sum, *The White Sheik* participates in the public shaming of women who read photoromances. This is evident in the film's reception; according to film critic Ezio Colombo, writing soon after its release at the Venice Film Festival in 1952, *The White Sheik* represented "a very widespread mentality of the time" precisely through its female protagonist and her "limited existence."[18] To quote Mario Dal Pra in an interview for *Corriere della sera*: "It is not by any chance that women are especially passionate towards *fotoromanzi*, [since] there is always in them a need for abandonment that is typically feminine."[19]

Italian film directors and critics parodied or mocked the photoromance industry and its female readership on the basis of cultural biases that were the very same ones used to attack film melodramas as products of entertainment, with respect to art cinema. In 1952, journalist Giorgio Capua, from the pages of the fan magazine *Hollywood*, claimed that "*fumetti* killed cinema" (by which he meant photoromances).[20] In the same article, he insisted that "fumetti" were to be blamed because they were responsible for diverting audiences from appropriate behaviors. According to Capua, rather than engaging in discussions on film form, as they did in the past, Italians now wasted their time in gossiping about the whereabouts of photoromance's *diva*.[21] The "evil of the century," as he calls it in another article, was responsible for the degradation of film viewers.[22]

And yet, *Hollywood* was devoted, for the most part, as its title conveys, to the discussion of American films and the private engagements and public commitments of movie stars (both Italian and foreign). In this sense, the rhetoric used in Capua's tirade with regard to the photoromance industry and its stars ironically corresponded to the same that had been employed to derogate fan magazines and the film industries that supported them. Indeed, those who loved Raffaello Matarazzo's weepies, starring film stars Yvonne Sanson and Amedeo Nazzari (often featured in fan magazines), had the same appreciation for photoromances. It is well known that his *Catene* (Chains, 1949) and *Tormento* (Torment, 1950) were titles of likewise lucrative products published in *Bolero Film* before being explosively successful films, and that both Matarazzo and *Bolero Film* were looked down on by film critics who promoted cinema as an art or as the political tool to emancipate the masses and build a national identity. In other words, if photoromances were threatening the predominant role occupied by cinema in the cultural hierarchy, they were in good company with genre movies.

Hollywood films, Matarazzo's melodramas, and photoromances were similarly blamed for escapism and as tools of capitalist domination. In a revealing comment to a reader's letter, the leftist film journal *Cinema Nuovo* explicitly rejected the idea that some attention should be given to the analysis of photoromances. Writing to Guido Aristarco, editor of the journal and well-known film critic, Dario Magno from Lucca narrated that he had borrowed from a fellow soldier a copy of a photoromance based on the film *La notte* (The Night), directed by Michelangelo Antonioni in 1962.[23] He noticed that the story emphasized conservative ideas that were absent in the film, such as the superiority of marriage over fleeting occasions of infidelity. In his conclusion, which is worth quoting at length, Magno complained about a typical disregard of popular audiences: "I imagine your resistance towards this kind of popular literature, and I agree with you. But don't you think that, in the context of complex interests in cinema that move beyond aesthetics to connect to sociological and political issues, it could be useful to examine features and nature of the influence that [this literature] exercises on your readers? I think it's unfortunate that crime and sci-fi fictions, comics and photoromances have so many clueless readers and that no critic would take them into consideration, on the other hand, so that to study their affect—and its mode—on the audience."[24] The interesting point is that not only did Magno blame *Cinema Nuovo* for ignoring the social and political relevance of "popular literature," but he also criticized the idea that its audiences were necessarily "clueless" and therefore not worth any critical support by the experts in the field.

Aristarco did not publish his response; instead, Magno's letter is followed by a message from the "Italian Film Circle." According to this message, a film series will soon promote "lo spirito del cinema di autore" (the spirit of *auteur* cinema): "Films that only from complete independence from the economic structure in place, which is too binding, they can get that degree of freedom and inspiration to influence deeply their time, the culture of their time, instead of being subjected to the worst myths."[25] This statement does not answer Magno's request directly, but rather sends a clear message: since photoromances are not independent from the market, they are not free and thus able to really have an impact on culture, in its historical development. In the Italian Film Circle's words, Magno is wrong in believing that pulp fictions actually mattered (i.e., they can have historical relevance) and, perhaps, he is as "clueless" as any other reader of photoromances. *Cinema Nuovo*'s negative account went hand in hand with the idea that consumers were helpless victims in the hands of the cultural industry.

This position was not unique among film critics and artists, even when they had something to do with its success, like screenwriter and director Cesare Zavattini. In fact, the engagement of figures such as Zavattini in the photoromance industry addresses a broader issue at stake here, and fundamental to the postwar period: the question of the *popular* as belonging to the working classes, to the nation, and to the People, in light of Antonio Gramsci's theorization, on one hand, and that of the indoctrinating role of the cultural industry, on the other hand, as in Horkheimer and Adorno's analysis.[26] Zavattini's ambiguous position toward the photoromance as *popular* reading exemplifies the conundrum that is inherent in the historical use of this term, particularly on the left, in the context of a postwar industrialized society. The binary between popular and mass culture was politically unsustainable, albeit it granted the industry complete power over its audiences who could not emancipate themselves without the help of the enlightened (male) intellectual.[27] It is well known that Zavattini was somehow involved in the birth of the photoromance as a medium (paternity then contested by Luciano Pedrocchi, editor of *Bolero Film*) and that he had authored a script on which the photoromance "La colpa" (Guilt) was based, published in the same magazine in 1962. The story of a young girl who is raped and gets pregnant was then published under a different author's name (Cesare Altieri), but a recent exhibition has shown that Zavattini was indeed willing to enmesh in a culture dictated by the market, if it was for an educational cause.[28] At the same time, the so-called father of Neorealism did not give much credit to readers and ultimately aligned with *Cinema Nuovo* in evaluating their intellectual abilities, as stated in an interview with Antonio Cifariello in the documentary *Il mondo dei fotoromanzi* (The World of Photoromances). Broadcasted by the Italian public channel RAI 1 in 1962, the goal of the film was precisely to undertake an objective inquiry into the factors that brought so much success to the magazines, as Magno had recommended to Aristarco. Among other intellectuals interviewed, Zavattini is the most explicit in his considerations on the naiveté of readers. He states, "the majority can identify themselves [in photoromances], find their own sentiments, which means that unfortunately these are problems of underdeveloped people."[29] For this reason, Zavattini continues, intellectuals should learn how to speak to these people, not only to the elites; however, they should never "vulgarize" literature.[30]

Throughout the decades, condescending attitudes toward photoromance readers such as that of Zavattini worsened into political condemnation. While Aristarco basically ignored the importance of the phenomenon, filmmakers like Giuseppe Ferrara argued that "i fumetti sono le regioni sottosviluppate dei nostri sentimenti" (photoromances are the underdeveloped regions of our feelings).[31] With the advent of radical movements, the sexual revolution, and second-wave feminism, photoromances signified the rise of consumerist culture and the role that the latter played in the oppression of women (specifically of the working classes). Critics maintained the argument that publishers mystified the capitalist system and embedded in readers' minds the patriarchal logic that sustained it. In the words of Arturo Quintavalle, "The photoromance has a specific, mythical function that is the projection of the ego against the superego, a projection that takes place within the limits established by the bourgeoisie: economic growth, marriage among equals, competition and, then, at the affective level: eternal feelings, paternalistic familial relationships, servile understanding of the woman inside the house."[32] Further, at a time when critics of popular culture were divided between "apocalyptic" and "integrated" to use Umberto Eco's 1964 expression with regard to the strenuous antagonists and the mildly accepting critics of the cultural industries, photoromances were singled out as *the* commercial product specifically responsible for—in the words of Italian writer and journalist Luigi Compagnone to the director of *Bolero Film* Luciano Pedrocchi—Italy's cultural backwardness.[33] Even to someone like Quintavalle, who was otherwise open to pop culture, no doubts were left when it came to reading photoromances politically: "For these kinds of comics, we can only talk about fascism."[34]

A WORLDWIDE SUCCESS

This univocal condemnation in national public debates is striking when one considers the global market in which photoromances thrived, beginning in Italy and across the Alps, and to the farthest shores of Latin America. Not only had photoromances been published both in Italy and in France since the late 1940s, but soon they were also exported to other European countries and to Argentina and Brazil, followed by Mexico, Columbia, Libya, Morocco, Tunisia, Sudan, Cameroon, South Africa, and the United States.[35] The personal tales behind the proliferation of photoromances in French- and Spanish-speaking countries are fascinating in and of themselves. After World War II, emigration of key figures in the Italian publishing industry during the Fascist period generated international business transactions between Italy, France, and Latin America. Two entrepreneurs are especially significant: Cino Del Duca and Cesare Civita, who acquired copyrights and created franchises of the two most important Italian photoromances, respectively, *Grand Hotel* and *Bolero Film*. Del Duca (brother of Domenico and Alceo, owners of *Grand Hotel*'s Edizioni Universo) moved to Paris in 1932 for political reasons, and from there he continued to work as founding member of La Moderna, publishing pulp fictions (romantic novels, adventures) as well as the first Italian youth comics *Il Monello* (1933) and *L'Intrepido* (1931).[36] In 1947, soon after his brothers created Edizioni Universo, Del Duca's Les Editions Mondiales launched *Nous Deux*, modeled on *Grand Hotel,* and publishing its photoromances in translation. As Sylvette Giet writes, the French magazine "frenchized" the Italian original, by translating toponymies and anthroponyms, modifying or eliminating names of writers and drawing artists.[37] Del Duca soon became the leader in the French market of women's magazines (the so-called *presse du cœur*, literally "heart's press"), producing fifteen different titles. As previously mentioned, he also maintained business in Italy, publishing the women's magazine *Intimità*. According to correspondence with Arnoldo Mondadori, he also had in mind a project for a German franchise named Mondial Verlag, which would have published a photoromance similar to *Bolero Film*. Eventually, Del Duca and Mondadori could not come to an agreement, but Mondial Verlag did publish a German version of *Grand Hotel,* with the title *Bei Dir*, in 1954–1955.

South America had its own counterpart to Cino Del Duca: Cesare Civita.[38] The two men's paths are similar insofar as they both were involved in transnational business relations, between Italy and their respective countries of residence. As Eugenia Scarzanella maintains, Civita created a publishing empire not only from his own efforts but also by leveraging a network of family and business relations that connected his company to the local Argentinian-Italian *and* Jewish community, on one hand, and to the Italian publishing industry on the other.[39] Born in New York, his parents both Italian, Civita began his career in Milan where, in 1936, he was the director of Walt Disney Italy and a top manager in the Arnoldo Mondadori Editore (from now on, Mondadori) corporation. After the promulgation of the Italian Racial Laws in 1938, Civita moved to the United States and then to Buenos Aires, with the goal of exporting Walt Disney characters to that country.[40] In Buenos Aires, in 1941 he created Editorial Abril with partners Alberto Levi and Paolo Terni, initially publishing children's books and Disney comics, and later expanding with an innovative women's magazine (*Claudia*), an automobile publication (*Corsa*), illustrated weeklies *Sietes Dias* and *Panorama,* and the comics magazine *Cinemisterio*, with the collaboration of famous graphic artists such as Hugo Pratt and Hector German Oesterheld. Around the same time, Civita's brother Victor created a branch in Brazil; a franchise opened in Mexico and distribution facilities in other Latin American countries. Editorial Abril thus became the largest editing corporation in Latin America. In 1948, Abril published the first issue of *Idilio,* which included two photoromances from *Bolero Film* in translation ("Amor dulce embriaguez" by Damiano Damiani and "Tormento" by Francesco Cancellieri), in addition to stories created and performed by Argentinean artists.[41] Abril soon expanded its market of photoromances in Brazil with the magazine *Capricho* and with another publication in Argentina, *Nocturno*, which published the same photoromances that appeared serially in *Idilio* in single issues. Mondadori had an exclusive copyright agreement for its photoromances and comics with Surameris, the in-house syndicate of Abril, following Civita's trip to Europe in 1947. These imports constituted the majority of photoromances published in both Argentinean and Brazilian magazines. Surameris and Mondadori may also have coproduced some stories, as some photoromances published in *Bolero Film* explicitly state in the opening titles.[42] The cultural importance of these business transactions is explained in Scarzanella's analysis. In her words, "the Italian *fotonovela* accompanied the last Italian immigration wave in Argentina and was vehicle of integration."[43]

THE PHOTOROMANCE IN SCHOLARSHIP

Despite their international success and cultural value, photoromances have been at best ignored in academia, in Jan Baetens's words, because they are stupid, poor, and repetitive; or condemned, because they are ideologically "highly suspect."[44] Italian scholars have dismissed photoromances as samples of "para-letteratura" ("adjacent literature") and excluded them from historiographies. It is enough to mention that in his six-hundred-plus-page history of publisher Arnoldo Mondadori, Enrico Decleva only gives half a page of attention to both *Bolero Film* and *Confidenze*, even though he contends somewhere else in the same book that periodicals were in fact pivotal to the well-being of the company.[45] In total, photoromance scholarship consisted until very recently of a few monographs and articles in Latin American studies of popular culture, French semiotics and cultural studies, and Italian literary studies. In the last ten years, Baetens is the first author to have undertaken a study of the "photonovel medium," while Anna Bravo's *Il fotoromanzo* (2006) and Silvana Turzio's *Il fotoromanzo: Metaforfosi di storie lacrimevoli* (Metamorphoses of Tearful Stories, 2019) are the first important historical commentaries on the cultural phenomenon of the photoromance in Italian. Sylvette Giet's feminist reading of *Nous Deux* and Isabelle Antonutti's broad analysis of Cino Del Duca's publishing empire are other important contributions to the field that move beyond depictions of photoromances as tools of indoctrination (and in the case of imported magazines from Western countries to Latin America, as instruments of cultural imperialism).[46] Alternatively, like pulp romances, these illustrated magazines are a means for women to find refuge from an everyday life of sorrow: a quite common perspective among Italian and French scholars such as Evelyne Sullerot, Ermanno Detti, and Serge Saint-Michel.[47] In *La presse féminine* (1963), Sullerot blames her male colleagues for not taking photoromances seriously and roughly dismissing them as bourgeois ideology (despite not having read them). According to Sullerot, women reading photoromance are not, for the most part, "in charge of their own lives" and thus, they find an escape in romantic stories that celebrate "the revenge of masochism"—that is, the success of the same behavior that made them accomplices in their own oppression.[48] These interpretations are largely based on the understanding that readers are feminine and passive receptacles of popular culture. In her report to the UNESCO on *Women and the Cultural Industries* in 1981, Michele Mattelart had questioned this idea and argued that women could be aware of the alienating structural features of the messages of the cultural industries, yet the visual-textual narratives continued to fascinate them. The question becomes, in Mattelart's words: "What mass masochism, what suicidal class attitude can explain this fascination?"[49] Her analysis concludes (once again) that romantic narratives function as compensation for women's dissatisfaction not simply as vehicles of capitalist ideology or patriarchy, or both, and that the mechanism of fascination may be due to the satisfaction that narrative devices can provide to delighted readers.[50]

However, Mattelart arrives at her conclusion, in Janice Radway's words, "on the basis of a performance of that text, which no individual in the group [of readers] would recognize."[51] With these words, Radway referred to common critiques of the effects of romantic pulp fictions on American female readers that did not take into consideration what the entire act of reading meant to the actual women who bought them. Radway's ethnographic study of women reading romances in Midwest America (1984) considered not only the individual's negotiation of the text, but also the social dimension of reading practices. According to Radway, the habit of finding space to read romances sustained a kind of mild defiance to patriarchy because it denied (albeit temporarily) the demands of a family, it was seen by readers as the signs of a woman's ability to do something for herself alone, and it provided the same readers with the opportunity to indulge in positive feelings about a heroine and women in general.[52] In the words of Joost van Loon, the desire of women reading romances is "at once an expression of women's agency and a discursively constructed node of (patriarchal) power-relations."[53]

In the case of photoromances, there are only a few studies that approach the question of their political and cultural relevance either by looking at its reception or through audience research methodologies.[54] To my knowledge, only Giet has considered the role of readers as active participants in the cultural and social experience of reading, although her analysis is limited to the case of *Nous Deux*. Milly Buonanno's inquiry on women's magazines of 1975 demonstrated an attempt to expand textual analysis into a sociological inquiry on the composition of readerships and their habits of consumption. Buonanno highlighted the necessity of considering the gendered object constructed by so-called women's magazines not as a universal subject but as a target audience, whose desires were nurtured and affected by the publishing system of production and consumption. The imagined "woman" that allegedly homogenized the readerships of magazines as different as *Grazia* and *Bolero Film* actually changed in relation to the different economic, social, and cultural background of the women who bought, borrowed, and shared the issues. By quantitative surveys, Buonanno showed that photoromances specifically targeted women of low income and education, who lived in provincial towns and identified as housewives or working class. Therefore, she argued (again, once again) that these particular magazines among the many considered *for* and *about* women were tools of domination in the hands of capitalism. Female readers were oppressed first as members of the working classes, and not only as women, by means of the ideological content spread via the romantic narratives.

Buonanno attempted to historicize the readership and thus to address the question of the texts' politics of gender more specifically; however, she dismissed the role played by readers in meaning making. Considering Stuart Hall's definition of "reading" as negotiation, Buonanno's account of the social and cultural dimensions of photoromances failed to investigate how Italian women negotiated their relationship with the texts.[55] Furthermore, given that magazines were also shared and discussed among readers, in the words of Henry Jenkins, "we have to think about negotiation differently—not in terms of how an individual negotiates their relationship with a text but rather how community members negotiate interpretations (and rules for forming interpretations) among each other."[56] I am not arguing here that Italian women who read photoromances necessarily understand the universal model of womanhood constructed and promoted in their narratives in ways that were radically different from those explained in Buonanno's or Sullerot's analyses; rather, that neither Sullerot nor Buonanno considered the importance of what the very practice of buying, sharing, finding the time to read, and talking about these stories meant for them. Instead, I agree with Giet who argues that the photoromance magazine *Nous Deux* becomes an "objet d'une consommation socialisatrice" (object of socializing consumption).[57] To put it another way, in light of current feminist scholarship in cultural studies, we cannot simply read photoromances as tools of capitalist and patriarchal domination while knowing that the women who read them actually enjoy them. In addition, since reading is one practice within the larger context of fandom, we need to understand the importance of a common identity and a shared culture in relation to individual responses to mass-produced cultural texts. Finally, I claim that we are bound to review the active role that fans have played and continue to play vis-à-vis not only the texts but also the industry.

THE PHOTOROMANCE AND CONVERGENCE CULTURE

In an article published in the *Washington Post* in 1979, American journalist Alan M. Kriegsman blamed the Roman publisher Lancio for invading the U.S. market with publications that were, in his words, "TV soap operas in magazine format."[58] "At long last," wrote the journalist, "we can read and watch television at the same time." Kriegsman ironically aimed to minimize the impact of these Italian-imported products on American culture while, in fact, he pinpointed the business and narrative strategies that made them a profitable, international product of consumption. In this book, I show that the success of photoromances was due to their belonging to a system of media convergence that (1) exploited storytelling across platforms, (2) branded characters and artists, and (3) nurtured fandom and readers' participation. These dynamics are at the core of what Jenkins has called *convergence culture*, at whose dawn, I argue, we should place the rise of the photoromance.[59] "Media convergence—the coming together of forms that were previously separate—has come to dominate contemporary understandings of the models through which popular culture is produced industrially," writes Matthew Freeman.[60] At the same time, Freeman points out, since the mid-eighteenth century magazines are devised as a strikingly interactive medium, "in much the same way as the internet in the contemporary media landscape."[61] As I show in this book, the photoromance fits the model of convergence culture because the magazine's content consists of the concurrent use of multiple formats and generic conventions, but also because the magazine's reception is based on the flowing of this content across multiple media and thus on the active engagement of readers across these platforms.[62] In this respect, the Italian case, where publishing groups had invested in other media since the 1930s, is distinguished by comparison to other European contexts.[63] Therefore, my focus in this book will be on unraveling how the dynamics of convergence culture developed in Italy, with the understanding that products as much as editorial strategies and business practices were adopted beyond the national borders. These interrelated aspects must be taken into consideration vis-à-vis the global market within which this hybrid medium thrived. Further, whereas scholars interested in convergence rarely address the gendered aspects of production and reception, my approach gives specific attention to the relationship between media productions and industries, and the discourses of gender and sexuality.

The photo-textual narratives of photoromances combined technical elements of the comic strips and the *cinenovella* or film-novel (a photo-textual object based on an existing movie), and they imported narrative tropes and generic conventions from film melodramas, the *feuilleton,* and romantic novels. Photoromances and comics were both financially and stylistically connected (as I previously mentioned, in Italy, the word for comics—*fumetto*—was frequently used to refer to both genres) (figures I.2–I.3). While from the business perspective Mondadori, Edizioni Universo, Les Editions Mondiales, and Abril all invested both in comics (or drawn romances) and photoromances, from the formal point of view, the latter imported from the former the use of captions and balloons as well as the element of closure, that is, the "phenomenon of observing the parts but perceiving the whole."[64] Similarly, in both cases, readers must create connections between panels (photographs, in this case) and fill in the gaps between them (the white lines that Scott McCloud calls "gutters"). The relationship with cinema was also important, if not even more determinant. First of all, there are striking similarities between film and photoromance narratives of the same period (going through several issues of *Bolero Film* at the Mondadori Foundation, I could hardly distinguish between stories that I knew from movies and those that I just read in the magazines). Furthermore, some film stars and stage performers, such as Sophia Loren, Gina Lollobrigida, and Vittorio Gassman, played also in photoromances, or appeared in the photo-textual versions of movies in magazines (the so-called *cinefotoromanzi* or *cineromanzi*).[65] In Italy and France, examples of film novelization have existed since the 1930s, once the rotogravure was imported from the United States.[66] However, the cinenovella used only a few still photographs and captions, while the cineromanzi (cineromances) were proper photoromances that employed (instead of original narratives and photos) still photographs taken on the set and film stills captured from strips as well as original dialogue from the script, to retell the film in its entirety, more or less faithfully. Cineromances turn a wide variety of films into readings for popular audiences who may or may not have been able to see them in the theater, including art films such as Juan Antonio Bardem's *Muerte de un ciclista* (Death of a Cyclist, 1955); politically engaged movies such as Mauro Bolognini's *La notte brava* (The Big Night, 1959); and Hollywood hits such as Alfred Hitchcock's *Notorious* (1946) (figure I.4).[67] Invented in Italy but short-lived in that country, where by the late fifties cineromances were not sold anymore at newsagents, the genre was also very popular in France, where fans could buy them until the mid-1960s (not only Italian translations but also original French productions). Agreements between publishers and producers bypassed the artists, whose intellectual and artistic work was not protected by copyright laws at the

Figure I.2

Cover of *Bolero Film* 3, no. 105 (1949). Courtesy of Gruppo Mondadori.

Figure I.3

"Disonorata" (Dishonored), *Bolero Film* 3, no. 105 (1949): 2. Courtesy of Gruppo Mondadori.

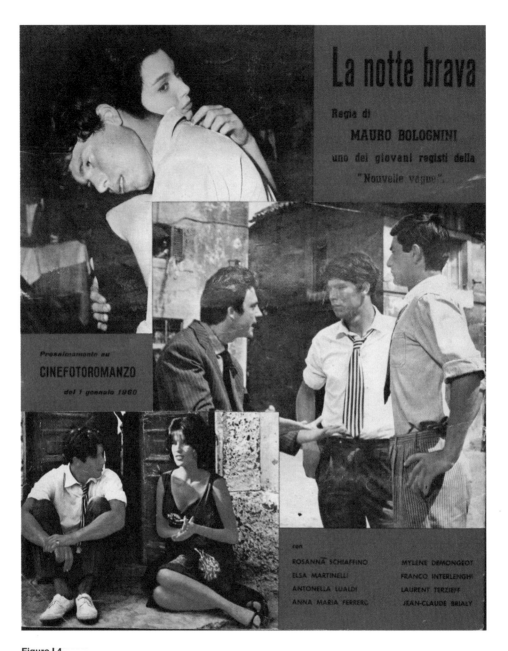

Figure I.4

Ad for *La notte brava* (The Big Night) directed by Mauro Bolognini, who is quoted as "one of the young directors of the 'Nouvelle vague.'" Back cover of *Cinefoto Romanzo* 4, no. 1 (1960).

time, despite the fact that stars were the main commercial attraction and that directors were increasingly regarded as a film's authors, in light of the so-called *politique des auteurs* of the Cahiers du Cinéma. In the case of obscure small publishers and foreign movies, it is not even clear whether permission to publish was at all established via legal routes. In between commercial extensions and bootleg productions, the "cineromanzo question" (as it is called in the Italian legal literature of the 1950s) thus anticipated convergence culture in yet another way, that is, by challenging restriction to public access in the face of unregulated appropriation of industrial products.[68]

Whereas cross-media strategies form the basis of the photoromance business, which promoted synergies between publishing houses and film producers, cross-media characters and fictional story-worlds and media branding are the basis of the profitable association with the record, television, and advertisement industries. Photoromances functioned as big containers of shared content: TV personalities starred in their narratives and columns, as well as in television series and advertisements; popular singers also appeared in the magazines as actors and interviewees, while their songs and records were thereby advertised (and often, lyrics were published along with the advertisements). According to Pedrocchi's 1964 letter to Arnoldo Mondadori, special editions of records by famous singers such as Gigliola Cinquetti were released "exclusively for *Bolero Film* readers."[69] Not only did the same character star in multiple media, but he or she was also associated with the same fictional world. For example, actor Franco Volpi took part in several TV series such as *Orgoglio e pregiudizio* (Pride and Prejudice, 1957) and *Il romanzo di un giovane povero* (The Romance of a Poor Young Man, 1957), both adaptations of nineteenth-century European novels. The same historical setting served as a background for many photoromances, such as Confidenze's "Gli occhi che non sorrisero" (Eyes That Never Smiled, 1960), in which Volpi costarred with actress Lidia Costanzo (who went on to become protagonist of the successful television crime serial *Le avventure di Laura Storm* [The Adventures of Laura Storm, 1965–1966]); and for the TV advertising for Martini and Rossi (which Volpi appeared in with another famous theater actor and regular presence in TV advertisement, Ernesto Calindri).[70]

In the pre-Internet era, Italian publishers also engaged individual readers as fans and stimulated collective forms of fandom to promote cultural consumption of media franchises (i.e., interconnected products of the publishing, film, television, and music industries). In particular, this book will examine *Bolero Film* and the Lancio series as two main case studies in point, vis-à-vis publishing innovations in participatory culture. In open letters and private correspondence, editors Pedrocchi (Mondadori) and Barbara Mercurio (Lancio) made a point to acknowledge and value customers' satisfaction and engagement. In the fifties and sixties, *Bolero Film*'s open contests and requests for submissions sustained and nurtured artistic aspirations of all kinds, such as becoming prospective writers, actresses, and celebrities. Among other initiatives, the magazine sponsored the music festival "Castrocaro" for "new voices" (very much in the same style as *American Idol* or *The Voice*), whose winners not only participated in the famous Sanremo Music Festival but also starred in at least one photoromance.[71] And Lancio was at the forefront of transnational markets in the 1970s, the first to do business in the United States, and the creator of in-house celebrities that ensured the success of its series by fostering an object-specific fandom still thriving today on social media, despite the company officially closing in 2011.[72]

Further, it is because of the peculiar historical situation in which Italy found itself in the postwar period that publishers happened to have the right (female) audience to make a profit, exploiting the liberties women gained through democracy and the capitalist system. The birth of photoromances cannot be separated from the socioeconomic changes that brought Italy from the postwar Reconstruction to the so-called economic miracle, but also fostered the kind of female emancipation that Angela McRobbie would later define "faux feminism:" deeply connected to modernization, grounded on consumption and sexual freedom, and yet traditional in its articulation of gender roles in the private and public spheres.[73] In Italy, the growth of a popular female audience of moviegoers and magazine buyers fostered the same kind of "faux-feminist" discourse. However, as opposed to other Western European democracies such as the UK, on which McRobbie bases her argument, Italian society and politics remained fundamentally patriarchal until the late seventies, on both the right and the left side of the political spectrum. From a gendered perspective, I claim in this book, photoromances threatened the status quo without promoting a radical break with tradition, by means of the modernizing power of consumerist culture, against the national political project of return-to-order (which officials across the political spectrum felt to be necessary to solve the social crisis caused by World War II), in spite of a male-dominated cultural sphere, and in opposition to a society ruled by Catholic morals. In this sense, I disagree with Baetens, Van Den Bergh, and Van Den Bossche in their compelling and yet binary analysis of the photoromance: a complex and rich phenomenon from a mediological and cultural-historical point of view, according to them, yet poorly made and ideo-logically backward.[74] In the chapters that follow, I will show that backwardness and silliness are actually more aptly the attributes of *representations* of female readership and fans of photoromances, in ways that reveal underpinning anxieties toward the democratization of culture, on one hand, and grassroot extensions of the products of the cultural industries, on the other.

Finally, to review photoromances in the paradigm of convergence means to realize that new media do not kill the old ones but rather, in Jenkins's words, "Each old medium was forced to coexist with the emerging media."[75] While the photoromance was blamed for "killing" cinema, at the time of its birth, the "death" of the photoromance normally is associated with the rise of television as a form of entertainment and, more specifically in Italy, with private channels broadcasting in the seventies.[76] Historians of the Italian press Lombardo and Pignatel claim that a general crisis of the illustrated magazine business was determined by the Kippur war (1973), when the price of paper rose 60 percent.[77] In some countries, the fate of photoromances is connected to polit-ical events, for example in Argentina, where the closing of Abril's *Idilio* followed the establishment of the military dictatorship (1976). In fact, still booming worldwide at the end of the 1970s, photoromances continue to be sold today in Italian newsstands, and the parabola of their success did not really decline until the mid-1980s.[78] More relevantly, I argue that, as the photoromance did not kill cinema but rather imported its generic conventions and plot devices and forced the latter to share the same popular audiences, in the same way, television soap operas inherited stylistic and narrative features from their photo-textual foremothers. While an in-depth study of continuities between the photoromance and the soap opera formats are beyond the scope of this book, my analysis of the Lancio fandom will take into consideration the nomadic and yet loyal fanship of photoromance readers from the seventies to today's digital platforms. The phenomenon of the contemporary Lancio fandom epitomizes the way in which the photoromance has had an impact on the development of popular culture in Italy throughout the postwar period, and how it participated in the "celebritization" of Italian society (that is, the permeation of celebrity culture to the depth of dominant social and cultural discourses).[79]

The Photoromance is divided into six chapters. In chapter 1, I examine the case of *Bolero Film* to demonstrate the prominent place that female readership had, in the midst of corporate demands and social changes, in the development of the photoromance. The degree to which this readership actually mattered (and thus to which we can talk about participatory culture before the digital revolution) depended on the power struggle between publisher Arnoldo Mondadori and editor Luciano Pedrocchi. My argument is that the success of *Bolero Film* was determined not only by how much women liked stories, characters, and photographs. The appeal of photoromances also lies in their media franchise extensions and as such they need to be studied in order to understand their cultural and social relevance.

Chapters 2 and 3 concern the interrelationships of magazines, female stardom, celebrity culture, and the film industry. Chapter 2 explores the connections between stardom, fandom, and the cineromance. Popular in 1950s Italy and France, cineromances are the precursors of 1970s American fotonovels, adult comic books that feature still images from movies or television series such as *Grease* (1978) and *Star Trek* (1977–1978). I argue that cineromances are hybrid texts in between commercial extensions and grassroots productions and thus at the origins of contemporary fan appropriations of popular movies. In the chapter, I focus specifically on Dino De Laurentiis' publishing branch Edizioni Lanterna Magica and discuss how the series *Cineromanzo gigante* and *Cineromanzo per tutti*, in their twofold identity of tabloids and storytellers, functioned as peculiar marketing tools for stardom, both nurturing the spread of celebrity culture and channeling rules of moral and sexual conduct.

Current studies in film and media history show that film novelization was both an extension of viewers' experience and a promotional tool. At the same time, existing documents regarding legal battles concerning cineromances in Italy problematize historical accounts of these magazines as straightforward product packaging. In chapter 3, I demonstrate that by looking into the literature on Italian copyright laws, we can not only address the legal question of film novelization on historical grounds, but also contribute in a unique way to the history of *auteur* cinema as tool of the industry, and to that of producers as authors of films. My claim is that at the core of judicial accounts on the cineromance was not the validation of the artists as copyright holders but the need for normative rules that could extend the disciplining power of producers (and of their main financer, the Italian government) on publications that were deemed to be influential among their female readership.

In light of their relevance as educational tools, chapters 4 and 5 examine the use of photoromances outside the realm of commercial entertainment, to advocate for political, religious, and social causes. In particular, I study the cases of the Catholic publisher San Paolo, the Information Agencies of the Italian Communist Party (PCI), and the Italian Association for Demographic Education (AIED), three organizations that similarly used photo-textual stories of love relationships as the means to promote their respective agendas. Catholic, Communist, and AIED photoromances popularized, respectively, the preaching of the Gospel, Marxist ideas, and sexual rights for both men and women. However, as I discuss in chapter 3, despite the evident attempt to engage with the commercial model in order to persuade female audiences, Catholic and Communist texts ultimately fail to address the social and cultural changes that determined the success of the photoromance formula. About a decade later, in the mid-1970s, AIED continued but innovated the use of photoromances for propaganda purposes, which were simultaneously adopted across the Atlantic by American agencies such as the Peace Corps in their efforts to educate Latin American populations about various health and social issues. In chapter 4, I show how the AIED campaign for "birth control in comics" demonstrated a deep understanding of what made the medium so successful among the general public by engendering the migration of celebrities into the space of civil activism.[80]

In chapter 6 I conclude my analysis of photoromances and their fandom by a netnographic study of contemporary social media platforms. Based on data collected through online surveys and communication with users and extensive reading of web posts on Facebook and other online materials, this study focuses on women users, readers, and collectors of photoromance series published in the seventies by the Roman company Lancio (while fans speak or understand Italian, they are not necessarily located in Italy, according to their Internet profiles). By looking at data comparatively to the historical analysis of the magazines themselves, I claim that Lancio's editorial strategies in the 1970s resulted in a distinct realm of celebrity culture and an object-specific fandom similar to that of American television soap operas. Lancio engaged in what Jenkins calls the logic of "affective economics," so that the customer is "active, emotionally engaged, and socially networked."[81] In this context, contemporary Lancio fanship (including digital archiving at the fringes of copyright laws) reveals the importance of a common identity and a shared culture to explain individual responses to mass-produced cultural texts.

This book is based on extensive archival and library research that I conducted at the Mondadori Foundation in Milan; the National Film Library (Biblioteca Luigi

Chiarini), the Gramsci Foundation, the Umberto Barbaro Library, and the Central State Archives in Rome; and the Harry Ransom Center of the University of Texas at Austin. But above all, it is the product of endless negotiations and passionate exchanges with collectors and fans whom I had the privilege to virtually encounter via email communication, social media, and electronic markets. Thanks to them, I was able to read (and enjoy) the photoromances that are the objects of this study, and to learn about the consumers who are the subjects that made it possible. In the process, I became an "acafan" (not simply an academic scholar but also a fan myself); it is from this position of personal attachment and intellectual curiosity that I eventually began to write the fascinating history of the photoromance and its audiences.[82]

1 CHASING THE AUDIENCE

Can we talk about convergence culture before the invention of the World Wide Web? And how does participation function in the pre-Internet era? The photoromance is, at the same time, "un film stampato" (a printed film), a "complete illustrated soap opera," a fan magazine, and a tabloid.[1] But how much was the audience involved in its making? While the presumption of a passive audience made leftist critics doubtful with regard to the political effects of these magazines, in the age of the massive industrialization of culture, some claimed to engage with their readership as educators, thus believing to be able to mold readers' behaviors via their magazines. The heteronormative discourse of the photoromance as low culture for women articulated the common sense of leftist intellectuals and Catholic politicians alike, demeaning female readers by considering them passive receptacles of corruptive ideas. In response to this discourse, and in the attempt to reconstruct the history of the Italian photoromance as a participant in the media system and as a product of the cultural industries, in this chapter I examine the role readers played in the making of the magazines accused of indoctrinating them.

In particular, I focus on the case of *Bolero Film* (*BF*) to demonstrate the prominent place that readership had, in the midst of corporate demands and social changes, in the development of its content (photoromances, columns, advertisements). In comparison to other magazines, such as *Sogno* and *Grand Hotel*, *BF* most interestingly shows the contradictions that derive from a publishing politics that both exploits and privileges readers/consumers. The degree to which readership actually mattered (and thus to which we can talk about participatory culture) depended on the power struggle between publisher Arnoldo Mondadori and editor Luciano Pedrocchi. In a way, the publisher acted as a Hollywood major producer would: to maximize profit, he added quality to entertainment by hiring the most respected professionals, by using the latest technologies in printing, and by investing in innovative marketing strategies (*BF* for example sponsored the music contest "New Voices" of Castrocaro Terme, a sort of Italian precursor to *American Idol*).[2] Ultimately, though, Arnoldo Mondadori's approach to publishing made customer satisfaction relevant exclusively in order to please advertisers. Instead, Pedrocchi's private correspondence and editorializing show an explicit recognition of the active role played by consumers, who could not be manipulated or fooled. As I explain in this chapter, this approach is reflected in the magazine's columns and in photoromances that represent *BF* fans (passionately engaged with celebrities and stories) and that foster the *BF* fandom, that is, that prompt readers to recognize themselves as part of a *BF* community.

These representations did not necessarily correspond to the historical reality of readers who were nomadic, according to data, since they usually bought other photoromances (but rarely read any other form of literature), went to the movies, watched television, and listened to the radio.[3] In this respect, *BF* is more specifically an insightful case for a study of the photoromance in the context of media convergence. By comparison to the French *Nous Deux*, for example, *BF* is inscribed not only within a system of social relationships but also within a network of cultural industries. Agreeing with Giet, I claim that by sharing copies of different magazines, and discussing them, readers could establish links among family members and neighbors, and particularly, between generations of women.[4] In addition, other media platforms exploited by *BF* under Pedrocchi's direction were linked to build consumer loyalty, in other words, to ensure that readers found in the magazine a place to satisfy their multiple demands and a community with which to share their interests. While published letters and representations of fans as characters in photoromances created models of identification, cross-media strategies maximized the magazine's potential to attract and maintain its clientele (who were also moviegoers, TV viewers, and music listeners).

The dispersed practices of cultural consumption across media favored advertisers who were, according to Fausto Colombo, "the receiver with whom [the publisher] really communicated."[5] However, I disagree with Colombo that the advertisers were the exclusive point of reference vis-à-vis production and show in this chapter how *BF* was informed by the association of convergence to consumer culture in its address to the readers. As Matthew Freeman describes in reference to early twentieth-century American culture, "the practice of guiding a fictional character across multiple cultural forms had become both a means and a source of branding consumerism to mass audience."[6] In the case of postwar Italy and its cultural industries, performers such as Mike Bongiorno (photoromance actor in *BF*, TV celebrity, and the face of various commercial products) mobilized Italian audiences as both media users and consumers. In this sense, *BF* becomes fertile ground for the study of the complex dynamics of "cross-media strategies as a historical industrial practice."[7]

This is not to say that ultimately, readers were just coopted by *BF* to buy products that they did not need. On the contrary, considering the magazine's trajectory from its birth in 1947 to its closure in 1984, which corresponded to the period of rapid growth in the Italian economy (approximately from the mid-1950s to the mid-1960s), the magazine's narratives and columns (together with advertisements) interpret the gradual changes happening in Italian society, especially with regard to gender roles, in the private and public spheres. Perhaps more savvy than erudite, more liberated than emancipated (challenging patriarchy in sexual conduct but continuing to fulfill their role as daughters, spouses, and mothers), the Italian women who made up more than 90 percent of *BF* readership could learn by means of *BF* how to take advantage of their increasing economic power to gain a new kind of perception of themselves and of their femininity. These new feminine fans, projected in the magazine's pages, studied in surveys, and discussed in production materials and correspondence, simultaneously challenged the patriarchal status quo while actively embracing the culture of consumerism, giving way to ambiguities never completely solved in the dynamics that tied them to the publisher, the editor, and the advertisers.

BRIDGING MEDIA

A modern style of entrepreneurship and mass production had characterized Mondadori since its inception in 1907.[8] Similar to other Italian publishers, the company identified with its president and founder Arnoldo Mondadori (1889–1971). Differently than its earlier competitors, Treves and Sonzogno, Mondadori had applied the American model of industrial organization since the early 1920s. In 1927, the headquarters of Mondadori moved from the province of Mantova (Ostiglia) to the metropolitan center of Milan. A network of agencies opened throughout the peninsula, while books and magazines were distributed abroad with the help of local agents. From the 1930s onward, Mondadori strategically diversified to create a large, "integrated" firm.[9] The company invested in illustrated magazines and cheap classics series, in addition to more expensive book editions, as well as in paper production.

Arnoldo Mondadori's ascent from printer to publisher fueled a legend: that of a self-made man whose ties with industrialists and whose clever managerial choices (above all, the deal with Walt Disney in 1935 to become the only official franchise of the American comic strips in Italy) allowed him to build a commercial empire that not only continued to function under the Fascist regime, but also was able to immediately recover after War World II, thanks to U.S. financial support. Key to Mondadori's editorial strategies within the framework of media convergence were its international distribution system, targeting of specialized audiences (children and women, in particular), and standardization of production. Also, Mondadori diversified its products by investing in periodicals, in addition to acquiring bestselling authors (from another publishing house, Sonzogno), signing Gabriele d'Annunzio at the height of his success in 1926, exploiting pulp fiction and comics, and publishing numerous translations (particularly in the 1930s). In direct competition with Rizzoli, Mondadori found its place in the tabloid industry by issuing the first women's magazine *Grazia* in 1938, which targeted middle-class female readers with a cheerful imperative of optimism. That same year, the Fascist Ministry of Popular Culture (MinCulPop) banned all foreign strips with the exception of *Topolino* (Mickey Mouse), which continued to be published until 1943, when the factory was occupied by Nazis and Fascists, under a different name (*Tuffolino*) but maintaining the same graphic in the title page and the original title (*Topolino*) for the magazine. This incident, among others, reveals the degree of freedom that Arnoldo Mondadori enjoyed, an ambiguous sign of both his independence and his entrenchment with the Fascist regime.[10] Such an ambiguous position and new political alliances allowed the publisher and his family to come back from their exile in Switzerland (where they escaped in 1943) and to retake control of the factory almost immediately, to rebuild the plant with the help of the European Recovery Program, and to import advanced machineries from the United States (such as color printer Cottrel), which especially strengthened output. In 1947, *BF*'s first number was issued at the same time as a new women's magazine (*Confidenze*) and the Italian version of the pro-American, conservative, and anti-Communist magazine *Reader's Digest* (titled *Selezione dal Reader's Digest*).

BF was not born a women's magazine but rather became one, in the course of its history and in the process of maximizing sales. Both children and women were not "culturally at the margins" as Angelo Ventrone argues with regard to the target audience of Edizioni Universo's *Grand Hotel,* but in fact, were highly profitable markets.[11] Mondadori's strategies also focused on selling *BF* (like other periodicals) on a global scale. In South America, franchises and affiliated publishers have been buying *BF* photoromances since the early 1950s; in North America, the magazine was distributed through subscriptions starting from 1949, reaching the Italian-speaking communities in the United States and Canada. In addition, *Grand Hotel* had already established a format in the 1950s that remain more or less the same thereafter.[12] Instead, *BF* continuously changed through the decades, in multiple ways: in the composition of front and back covers, including the title, which in 1966 becomes *Bolero Film Teletutto* and then, in 1967, *Bolero Teletutto*; in the number of pages and therefore, of columns and photoromances; in the kinds of stories and of settings of photoromances; in the products and services advertised.[13] Here, I claim that the magazine transformed in response to mutations in the social and cultural habits of readers and to their preferences with regard to entertainment and narratives, as well as on the basis of modifications and developments in the media system.

Structural configuration in the industry runs parallel to aesthetic hybridization and intertextuality. *BF* "poaches" (in Jenkins's terms) from literature, cinema, theatre, and television with the same irreverence attributed to its fans.[14] The magazine turns literary classics (Italian and foreign) into popular culture, casting respected actors in the main roles, and advertising the issues via newsreels in the movie theatres (as well as on the pages of its own magazines). In addition, *BF* extends consumption and bridges content across different media, within the photoromance medium and throughout the issue, in the relationship between columns and the photo-textual narratives. For example, the photoromance "Sconosciuto amore" (Unknown Love, 1949)—the first "romantic and musical story"—integrates music into the narrative world of the photoromance, to inaugurate a genre that would continue successfully in the 1960s by capitalizing on the popularity of singers on television and at the music festival of Sanremo.[15] The lyrics of the song "Unknown Love" (by G. C. Testoni) were published in the same issue of the first episode, captioned by the announcement that the "beguine" song could be heard for the first time on the radio stations Rete Rossa (Red Network) and Rete Azzurra (Blue Network) the following Sunday.[16] Radio, music, and the photoromance thus work in a coordinated effort to attract both consumers' time and attention, over the narratives and beyond the magazine. In this respect, *BF* is peculiar by comparison with the other two main competitors in the photoromance market, *Grand Hotel* and *Sogno*, in the way that Mondadori fully exploited cross-media strategies beyond the branches of its business, in anticipation of current structures in media conglomerates.

To explain how celebrities in photoromances serve the purpose of branding consumerism, while also embodying and promoting social types, the example of the American-born TV personality Mike Bongiorno is useful.[17] "National Mike," also known as "the King of Quiz," was the host of successful TV programs such as *Lascia o raddoppia?* (Leave It or Double It?, 1955–1959, considered the Italian version of *The $64,000 Question*) or *La fiera dei sogni* (Dream Fair, 1963–1966) as well as of many editions of the "Festival della Canzone italiana" (Italian Song Festival) in Sanremo (a national beloved music competition). In addition, Bongiorno starred in *BF* photoromances and advertised the detergent Dash and L'Oreal hair products in the televised commercials called *caroselli*. In many stories as in the commercials, Mike (as he is familiarly called in the magazine) plays himself, and fans recognize him;[18] even when he interprets a fictional character, he acts always the same type: courteous, kind, and selflessly acting for the well-being of others, particularly women.[19] Indeed, his character and demeanor correspond to that of the "everyday man" described in Umberto Eco's famous 1961 essay titled "Phenomenology of Mike Bongiorno."[20] Eco claims that in his average look and conformist behavior, Mike-the-character ("un personaggio," in his words) is not a "superman" who appeals to the consumer because he offers an impossible model to attain. Italian audiences like Mike because he is "a living and triumphant example of mediocrity."[21] To Italian women, Mike represents "an ideal lover, subdued and fragile, sweet and kind."[22]

I would extend Eco's semiotic framework to consider Mike not just as a character but as a *migrating* character, across media platforms (publishing, television). In this perspective, I think there is something to add to his interpretation. In his migration, Mike maintains the same constitutive features of wholesome celebrity for the family (both children and adults); his fame does not keep him from acting properly and being relatable. In *BF* photoromances, his kindness and disinterested eagerness to help women stand in opposition to the behavior of the Italian male characters, the latter perhaps more virile but also ruthless and violent. Carried over in the TV commercials, Mike's gendered identity promotes consumerism: the product he advertises is being offered (with courtesy) as a gift to the feminine consumer. Whether driving women in expensive vehicles to provide them with emotional support in a moment of need in the photoromances or landing in a helicopter to bring a new detergent to other women, also in need, in the commercials, Mike plays the accessible object of female desire that is associated with modern lifestyle and technology, in both situations. As an American man in the context of the heteronormative society of 1950s–1960s Italy, to which the readers of *BF*, primarily women, belonged, Mike is the masculine champion of modernity, representing the appeal of Americanism to a feminine audience.

Furthermore, the social type Mike embodies is a foil to the one of Italian masculinity in crisis, typical in Italian films of the period, especially comedies. In this context, Mike-the-character provides to both masculine and feminine fans an alternative model of both political redemption and social integration. For example, in the photoromance "Una strana storia" (A Strange Story, 1965), Mike reevokes an episode of his life during War World II. According to an ad published in *Bolero Film*, "when he [Mike] was hunted by the German police, he found refuge in an abandoned house where a woman lived and thus he could save his own life."[23] A very similar episode takes place in the film comedy *Una vita difficile* (A Difficult Life, 1961), directed by Dino Risi, in which the main protagonist Silvio (played by Alberto Sordi) is saved from the Nazis and hosted by Elena (interpreted by Lea Massari) in an empty barn. Likely, the same story resonated with many Italian male readers and viewers who lived through the war. Mike was a soldier, but he was no hero. Like Silvio, he was saved by a woman, an event that could be interpreted ambiguously as both emasculating and serendipitous. But while the situation that Alberto Sordi and Mike Bongiorno live through is similar and relatable, their characters are very different, particularly in the social and gender models that they respectively embody. Like the typical protagonist of a "commedia all'italiana" (Italian-style comedy), Silvio is a pathetic, self-centered, and cynical man—an outcast in a modernized Italian society. Mike, on the other hand, is a man who has suffered and whose story may help readers to make peace with themselves and, moreover, to move forward. In the case of Silvio, desertion is a means to satirize the masculine hero; in the case of Mike, it is the guilt that needs to be forgiven. As the advertisement explains, the photoromance narrative aims "to forget the past and give hope for the future."[24] Italy's transition to a consumerist society, which Silvio openly rejects in *A Difficult Life*, is "the future" that Mike embraces as one of its branding characters.

TRANSMEDIALIZATION

From the point of view of photoromance production, *BF*'s approach to both cinema and comics signals a process of *transmedialization* rather than adaptation of the old medium into the new medium. As Jan Baetens explains, transmedialization is "less an *event* than a process" and "is less concerned with the shift from one medium to another . . . than the result of a wide and variegated range of relationships within a much larger network of related media, which all play a role in the process of trans-medialization."[25] Pulp fiction, cinema, and comics all converge in the first issue of *BF* (published in 1947), which on the cover featured the photograph of an upper-middle-class couple, protagonists of the photoromance "Catene" (Chains). These characters (like those of pulp romances) inhabited the exotic (and geographically foreign) narrative world that was out of reach of the working-class readership, feeding the fantasy of social mobility through marriage that was forcefully under attack by many. While "Chains" may appear as an adaptation of a novel by *feuilleton* author Carolina Invernizio or by romance writer Liala, the second photoromance included in the issue resembles (in setting, plot, and character) Raffaello Matarazzo's movie of the same title, *Chains* (1949), a story of motherly love and couple betrayal in a working-class family of a provincial town in Italy.[26] Consistently, one of the two photoromances published in each issue of *BF* from the late 1940s to the early 1950s was set in Italy, in a low-income urban or rural environment, frequently in Southern Italy, and told stories of personal and social injustice, of forced emigration, of unwanted pregnancies, and of *banditismo*, featuring at least one scene of brutal violence, often a murder.[27] The realist rather than escapist narratives of these *BF* photoromances recalled those of films such as *Il lupo della Sila* (Lure of the Sila, dir. Duilio Coletti, 1949), *Il brigante di Tacca del Lupo* (The Bandit of Tacca del Lupo, dir. Pietro Germi, 1952), *Tormento* (Torment, dir. Raffaello Matarazzo, 1950), and *Non c'è pace tra gli ulivi* (Under the Olive Tree, dir. Giuseppe De Santis, 1950), featuring characters such as mothers, *briganti* (bandits), abandoned children, and unjustly accused wives. To bind them, the same "melodramatic imagination"—to use Peter Brooks's definition, which brings to the surface the "moral occult" (the ethical dilemma)—expressed innocence, guilt, and repentance through the language of violence.[28]

BF's convergence with cinema also had to do with production techniques, which set the magazine apart from other photoromances. In his analysis of the case of *Grand*

Hotel, Ventrone argues that the photographer and the director were secondary to the writer, since shooting took place only after each episode was already completed in a storyboard. Based on the testimony of Director Matteo Macciò, Ventrone's account contends that both the photographer and the director were not creatively intervening on the written text, but only dealt with practical aspects concerning the actors, lights, and so on. On the contrary, according to writer and director for *BF* Dante Guardamagna, production of a photoromance had much in common with that of a film, with the only difference being that characters did not move or speak.[29] Scripts were structured according to scenes and characters; they included indications for direction (such as close-ups, long shots), mise-en-scène (interior/exterior), and photography (daylight/night time). However, the script was only the starting point for a visual text that was realized on the set and completed in the editing room. The director was in charge of composing the frame, giving indications to actors on how to express their lines, and even acting out the line for them. According to Guardamagna, "the idea was that readers received a printed film from us."[30]

In fact, the photoromance is not a photographic rendition of a comic book, but it is also something other than a printed version of a film. As Guardamagna also indirectly confirmed in the interview, the ultimate product combined practices from multiple media (film, photography, comics): a set with rented furniture, both professional and nonprofessional actors, and the clapperboard; a day of work that produced between fifty and ninety shots; graphic designers in charge of writing dialogues over photographs (initially by hand) using a transparent sheet of paper over the grid, but also of retouching single images and creating photomontages. For each photo to be used, photographers could take up to twelve shots, which means a total of 150 to 800 photos per day (good, useful, needed) and shooting could last up to ten or twelve days. Approximately six hundred photos were selected for each script to be published over about six months.[31] At the Mondadori Archives, the large number of negatives collected for each photoromance are grouped in packages of fifty photos, up to 800 for each photoromance. These also include several takes of the same shot, just slightly different in posture or composition and so-called *negativi di riserva* (extra negatives) or *diversi* (different) ones, some of which reveal crew members working with lights or other objects. One of the packages of negatives that I examined (for the photoromance "Donne tra le sbarre" [Women behind bars], published in 1959) presented some examples of photomontage, in which a cut image from one shot is superimposed on another. Possibly, this technique worked as a substitute for zooming in printing or, to put it another way, to create close-ups in post-production. In addition, looking at the original shots back to back with the printed version, it is possible to see how moving scenes that were difficult to render in still photographs could be recreated at the editing stage. For example, a car accident is reconstructed by editing long and medium shots taken at different times: first an image of people riding in a car, then a very long shot of the same car upside down in the street. Close-ups are then used to visualize the final scene from different point of views to instill some dynamism into the static shot. The performative aspect of photoromances is also evident in the script, and changes in graphic design functioned as a means to make them less wordy. While photoromances in the beginning included extensive captions and very little dialogue, the proportion progressively reversed during the 1950s (figure 1.1). Later on, makers of photoromance kept captions to a minimum, limiting verbal communication to dialogues (figure 1.2).

Stylistic choices speak of technological innovations. In 1949, Arnoldo and Giorgio Mondadori traveled to the United States looking for loans and tools. They came back to Italy with both, including a new Cottrel five-color offset printing press and a Champlain rotogravure press, which allowed better image quality.[32] Within a few years, *BF* had moved from Novara to Verona, where the new Mondadori plant increased quality and output. From around the mid-1950s to 1966 (when the magazine transitioned from *BF* to *BF Teletutto*) transmedialization extended to the relatively new medium of television, in addition to radio and cinema. Because of its serial form, the photoromance was directly connected to the so-called *sceneggiato* (TV serial) since its inception in the mid-1950s, as well as the choice of literary classics to be used as narrative sources.[33] In addition, photoromances based on original stories were shortened or prolonged according to ratings, similar to how ratings determine whether television series are renewed or ended. In the words of Guardamagna, "If readers did not like them [particular photoromances], they had to be cut, but if they did (and weekly sales established whether they were . . .), they should NEVER end. Or at least last longer."[34] For this purpose "we could extend an episode, with enlargements that took the typical page of six or eight photos to three and even going from episodes of four pages [tables] to three pages."[35] Given that Guardamagna's testimony may or may not be reliable, generalization should not be based on it. However, in reading through several issues of *BF,* I noticed that some episodes are clearly "inflated"; the use of several close-ups can create an episode in which the plot does not really move forward but

Figure 1.1

"Addio Daniela!" (Goodbye, Daniela!), *Bolero Film* 3, no. 116 (1949): 2. Courtesy of Gruppo Mondadori.

Figure 1.2

"È successo a Milano" (It Happened in Milan), *Bolero Film* 17, no. 858 (1963): 18. Courtesy of Gruppo Mondadori.

rather represents, for example, in one grid a single encounter between two people. More generally, Guardamagna introduces the question of whether or not the audience actively participated in the making of the magazine.

KNOWING THE READER

So far, my reading has highlighted exclusively how cross-media strategies and business synergies functioned within the cultural system of representations and self-representations. I have discussed how *BF* converged literature, film, TV, and radio to make cultural products that engaged readers across multiple media channels with the goal of ensuring their loyalty. Readers were not only the target of these practices but also the subjects that fostered their development. In the early 1960s, in order to gather information on its readership, Mondadori Publishing commissioned the major statistical institute in Italy, Doxa, to complete a study on eight of its periodicals: *BF*, *Epoca*, *Grazia*, *Arianna*, *Confidenze*, *Storia illustrata*, *il giallo Mondadori*, and *Topolino*. Published in 1963, the study titled *I lettori di otto periodici italiani* showcases and analyzes data researchers collected by interviewing customers at newsstands (from April 22 to May 16, 1962) and subscribers (from June 10 to July 10, 1962). Here, I will only consider the data for *BF* readers (868 out of a cross-section of 6,349 respondents). This data includes information about readers' purchasing power and ownership of durables such as cars and appliances, as well as about their reading practices and consumer behaviors (faithfulness, regularity, frequency, time for reading, keeping vs. borrowing/lending magazines, number of readers per copy, readings other than magazines, movie-going frequency, vacations). The results are framed in the study's introduction by a statement regarding the "valore pubblicitario" (advertising value) of each magazine. According to this statement, the Doxa survey was conducted with the utmost scientific rigor to ensure precise, clear, and valuable information for advertisers seeking the best venues for their campaigns.[36] For this reason, I argue that data included in the volume not only describes the readership but also sheds light on the publisher's interests in its composition and expectations in order to foster business relations with advertisers and, at the same time, the magazine's commercial success.

In 1962, *BF*'s buyers are almost exclusively women (92.6 percent).[37] The image of the average female reader of BF that the survey established corresponds to the middle-class consumer who is the protagonist of the economic boom of the late 1950s to early 1960s. In fact, the same female middle-class consumer is also the main subject of the advertising campaigns published in BF. In conjunction with the increasing number of ads for beauty products and household items (as well as breast enlargement services, weight-loss programs, birth control methods, and more), the number of columns regarding fashion and household management increases in *BF* through the 1960s, thus feminizing the target reader according to traditional heteronormative models of gender. From the economic perspective, *BF* represents the average readership in the country with regard to durable goods, while readers of other magazines such as *Grazia* own durable goods in higher proportion with respect to the median Italian family. According to the survey results, almost half of the families purchasing *BF* have at least one person with an "occupazione fissa" (stable job), only a few of them have cars (15 percent) while most of them have a radio (74.3 percent), and about half own some appliances such as a refrigerator (42.2 percent) and a TV (38 percent). As stated in the volume: "[readers of BF] constitute a market that can absorb some or all appliances under consideration. Considering these percentages and at the same time the income bracket, it is possible to rationally plan campaigns to sell specific products, as a first or repeated purchase."[38] In fact, some data is collected to understand the projected condition of readers and their families, for example, asking whether there is *an intention* to buy furniture in the future or to make house renovations. Exactly 32 percent of *BF* readers say that they had such a plan and 32.5 percent of TV owners say that they had bought the appliance less than five years prior. The conclusion, according to Doxa, is that *BF* readers show signs of "the good path on which families are walking on their way to socio-economic elevation."[39]

Documents collected in the Arnoldo Mondadori Archive at the Mondadori Foundation show the relevance of these results to the politics of *BF*. In 1964, Pedrocchi writes about *BF* readers in line with Doxa's analysis with regard to Gigliola Cinquetti's record that was released exclusively to *BF* readers by Mondadori's own music label. According to Pedrocchi, sales were exceptional even though the record cost a "good 2000 lira": "A rewarding experience since it demonstrates that among readers of the weekly magazine are those who have great purchase opportunities."[40] This letter is illuminating vis-à-vis the stereotypical image of *BF* readers that I discussed in the introduction: the so-called *servette* (little servants) who would be the target audience of the magazine were rather economically independent and ready to spend on entertainment. In fact, in the available correspondence, Pedrocchi comes across as mainly concerned with the fickleness of *BF* readers, not with their purchasing power.[41] The Doxa survey also supported this position by showing that Italians were able to spend but were not exclusive in their choices. According to the data, 98.9 percent of *BF* readers are not subscribers but 86.1 percent read each issue faithfully (and more than two-thirds read each issue more than once), and while 81.2 percent did not read books, 50.1 percent read other photoromances. These nomadic readers fall into the category of consumers who may take their business elsewhere when dissatisfied with the product. Cinquetti's record testifies to the effort to make readers feel privileged and thus valued customers by granting them access to exclusive products of Mondadori's industries.

A sample of a survey distributed to *BF* readers by the publisher itself shows how important it was to monitor satisfaction and frustration among consumers.[42] The survey included the following eleven questions:

1. Which photoromances do you like the most at the moment?
2. Do you like crime fiction and modern adventure photoromances?
3. Do you think that *Bolero Film* is better since the inclusion of a photoromance in color?
4. Would you like *BF* to publish a costume drama photoromance?
5. Among male characters that appear today, who do you like the most? And among the female ones?
6. Are you interested in song lyrics?
7. Are you interested in radio and tv listings?
8. Do you buy other magazines?
9. Do you work?
10. Are you a student?
11. Are you single?[43]

It is unfortunate that the Mondadori Foundation do not hold any copies of completed surveys or any collected data that could provide information on the results. The eleven questions themselves, however, are relevant to discuss editorial strategies. At first glance, the survey simply seems to assess readers' preferences and demographics. A closer look reveals that questions clearly are intended to test two main strategies underway: developing cross-media content and experimenting with different genres. Questions 6 and 7 more specifically seek data on readers' interests in media other than publishing, specifically, music, radio and television. To be noted song lyrics and radio and TV listings appeared in *BF* at the time of the survey; therefore, these questions can be interpreted as a way to probe customers' satisfaction in these items. Furthermore, television (which in Italy consisted only of national public broadcasting, until the 1970s) had become increasingly important both as a form of entertainment in Italian society and as a subject of interest for *BF* to cover. In 1964, when the survey was distributed to readers, *BF* had recently expanded the number of pages dedicated to television and was casting TV celebrities in the photoromances, while proportionally reducing its coverage of cinema and film stars. Given that several TV shows were also music programs, and that singers appeared frequently on television and in TV advertisements, the survey's attention to these media reflects certain changes in the magazine that needed to be tested. Questions 3 and 4 instead address innovations undertaken with regard to genres while shedding light on the implementation of practices that built on readers' responses. In fact, a "action-photoromance" about a secret agent (Tom Dollar) featuring some pages in color had recently been introduced in the magazine; this venture may have been related to the success of the American James Bond movie saga (which began in 1962) or the national TV series *The Adventures of Laura Storm* (1965–1966), starring Lauretta Masiero as a journalist-detective and Oreste Lionello as her right-hand photographer.[44] To be noticed, Tom Dollar would be later adapted for the big screen in a movie by the same title (*Tom Dollar*, 1967), a French-Italian joint production starring the same French actor (Maurice Poli) and directed by Frank Red (aka Marcello Ciorciolini).[45]

These questions are useful to understand how Pedrocchi perceived the magazine's readership, whose level of sophistication was higher than in the average perception of *BF* consumers, derogatorily identified with the lower classes. In another letter to Arnoldo Mondadori, dated June 26, 1965, Pedrocchi expressed his concerns regarding customers' frustrations due to the quality of paper, the number of photoromances published per issue, and the number of pages, with respect to the cost of one issue. In the conclusion, he shared his own frustration with Mondadori: "We cannot keep considering Italy a country in medieval conditions, with a small percentage of intellectuals and everyone else as savages. And *Bolero* proves that, since we lost readers after we promised (and did not maintain) great things when we hired the price from 70 to 72 lira (for 4 numbers), and *Confidenze* proves that because of the irresponsibility of its managers. Popular magazines are the most difficult to handle because they talk to an audience that remembers what was promised, who has demands, an audience that is by no means a creature of habit and, therefore, easier to abandon you."[46] A few weeks later, Pedrocchi sent another letter to Mondadori in which he complained about the latter and *BF* co-director Adolfo Senn neglecting readers' expectations. In his words, "Luckily, I did not talk to my reader about the new paper, against your will and Dr. Senn's. I sensed that, or better, my experience told me that, I would have lost my reputation. Today the publishing industry would have had a laugh about that."[47] Seemingly isolated in the company, which reflected the established notion of audiences' passivity, Pedrocchi shared his frustrations on a few occasions with readers themselves in the pages of *BF*. For example, in a rebuttal to the accusation that *BF* was spreading propaganda in favor of voting "YES" at the referendum regarding the divorce law in 1974, he wrote: "Certain press believes that the Italian people consists of half-wit individuals, ready to change their political ideas even according to the wishes of a well-known Milanese actor. . . . Our friends and readers know that this is not true. I understand their outraged letters for the hideous slander and I understand also the harsh opinion on the credibility of certain press."[48]

With these words, Pedrocchi expressed his editorial approach, which was to give complete support to readers' opinions and recognition of their agency. Furthermore, Pedrocchi's statement challenges the idea that photoromance fans lack rational skills and are blinded by their proximity to celebrities.

INTERACTIVITY, PARTICIPATORY CULTURE, CONSUMERISM

In this light, we can look at the different tactics by which Pedrocchi supported participatory culture to engage readers and sustain their loyalty. First of all, celebrification and celebrity culture were at the core of *BF*'s structure. TV personalities, singers, and film stars regularly appeared in columns about recent news, were featured in interviews, and even offered advice on every part of life, from housekeeping to love relationships. Frequently, the authors of the articles claimed that fans had commissioned the interview or asked for the advice, thus constructing the world of celebrities at the service of their fans. Moreover, consumers of *BF* were constantly offered the opportunity to become celebrities themselves: to audition for a part in a photoromance, to sign up for a music competition, or to send in their photos for consideration by a film producer. Eventually, however, *BF* defied the idea that the show business (and the film industry in particular) was the only or ultimate source of fame. Since the very first issue, the column "La posta di Ciak" (Ciak's Mail) most clearly exemplified how *BF* was committed to helping fans get closer to their favorite celebrities, and even nurtured readers' artistic aspirations, in some occasions, while also supporting the idea that the reward that came with consumer loyalty was much more valuable. Anonymous and knowledgeable, Ciak answers readers' questions about film stars (including providing their mailing addresses), accepts requests for autographed pictures, and gives candid advice about readers' own potential for stardom (as performers as well as writers). Upon request, Ciak (who identifies as a man) is willing to send manuscripts and photographs to Pedrocchi (or so he says); when he thinks that a reader does not have what it takes, he candidly rejects the request. When Ciak discourages readers' aspirations, he does not do it because he does not trust their capabilities but because he does not seem to appreciate the glamour of the film industry very much. With the same skepticism of Luigi Malerba's ironic portrayal of a female fan in *Le lettere d'Ottavia* (Ottavia's Letters, 1956), Ciak's bitter perspective paints the world of cinema as the place where young women are lured and betrayed.[49] Unlike Malerba, however, Ciak does not satirize his female readers and their aspirations, but rather makes a point about the positive aspects of ordinary lives. In sum, in his view, readers have the potential to become stars but they are better off as fans. Above all, Ciak idolizes the *BF* community of readers, whom he calls *propagandisti* (promoters, literally "the propaganda-makers"). Issue after issue, he selects pictures that readers have mailed per his request: a group of male fans in Reggio; a young boy with his parents in Bari; a "beautiful *propagandista*" from Imperia; a group of "happy and enthusiast *propagandisti* of bolero film" from Milan; or from Sardinia, "five pretty and cheerful *propagandiste* di bolero."[50] In 1949, way before Andy Warhol's oft-repeated quote "In the future, everyone will be world-famous for 15 minutes" (1968), Ciak already celebrated the notoriety that, in Graeme Turner's words, "may or may not have arisen as a result of personal significant achievement."[51] From this perspective, Ciak's campaign was forward-looking: the following year, the cover of the first issue of another Mondadori periodical, the tabloid *Epoca* (October 14, 1950) reinforced this point. Featuring a close-up of nineteen-year-old Liliana, a shop assistant in a Milanese ice-cream place, over the caption "Liliana, Italian girl," the issue includes a photo-story that recounts her outing on Lake Como with her boyfriend. The text stated: "We choose Liliana and a Sunday afternoon on the lake because the ice-cream girl and her day off are part of daily life, and this is the magazine that tells your story, that comes looking for you in a crowd, picks out your face and brings it to the surface, in other words makes you a protagonist of the time."[52] What *Epoca,* "Ciak's Mail," and Neorealism shared, albeit the different settings, was the celebrification of ordinary life. In addition, "Ciak's Mail" demonstrated that fandom was vital to turn the recognition of celebrity into a productive business. *BF* generated a community whose members could be proud rather than ashamed of liking photoromances, and thus more likely to transform from casual into loyal readers.

The case of the "Concorso Voci Nuove di Castrocaro Terme" ("New Voices Contest," from now on, Castrocaro, created in 1957 and sponsored by *BF* since 1962) further supports the commitment to celebrifying readers, while revealing the link between this process and that of branding consumerism, at a different stage in the history of the magazine.[53] Castrocaro was a contest for unknown singers with little or no experience, similar to contemporary reality shows such as *American Idol*.[54] When *BF* became the official sponsor of the competition, the first to benefit were of course its loyal readers, who were invited to send their applications (in order to enter local auditions), but also to enter a contest with prizes such as a Lambretta motor scooter and a television.[55] A few participants in this contest were selected and paired with a singer at Castrocaro and could hope to win their prize if the singer with whom they were matched won the competition. Again, *BF* was in charge of advertising not only Castrocaro but also the *BF* community and the privileges that came with its membership. In 1965, the Editorial Board published an article titled "Sei nostri lettori in gara a Sanremo" (Six of Our Readers Participate in Sanremo), claiming that six contestants in the national music festival that took place in Sanremo not only were previous participants of Castrocaro but also *BF* readers. "When these guys cut the application form out of *BF* [to participate to Castrocaro], they were totally unknown," the article reads. "Today their names appear in the cast of the biggest song competition in the world."[56] Other media made evident that *BF* played an important role in turning ordinary boys and girls into celebrities, and that loyal readership was the means to success. In one episode of the newsreel series called *Caleidoscopio Ciac*, the commentator reveals the modest cultural, social, and economic background of Castrocaro's contestants, who were also from different parts of Italy: Luciano Tomei from Naples, a student of music who reads philosophy; Anna Identici from Cremona, a clerk who likes to read poetry as much as comics; Anna Marchetti, a factory worker from Ferrara (same hometown as the famous singer Mina, the commentator points out); and the winner, Vittorio Inzaina, a bricklayer (according to the commentator) "whose life resembles a popular, tear-jerking novel."[57] At the end, the voice-over adds the stakes of the festival: "Thanks to Castrocaro and *BF*, the first moment of notoriety comes for one [the winner], which can turn into fame and, why not, into a full bank account."[58] The last point makes reference to the cash prize for singers, but also to those goods that readers could win if they entered the prize contest. In the sequence, a shot shows the list of names paired with the singers in the competition and the prize they could hope to win if their "idol" won.

Castrocaro winners, fans, and consumer culture are all thus connected in the process that brings fame to readers when they can sing but also, in any case, because they can buy. An interesting dramatization of this dynamic is in the photoromance "Caterina," published in 1965, which also more specifically addresses the question of the celebrity status of the ordinary girl. The 1950 cover of *Epoca* featured an ordinary girl who was a shop-assistant but also a fiancée. Caterina works in a department store and is the only child of a single mother. In the narrative, her confrontation with a music celebrity (singer Bruno Filippini) questions the passivity of consumers, sketching a new model of femininity defined by her taste in popular culture and her freedom of choice in sentimental matters. This gender model and the character are perfectly inserted into a context of media convergence: Caterina listens to the same music as the youth starring in then-contemporary Italian movie musicals in which famous singers like Adriano Celentano and Mina often portrayed themselves (Caterina likes Celentano and rock and roll). Also called *musicarelli*, these romantic comedies starred singers who played their music in television advertisement and shows.[59] Singers, products, and films appeared simultaneously in the pages of *BF*, which provided an entrance to a narrative world that extended across media platforms and was not necessarily accessed by fans in a strict chronological order. In fact, Caterina looks like Caterina Caselli, who participated in Castrocaro in 1963 (although eliminated) but was later discovered as a singer, in 1965 (when "Caterina" was published). In 1966, Caselli successfully performed at Sanremo the hit song "Nessuno mi può giudicare" ("Nobody Can Judge Me," originally written for Celentano), also the title of a movie musical that came out the same year, in which she plays a shop assistant in a department store.[60] The female protagonists in *Nobody Can Judge Me* and "Caterina" are close to each other insofar as they both embody a feminine type increasingly prominent in Italian society; not really an intertextual connection per se, as much as a symptom of a convergence culture in which successful narratives and fans' demands contributed to transmedia storytelling and the migration of the same characters across platforms. The Caterina type falls in love but does not necessarily want to get married; she keeps her hair short but not her mouth shut, she flirts but is not a coquette, and she "does not want to be judged" (interestingly, the song was initially intended for a male singer, but was a success as soon as it was sung by a young woman). Caterina's irreverence toward stereotypical models of femininity is shown in episode 19 when, while at work, she meets Filippini, who had won first place at Castrocaro in 1963 and participated for the second time in Sanremo just a few days before the episode was published. In fact, the cover of the same issue announces the publication of all the song lyrics from the competition, including Filippini's melodic tune "L'amore ha i tuoi occhi" (Love Has Your Eyes). Extensive space is given to Castrocaro news, while an ad promotes the sale of records with all the Sanremo songs to be mailed directly to readers' homes. The episode opens with an image of Filippini as he enters the department store where Caterina works and is welcomed by a crowd of *tifosi* (fans) wanting to buy his record and asking for his autograph. But while one of her colleagues, a blond girl named Susy who helps the singer get through the many requests, "is a masterpiece of initiative and vanity," according to a caption, Caterina "keeps it to herself and ignores him."[61] Prompted by the singer, she admits that she does not like "little motifs, affected and bland," but rather enjoys songs that are "truer," with grit, and that can be more entertaining (such as those of Celentano) (figure 1.3).[62] The scene provides readers with a model of femininity based on a woman who is confident in her social behavior and independent in her choices of consumption, but also proud of her condition as worker and not at all blinded by celebrity culture. In her conversation with Filippini, Caterina proudly states, "Work is work and must be taken seriously." She adds, "I cannot stand them [singers] when they act like divas, when they think like they are God Almighty. There are many people more important than them!"[63] Eventually, the episode concludes with a note on the impact that fans like Caterina can have on the industry. In fact, Filippini promises to write a new kind of song in the future, one that will be inspired by a girl like her.

FEMALE FANS AND THE POWERS THAT BE

The case of "Caterina" shows that media convergence (music + photoromance) refers to fans' active participation as much as it does product promotion across media platforms (for example, Filippini's record).[64] Many other photoromances do the same by featuring singers as side characters in stories about aspiring female singers or female

Figure 1.3

"Caterina," *Bolero Film* 19, no. 926 (1965): 12. Courtesy of Gruppo Mondadori.

fans, similarly, as I mentioned, to the Italian-style musical, also functioning as both sources of entertainment and means to promote the artists. From a gendered perspective, it could be argued that the link between media convergence and consumerism can provide some agency, as portrayed also in "Caterina," especially in a country like Italy where the government had a monopoly on television broadcasting and the Catholic Church exercised great control on the morality of both publishing and cinema. According to Sandra Falero, the idea of audience rights or "audience sovereignty," which is usually referred to only in the context of contemporary digital participatory culture, could be traced back and connected "to larger political ideas about autonomy and power."[65] In other words, we can frame the previously mentioned strategies of engagement, promoted by the magazine, to the Italian context, in which political freedom and industrialization allowed working-class women to gain economic power, on the one hand, while continuities in social and gender dynamics limited their actual emancipation, on the other. Consider for example how, in the Doxa survey, more than 90 percent of buyers were women, while at the same time, more than 80 percent of respondents identified the man in the family as the head of the household. In face of these limitations, a sample reading of *BF* issues from the late fifties to the late sixties shows that *BF* defied traditional gender roles and sustained the modernization of social and sexual conduct.

According to Maurizio Cesari, photoromances followed the directives of the Christian Democratic government, whose information agency was in charge of controlling the press.[66] In his view, the press was biased in defense of Catholic values and the politics of Christian Democracy, which especially addressed the new electorate of women: publishers sided with the government in repressing moral and social behaviors that could potentially destabilize its hegemony. Contrary to Cesari's conclusions, my reading of *BF* suggests a different kind of alignment that favored the public over the national government. I am not claiming here that *BF* served the feminist cause of radical movements; however, if Cesari had actually browsed through its pages, he would have probably caught the nuances that are missing in his categorical judgment. In a way, given its history, Arnoldo Mondadori and his company continued to ambiguously thrive (as they did under Fascism) in line with the government and in favor of profit. From the unwed mothers of the late 1940s to the single working girl of the 1960s, women in photoromances do not conform to the Christian Democratic model of femininity, of motherhood and companionship, because of the ways in which they handle their sexual desires and behaviors. The so-called sexual revolution, in fact, as Dagmar Herzog demonstrates in his history of sexuality in Europe, was ambiguously fueled both by social movement activism and by consumerist culture and medical-technological inventions (i.e., commercial products), such as the birth control pill.[67] In this sense, to highlight the magazine's progressive attitude with regard to sexuality does not necessarily mean to claim its radical political position, but rather to understand its modernity. Through the decades, columns became increasingly open to discussing female sexuality and to promoting, rather than holding back, the tide of modernization. It is fair to say that the individuals in charge of these columns acted as experts and were generally conservative in their understanding of gender roles. Indeed, female characters in the photoromances as much as the authors of weekly columns supported aspirations for pure love to be crowned by marriage, which was still the ideal accomplishment for women. However, photoromances, columns, and advertisements also promoted a model of woman whose sexuality was not denied but rather embraced as empowering: efficient at home, this ideal woman of *BF* also achieved her professional goals; she was desired by men and used beauty to her advantage.

These seeming contradictions are rather characteristic of a gender discourse developed in Western European Democracies in conjunction with processes of socioeconomic modernization and with the development of the neoliberal discourse of self-improvement. According to Angela McRobbie, the "double entanglement" of this "postfeminist" discourse consists in "the co-existence of neo-conservative values in relation to gender, sexuality and family life, with processes of liberalisation in regard to choice and diversity in domestic, sexual and kinship relations."[68] Between the late 1940s and the early 1960s, Italy's transformation from a predominantly rural country into a modern industrial one was grounded in the reestablishment of traditional gender roles in the family, as part of a return-to-order process felt to be necessary to solve the economic and social crisis caused by World War II. At the same time, socioeconomic modernization meant increased liberties for women, both in terms of economic power and sexuality. Rather than unequivocally supporting the project of nation-building, *BF* gives increasing space throughout these decades to characters like Caterina, a single girl, and introduces new columns that engage in conversations with readers about their sexual conduct and love aspirations, in conjunction with advertisements that pitched the essential products for the modern woman such as the seductive shampoo, the efficient washing machine, and the powerful bra. In this respect, the case of *BF* fits within a feminine culture that Hilary Radner has defined by the tendency "to evoke choice and the development of individual agency as the defining tenets of feminine identity."[69] This culture, also called by Robert Goldman "commodity feminism" in reference to American advertising of the 1970s and 1980s, can then be understood as a "set of practices and discourses" focused on (1) reclaiming girlishness "as a new ideal promising continual change and self-improvement a sign of individual agency" and (2) rewriting sexual availability of women as a form of personal empowerment.[70] While Radner argues that commodity feminism (which she calls "neo-feminism") constitutes the main discourse articulated in the girly films (chick flicks) of the last twenty years, I claim that *BF* reproduced a similar paradigm in its targeting of female audiences, however, complicated by the contradicting discourses of gender and sexuality, as explained in McRobbie's analysis, as well by the conflicting positions peculiar to Italian society, still fundamentally patriarchal despite the changes.

The magazine page is the space where such contradictions and conflicts are visualized in the relationship between texts and photos, as well as between different media sources. For example, in a page of a 1963 issue, a woman's letter in the column "Chi sono?" (Who Am I?), a photograph inserted in the letter, and a large advertisement at the bottom of the page speak of sexual availability as a form of empowerment that could be both beneficial and damaging to a woman (figure 1.4). The column "Who Am I?" is in itself an interesting object of study. Agony aunts were a typical presence in women's magazines where, as Milly Buonanno claims, "the commercial project and the educative project are admirably fused together."[71] In "Who Am I?," counseling is offered by "a bit wiser and more expert friend" named Enrico, who is at the same time conservative and progressive.[72] This coexistence of traditional gender norms and modern behaviors, which Buonanno does not consider, are in fact (as I previously explained) a defining feature of the pedagogical model offered in *Bolero Film*.[73] Enrico's answers vary from the appraisal of true love to statements of emancipation such as "your partner, not your boss" and, in response to a man's letter, "a woman is a free subject and complex as you [man] are, not an object for your whims."[74]

In the letter I consider, titled "Il solito onore" (The Usual Honor), a twenty-two-year-old Neapolitan woman writes that she is enraged with her boyfriend (who is twenty-three) because she is pregnant but he does not want to know anything about it.[75] If he wants to leave her, she writes that she would be ready to kill him in order to defend her honor. The cultural, social, and legal issue hinted at in the letter is the

CHI SONO?

IL SOLITO "ONORE"

La lettrice che si firma «Cuore disperato A. F. di Napoli» mi scrive: «Caro Enrico, sono una ragazza di 22 anni, fidanzata da sei mesi con un ragazzo di 23. Sono in stato interessante da due mesi e lui non ne vuole sapere niente. Se lui mi vuole lasciare io le levo da sopra la terra, io la ammazzo e mi difendo il mio onore perché dopo tutto io con lui ho imparato certe cose d'amore».

Che quel giovane sia un gentiluomo non direi proprio, così come credo che tu debba fare il possibile perché lui riconosca e affronti la sua responsabilità. Fin qui, ma non un passo più avanti, sono d'accordo con te.

Infatti, mi pare che all'onore potessi pensarci un pochino prima: non sei una bambina e inoltre mi pare che siate andati davvero in fretta. Lo amavi, d'accordo; ma sei proprio sicura che questo basti per giustificare ogni cosa? Quanto alla tua dichiarazione «io ucciderò», vorrei prenderla come un semplice sfogo, ma purtroppo tanti fatti di cronaca

Stefania Sandrelli e Alfio Puglisi nel nuovo film di Germi «Sedotta e abbandonata», ispirato all'«onore» come è inteso in Italia.

mi convincono che questo assurdo delitto d'onore è in certi ambienti ancora giustificato e anzi imposto.

Parlare del lato morale della cosa è assurdo, tanto è evidente l'abisso in cui piomba un assassino; in un Paese in cui giustamente è stata abolita la pena di morte anche per i cri-

mini più gravi, ecco che una corrente di opinione pubblica giustifica il delitto per «motivi d'onore». È una vergogna ed è proprio questa mentalità una delle cose che più danneggia il Sud negli occhi di tanta gente. Finora hai commesso uno sbaglio, ma se davvero volessi mettere in atto la tua minaccia diventeresti una criminale, una belva che si arroga il diritto di troncare una vita umana. Troverai, d'accordo, qualcuno che ti comprenderà e ti giustificherà, ma non avrai diritto né alla clemenza di Dio né a quella della gente perbene.

Pensaci finché sei in tempo, dato che finora hai dimostrato, a tue spese, di pensare assai poco.

RISPOSTE LAMPO

(MILENA S., IMPERIA). La tua relazione oltre che illecita è vergognosa. Esci subito da quell'immonda situazione, prima che tutta la tua famiglia ne rimanga coinvolta.

(MARIA B.I., FRANCIA). Sono d'accordo con te nel ritenere eccessiva la schiavitù in cui ti tengono i tuoi e trovo che almeno i tuoi fratelli potrebbero essere un po' più generosi.

(UNA RAGAZZA IN TORMENTO). Non bisogna esagerare con i pregiudizi: è assurdo pensare che tutti i meridionali picchino le mogli e le tengano segregate in casa. Ma siete ancora così giovani che avrete tempo di conoscervi meglio; e

anche i vostri genitori potranno modificare il loro parere.

(ESTER, MILANO). Non credo assolutamente che un ragazzo voglia prenderti in giro, solo che tu sei proprio una ragazzina. Se il suo sentimento è veramente forte non si sgegnerà anche se gli chiederai di attendere almeno un anno ancora.

(LETTRICE INNAMORATA). Il tuo pessimismo è eccessivo. Certo, una ragazza deve stare sempre un po' sulla difensiva, ma non partire col presupposto che tutti gli uomini cercano solo l'avventura.

(GIORGIA SOGNATRICE, TRIESTE). Come giudicare del valore di un quadro che non si è visto? A Trieste non mancano

antiquari e intenditori d'arte in grado di darti un giudizio competente.

(GIOVANNI L., PORTOSA). Spiacente per te, ma comprendo la tua insegnante che ti considera un ragazzino. L'infatuazione per la giovane professoressa non è cosa nuova; ma non è nuovo nemmeno il finale, triste e romantico, di un amore impossibile.

Se avete dubbi o perplessità su questioni che riguardano voi stessi o gli altri, rivolgete le vostre domande alla rubrica «Chi sono?», BOLERO FILM, via Bianca di Savoia 20, Milano. «Chi sono?» sarà per voi il salotto da amico un po' più saggio ed esperto al quale ci si può rivolgere fiduciosi per ottenere un consiglio o per un chiarimento.

LUCIANO PEDROCCHI Direttore responsabile - Redaz. Amministraz., Pubbl.: ARNOLDO MONDADORI EDITORE, v. Bianca di Savoia 20, Milano, telefoni 851141-851271 (8 linee) - Redaz. romana: v. Veneto 116 - tel. 444221 - ABBONAMENTI Italia annuo L. 2900; sem. L. 1500; Estero annuo L. 4800; sem. L. 2500. Per il cambio di indirizzo inviare L. 40 insieme alla fascetta recante il vecchio indirizzo. Numeri arretrati L. 100 - Inviare l'importo a: Arnoldo Mondadori Editore - v. Bianca di Savoia 20, Milano, tel. 6392241 servendosi preferibilmente del C. C. P. n. 3/34552. Gli abbonamenti si possono fare presso i ns. Agenti nelle principali città e nei seguenti negozi e Mondadori per voi e: Bologna, via D'Azeglio 14; Catania, via Etnea 271; Cosenza, corso Mazzini 156/e; Genova, Via Carducci 5r; Milano, Corso Vittorio Emanuele 34; Milano, via Vitruvio 2; Milano, viale Beatrice d'Este 31; Milano, Corso di Porta Vittoria 51; Napoli, via Guantai Nuovi 9; Padova, via Emanuele Filiberto 5; Pescara, C.so Umberto I 14; Pisa, viale Principe Amedeo 21/23; Roma, Lungotevere Prati 1; Roma, via Veneto 140; Roma, (CIM.P. Vetro) via XX Settembre 97/c; Torino, via Monte di Pietà 21; Trieste, via G. Galina 1; Venezia, calle Stagneri, San Marco 5207; Venezia (Mestre), via Carducci 48; Viareggio, (Galleria del Libro) viale Margherita 83. PUBBLICITA: Tariffa inserzioni in bianco e nero. L. 620 mm colonna. Manoscritti e foto non richiesti non si restituiscono - Tutti i diritti di proprietà artistica e letteraria sono riservati - Stampa: Officine Grafiche Arnoldo Mondadori, Verona - Pubblicazione registrata presso il Tribunale di Milano n. 3547 del 14-10-1955 - Spediz. in abbon. post. Gr. 2c.

CONTROLLO DIFFUSIONE

BOLERO FILM, September 22, 1963 - Bolero film is published weekly by Arnoldo Mondadori Editore, via Bianca di Savoia 20, Milan, Italy. Printed in Italy. Second class postage paid at New York, N.Y. Subscription $ 7.70 a year in USA and Canada. Year 17th, number 855. Corren. Argentino central B. Franqueo pagado. Concesion 4981.

nei vostri capelli un richiamo che dice...

...amami

Un fascino sottile, avvincente si sprigiona dai vostri capelli... sono morbidi, profumati, dolci da accarezzare... amami è lo shampoo che dà alla loro naturale bellezza quel risalto che incanta, che seduce. Delicato e completo nella sua formula alla lanolina, amami condiziona l'equilibrio fisiologico dei vostri capelli, rendendoli docili, pronti alla piega.

amami SHAMPOO

shampoo amami per essere amata

Figure 1.4

Bolero Film 17, no. 855 (1963): 4. Courtesy of Gruppo Mondadori.

so-called *delitto d'onore* (honor killing), protected under the Italian law, which gave only a light punishment to a man who killed his wife (daughter or sister) because he discovered her "illegittima relazione carnale" (illegitimate sexual relations).[76] The delitto d'onore is also the center of the film comedy *Divorzio all'italiana* (Divorce Italian Style, dir. Pietro Germi, 1962) as a symptom of backwardness and the object of satire.[77] In the film, the news about a woman who killed her husband because of his unfaithfulness inspires the protagonist to do the same with his wife; the bitter irony lies in the fact that the Italian law understood the murderer exclusively as masculine and did not provide for the case in which the killer was a woman. A few years after the previously mentioned letter was published in *BF*, another movie titled *La ragazza con la pistola* (The Girl with the Pistol, dir. Mario Monicelli, 1968) would tell the same story of a woman wishing to kill the man who took her virginity. Also a comedy, *The Girl with the Pistol* interprets the social reality by showing the contrast between the anachronism of honor and the woman's emancipated character.

Fictional representations in comedies, Italian style, are satirical expressions of Italian society that aim at critically unpacking its anachronisms. While characters in these films are verisimilar, in their comedic form their stories narrowly convey a masculine perspective on issues of female sexual conduct.[78] Like *Divorce Italian Style* and *The Girl with the Pistol*, the letter in "The Usual Honor" engages with the same topic of honor in a serious tone, which is not only a matter of generic conventions. This is better explained by considering how the experience of the Neapolitan woman and reader of *BF* was not a unique case, not only privately but also in public debate. In 1959, Gabriella Parca, a writer for *Sogno* and *Bolero Film* who was also in charge of a letter column in other photoromance magazines, *Luna Park* (Carnival) and *Polvere di stelle* (Star Powder), edited a selection of women's letters from a sample of eight thousand that she received throughout her career, publishing them in the volume *Le italiane si confessano* (Italian Women Confess, [1959] 1966). As testimony to the pervasive relevance of honor in the everyday lives of Italian women, a distinct section in this collection is dedicated to the "prova d'amore" (love proof), meaning, a man's request to have premarital sex. In the letters, the man usually abandons the woman after she has agreed to his request and had sex with him, as in "The Usual Honor." The typical double standard to which women were subjected (premarital relations as both a duty and a sin) makes the particular interpretation of this situation (i.e., the woman being the subject rather than the object of the honor killing) not a laughable cliché but a desperate gesture.

In his answer to the letter published in "Who Am I?," Enrico begins regressively by blaming the woman for her carelessness; he argues that she should have thought about her honor earlier. Then, acting as the "wiser friend" Enrico addresses the question of revenge and argues that honor is a symptom of an old and anachronistic way of thinking, which damages the image of Southern Italy. His answer sides with the educational message at the core of Divorce Italian Style and of *Sedotta e abbandonata* (Seduced and Abandoned, 1964), also directed by Germi and a sort of sequel to the first film, in its critique of Southern Italian culture and plot centering on a premarital relationship not *honored* by marriage. A still from *Seduced and Abandoned* is printed below Enrico's answer in the magazine as an illustration, with a caption that states how the film was "ispirato all 'onore,' come inteso in Italia" (inspired by "honor," as it is understood in Italy). *Seduced and Abandoned* had not been released yet when the letter was published by *BF*; thus, on the one hand, one may wonder whether the photo and perhaps even the letter are only a stunt to advertise the movie. On the other hand, these two texts together make visible the intertextual structure of the magazine's page, completed by the advertisement printed at its bottom. In the ad, the young actress promoting a beauty product vaguely resembles Stefania Sandrelli, starring in both of Germi's films. Shot as she leans against the bed with her shoulders uncovered, with the blurred image of a man (completely dressed in a suit) behind her, this photo lures readers with the glamour of the same behavior that "Who Am I?" scolds and *Seduced and Abandoned* turns into comedy. Seduction is visually expressed as well as linguistically conveyed in the slogan that says "in your hair, a call that says . . . love me [amami]."[79] "Amami," the name of the shampoo promoted in the ad, is the desired tool of desire that will allow the woman to get the man she is supposed to reject, according to patriarchal rules, as in a famous scene in *The Girl with the Pistol*, when the female protagonist has finally convinced the man with whom she is temporarily sharing the apartment to make a move, only to violently reject him and say, in her defense: "a man must try, a woman must defend herself."

By the late 1960s, right around the time when *BF* was renamed *Bolero Teletutto*, contradictions between the traditional ideal of honor and the modern imperative of choice are eventually smoothed to more openly support women's sexual emancipation against legal and social backwardness.[80] In the 1968 photoromance "Article 560 Concubinage," for example, cohabitation is presented in a positive light, despite being forbidden by law, and having a premarital relationship is also portrayed as a fair option. In a dialogue between a female character who had sexual experiences before the marriage (with a man other than her husband) and her mother, the latter goes as far as to vindicate women's rights to have pleasure and to attack men for their customary abuse of power. "Be sure that when he was in Germany he had his adventures," the mother says to her (the man in question was an emigrant in Germany when the "illegitimate" sexual encounter happened). "And so? Men are allowed anything: they can do their business and poor women must stay subjugated to wait that they decide *to do what's right!*"[81] Most relevantly, the fictional representation of sexual emancipation finds resonance in readers' experiences, for example, in the "true stories" told by Franca Antonini but "from the live voice of a reader" and published about two years earlier.[82] In one of these stories, titled "Frigid by Mistake," Antonini describes a woman who overcame her sexual problems by openly discussing them with her husband; while another, titled "The True Frigid," debates the impact of past experiences, education, and repression of female sexuality. Antonini does not come across as feminist in her interpretations of readers' stories, and her perspective on their experiences is quite conservative (she at some point sings the praises of virginity). At the same time, the column does acknowledge the rights of women to a satisfying sexual relationship (although still within marriage) and the uniqueness of female sexual desire at a time when frigidity was a common stigma. Recognizing this right, the "true stories" find correspondence in a product advertised on another page in the same issue: a contraceptive system, based on a natural method and approved by the Catholic Church, which will allow women to have children only when they want them, "to safeguard the happiness of your married life."[83] In sum, the various components of the magazine (photoromances, columns, and advertisements) converge to construct an ambivalent but consistent picture of Italian women.

In conclusion, while the actual degree of readers' participation in the making of the magazine is hard to measure, my analysis shows that through links between texts within the issues and by means of connections across media platforms, *BF* casts their readers as subjects of representation as much as objects of study. Whether the true stories told in the series in fact really happened is not possible for us to say with certainty, the same way that readers' letters could be (and probably were) edited before being published in "Who Am I?" What is more relevant here is that these columns make a point about the value of such contributions, about the fact that their choices and demands mattered (especially those of women). Further, these columns cannot be understood apart from the photoromances when drawing some conclusions with regard to the engagement of the latter with their audiences. To consider photoromances as tools of domination and indoctrination not only means to dismiss the evident involvement of readers as fans, but also to overlook the actual dynamic structure of the magazine, in which each tool of communication intertexts with the other. Ultimately, the success of *BF* was determined not only by how much readers liked the stories and the characters of photoromances, how photography could attract their attention, and how writing could capture their imagination. The appeal of photoromances also lay in their structure of media franchise, and as such they need to be studied in order to understand their cultural and social relevance.

2 MORE THAN ROMANCES

"I am a fotonovel, where all media converge, the newsiest novelty since the novel, and the comeliest since the comix. I speak all tongues and can tell all tales—in color!"[1] These words are placed at the opening of *Grease*, the first of a series of paperback-sized photoromances based on Hollywood films and printed on glossy paper in a book format. Published in 1978 by Herb Stewart and his business partner Laszlo Papas of Fotonovel Publications, *Grease* employs for the first time in history the term *convergence* in reference to the photoromance. Despite Stewart's claim in an interview with the *Washington Post*, however, it is not the first time that a film was used as a source for these adult comics.[2] A small Italian publisher named Victory had already issued a fotonovel titled "La Valle del Destino" (The Valley of Destiny) in 1952, from Tay Garnett's 1945 film *The Valley of Decision* with Greer Garson and Gregory Peck.[3] After Victory's first attempt, other obscure Italian companies quickly proliferated in the business of cineromanzi or cinefotoromanzi (from now on, cineromances), that is, weekly or monthly publications of photoromanced versions of films, both new releases and classics. Two main trends developed within the same market. The first was quality publications with bright, colorful covers that feature both frame enlargements and film stills, often in large format, intended to appeal to movie fans (figure 2.1). And the second was pocket-sized booklets of up to eighty pages, filled with hundreds of poorly printed and at times even blurred images, organized in regular grids and covered by substantial amounts of text, both dialogues and captions. Much in the same manner as exploitation cinema, in this cheaper format the cineromances milked the growing popularity of melodramas and pulp romances. Both familiar and obscure film titles appear in the list of printed issues, featuring recognizable taglines such as "In the

Figure 2.1

Cover of "Duello al sole" (Duel in the Sun), *Cineromanzo per tutti*, no. 8 (1954). Based on the film by the same title, dir. King Vidor (1947).

Vortex of Sin," "Deadly Seduction," "Fatal Meeting," "The World Blames Women," "Love That Chains Us," and so on and so forth (figure 2.2).[4] Most of these small Italian publishers had franchises in France, where the same titles and the exact same photo-textual narratives were published, usually, within a few years (figure 2.3).[5] By the end of the fifties, the genre had already disappeared in Italy, while it continued to thrive in France for a few more years, until the mid-1960s.

Stewart and Papas thus did not really invent a new genre but rather resurrected and refashioned an old one according to the tastes of American film buffs and comics lovers. Cineromances are not a completely new genre either, and instead perfect previous offerings in the realm of fan magazines. Interviewed for the *Washington Post*'s article about Stewart and Papas's venture, Professor Jack Nachbar of Bowling Green University observes, "Movies and prints have been feeding off each other ever since comic strips and movies developed simultaneously at the end of the 1890s." Before the emergence of the Italian cineromance, the U.S. magazine *Photoplay* (founded in Chicago in 1911) provided readers with the plot of one or more films, including some dialogues, and illustrated by still frames of significant scenes and stars. In France, there are examples of film novelization since the 1910s, which Baetens groups into three different formats: illustrated screenplays; illustrated or non-illustrated short story novelizations; and experimental filmic storytelling (figure 2.4).[6] In Italy, the so-called *cinenovella* (film-novel) is introduced in the 1920s as a weekly or monthly issue complementary to fan magazines and other publicity materials such as *fotobuste* (medium-format publicity stills furnished with a minimal amount of writing) and posters, at the time of the arrival of the rotogravure in Europe from the United States, which allowed publishers to produce magazines at lower cost with many photographs of higher quality.[7] However, when the cineromance was born in Italy in the postwar period, it emerged only formally from the tradition of film novelization, and was developed as a new niche market managed by publishers who did not previously invest in the cinenovella genre. In France, where the genre boomed only after the arrival of Italian imports, the established film-novel magazines such as *Mon Film* (My Film) shifted to the new formula and began producing their own photo-stories.[8]

At the core, all of these examples of illustrated film novelization serve similar purposes, as explained by Raffaele De Berti: to advertise films (inviting readers to movie theatres); to prolong the film-viewing experience (providing photographs of stars and reminders of key scenes); and even to substitute for it, in places where movie theatres

Figure 2.2

Cover of "Nel gorgo del peccato" (In the Vortex of Sin), *I vostri film romanzo* 1, no. 10 (1954). Based on the film by the same title, dir. Vittorio Cottafavi (1954).

Figure 2.3
Cover of "La femme aux deux visages" (The Two-Faced Woman), *Les films du coeur* 1, no. 7 (1959). Based on the film *L'angelo bianco* (The White Angel), dir. Raffaello Matarazzo (1955).

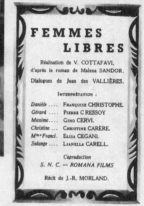

FEMMES LIBRES

Réalisation de V. COTTAFAVI,
d'après le roman de Malena SANDOR.

Dialogues de Jean des VALLIÈRES.

INTERPRÉTATION :

Danièle .... FRANÇOISE CHRISTOPHE.
Gérard .... PIERRE CRESSOY
Maxime.... GINO CERVI.
Christine ... CHRISTINE CARÈRE.
Mme Franci. ELISA CEGANI.
Solange .... LIANELLA CARELL.

Coproduction
S. N. C. — ROMANA FILMS

Récit de J.-R. MORLAND.

FEMMES LIBRES

DANIÈLE FRANCI était jeune encore, mais un destin implacable, une nature passionnée, entière, facilement égarée par l'appel du bonheur, avaient ruiné sa vie. De quel prix allait-elle payer ses erreurs ? Elle était maintenant entre les murs d'une prison. Atterrée, elle évoquait son passé, pourtant proche, mais où il lui semblait voir évoluer une autre Danièle, à jamais perdue...

— Je suis un être accablé, fini, murmurait Danièle. Et cependant le temps n'est pas si loin où je me sentais jeune, enthousiaste, prête à lutter, décidée à défendre ma liberté à tout prix...

Danièle avait toujours vécu à Rome, dans l'intérieur bourgeois, aimable, confortable, de ses parents, lorsqu'elle se fiança à l'un de ses camarades de travail, Fernand. La famille Franci considérait ce mariage avec plaisir. Fernand était un jeune ingénieur très capable, dont la situation était déjà brillante. M. Franci, très traditionaliste, parfois même sévère, tentait d'élever de façon assez rigoureuse ses deux filles, Danièle et sa sœur plus jeune, Christine. Danièle, qui poursuivait ses études d'architecte, opposait aux vues de son père ses opinions de jeune fille moderne, équilibrée, loyale, mais éprise de liberté. Des scènes assez vives, qui désolaient la douce Mme Franci, dressaient souvent Danièle contre son père.

Aussi M. Franci était-il désireux d'unir le plus rapidement possible Danièle à Fernand. Il pensait qu'un mariage raisonnable, heureux, assagirait l'indépendante Danièle.

Précisément, lors de la petite fête de famille qui célébra l'obtention de son diplôme d'architecte, Danièle arriva chez ses parents avec un groupe d'amis fort aimables, mais qui ne correspondaient certes point à l'idéal des Franci. Il y avait Serge, le peintre totalement inconnu et plein d'avenir ; et Solange, sa femme et son modèle qui, cependant, trouvait moyen de mener de front ses obligations ménagères et conjugales et sa carrière d'écrivain débutant. Il y avait le fantaisiste Michel qui, après avoir tâté de plusieurs métiers artistiques, s'était jeté, pour gagner la vie de son ménage, dans la fabrication des parapluies ; il en faisait de très jolis, de couleurs vives, car les parapluies mornes attristaient sa femme, la rieuse Anne-Marie. Cette petite équipe joyeuse et bohème stupéfiait M. Franci. Il préférait évidemment Fernand qui, lui, du moins, était sérieux.

M. et Mme Franci et leurs amis — avocats, notaires, hauts fonctionnaires et leurs épouses — entourèrent affectueusement Danièle et la félicitèrent à la fois pour ses succès d'architecte et ses fiançailles.

— Et quand allez-vous marier ces jeunes gens ? s'enquit aimablement Mme Angeli, épouse d'un avocat fameux en désignant Danièle et Fernand.

— Le plus vite possible ! affirma avec empressement M. Franci.

Dès le surlendemain, une légère dispute éclata entre les fiancés. Ce jour était celui du vernissage de la première exposition de Serge. Danièle tenait absolument à être auprès de ses amis Serge et Solange en des circonstances aussi importantes pour la carrière du peintre. Fernand déclara qu'il ne pourrait accompagner Danièle : il jugeait indispensable d'assister à une commission des Travaux Publics. Contrariée, dépitée, Danièle se rendit seule à la galerie. Elle y retrouva, auprès de Serge et de Solange, le fidèle Michel accompagné d'Anne-Marie. Soudain, Danièle avisa, à la place d'honneur sur la cimaise, le portrait que Serge avait fait d'elle. Danièle aimait beaucoup cette toile, d'une facture très hardie, mais elle n'eut pas souhaité la voir livrée au public. Serge avait dit à Danièle :

— Je te peins comme je te vois !

Or Serge ne voyait que trop bien Danièle : très différente de la jeune fille encore effacée, indécise, que Danièle était le plus souvent, la femme du portrait rayonnait d'ardeur, d'audace et même d'avidité. Danièle pensait que cette toile imprévue et fort belle révélait trop nettement sa nature secrète.

— Si j'avais su, sourit Danièle en contemplant son portrait, je ne serais pas venue aujourd'hui !

— Plains-toi donc ! bouffonna Serge. Tu as sous les yeux la vraie Danièle, la Danièle inconnue qui a ouvert ses ailes, bien décidée à surmonter tous les obstacles qui se dresseront entre elle et le bonheur !

Mais Serge, appelé par un groupe de visiteurs, s'éloigna avec sa femme. De leur côté, Michel et Anne-Marie conversaient activement avec des journalistes auxquels ils faisaient l'éloge de Serge. Danièle se trouvait seule devant la Danièle du portrait. Et, soudain, elle sursauta en percevant une présence auprès d'elle : un jeune homme très beau, à l'expression attentive et un peu ironique, considérait alternativement la jeune fille et le portrait. Danièle se sentit gênée. Et, parce qu'elle était gênée, elle arbora un air désinvolte qui fit sourire franchement le jeune homme.

— Vous connaissez l'auteur de ces toiles ? demanda l'inconnu.

— Très bien, répliqua fermement Danièle. C'est un excellent et charmant camarade.

— Il semble très bien vous connaître aussi, repartit le jeune homme.

— Vous croyez que je suis ainsi ? s'écria Danièle.

L'inconnu ne répondit pas. Il n'avait pas renoncé à son sourire désabusé et charmant. Danièle se demanda où elle avait déjà vu ce visage à la fois séduisant et inquiétant.

— Vous peignez, vous aussi ? reprit le jeune homme.

— Euh, oui, à ma façon. Je suis architecte.

— Je n'ai pas vu les autres salles, reprit l'inconnu. Voudriez-vous avoir la bonté de m'accompagner ? J'avoue que c'est un genre de peinture un peu agressif pour une personne seule !

Médusée, intéressée aussi, Danièle accompagna le jeune homme dans sa visite. Ils contemplèrent quelques toiles, puis Danièle interrogea à son tour :

— Et vous ? Vous vous intéressez à la peinture ?

— Pour ne rien vous cacher, sourit le jeune homme, j'avais rendez-vous au bar d'en face. Comme je suis arrivé affreusement en retard, il n'y avait plus personne. Alors, je suis entré ici...

— Pour tuer le temps ! conclut Danièle.

Aussitôt elle constata que l'inconnu tuait le temps, non pas en examinant les toiles de Serge, mais en contemplant Danièle avec attention. La beauté de Danièle attirait souvent les regards. Mais cette fois la jeune fille, bien qu'elle fût habituée à lire l'admiration dans les yeux des hommes, se sentait bizarrement troublée.

— Je pense à vous ! dit le jeune homme sans ambages. Je me demande qui vous êtes, ce que vous souhaitez...

— Ne cherchez pas trop ! trancha Danièle, prudemment. Je ne suis qu'une petite bourgeoise qui a son diplôme d'architecte et qui va bientôt se marier. Oui, je suis fiancée à un collègue de travail, un ingénieur...

— Ah ! sourit l'inconnu. Et c'est sérieux ?

— Je me demande qui vous êtes, ce que vous souhaitez ! dit Gérard à Danièle.

were not available or among viewers who did not have the financial means to pay for tickets.[9] In the context of 1950s Italy, the introduction of subscriptions in addition to sales at the newsstands meant a more capillary distribution. In some rural areas in Southern Italy, according to Italian director and cineromances collector Gianni Amelio, "there was no cinema, let alone a newsstand," but thanks to home delivery, his mother (and he) could still get copies of cineromances, even in the remote Calabrian village of San Pietro Magisano.[10] However, while for De Berti these are simply features of the mode of production, I agree with Leonardo Quaresima that they can also be considered clues to how film novelizations had functional value for their audiences—in responding to and satisfying their demands and interpreting their "voices."[11]

At the crossroads of national culture and foreign appropriation, cineromances (like fotonovels) epitomize the commercial nature of cinema and the role of film viewers as consumers. Hundreds of titles from small-budget Italian melodramas to Hollywood blockbusters and *auteur* films are published per year. As Giuliana Muscio highlights, these magazines eliminate the gap between "high and low, between independent and major."[12] Or, in the words of De Berti, film novelization is "a typical phenomenon of modern industrial culture," a product of technological innovation and accessory to the development of mass consumption.[13] However, neither Muscio nor De Berti further investigates the role that consumers played as active elements of the dynamics of production and distribution of cineromances.[14] Also, neither is interested in studying how the gendering of the same audiences is constitutive of their business (and in this sense, fotonovels are different from cineromances, as I explain later). Muscio sustains that fan magazines stimulate film consumption but also foster a "desire for cinema, for stars, for stories and images."[15] In my view, to unpack the dynamics of such "desire," that is, of the bond that ties female fans to the cineromance industry, also means to understand how these publications innovate the publishing market *as* (not despite being) feminine readings, in the wake of photoromances' success.[16]

Cineromances look like photoromances (and often were referred to as such) not only in their style, but also in their approach to fanship and in the way they reflect a development of the Italian media system toward active consumption across media

---

Figure 2.4

Example of illustrated short story novelization: "Femmes libres" (Free Women), *Mon Film*, no. 482 (1955). Based on *Una donna libera* (A Free Woman), dir. Vittorio Cottafavi (1954).

platforms; in this sense, the film-novel is a precursor to the cineromance since it also stimulates viewers to read and readers to watch. Furthermore, when talking about cineromances we can play with Jenkins's idea of transmedia storytelling since printed magazines tell stories that branch from films and yet are not exactly the same (rather, they are unique extensions); they are meant to be autonomous points of entry in the narrative world (one can read the cineromance without having watched the film, and vice versa).[17] Using the term *transmedia storytelling* rather than *adaptation* highlights the open flow between narratives (not their codependence) and often their concurrent production, as when cineromances are issued before or in conjunction with the film's release. The narrative world in which printed illustrated stories and films coexist does not place them in competition or in succession, and each magazine opens up further possibilities for consumption, for example by means of previews of other films and magazine issues. Also, the construction of narrative worlds is fundamentally tied to individuals, that is, to movie stars who migrate from one medium to another, from the film to the cineromance, and from the cineromance to the magazine columns (and let's not forget that often magazines published lyrics of the main songs in a film's soundtrack, complete with all the information about the record label that produced them, thus creating further bridges with another industry). As I show in this chapter, these strategies of media convergence are gendered to maximize the products' success and the effects are useful to further deepen our understanding of female fanship of this period. In particular, the relationship between a star's images across platforms and her role as gender model for an increasingly modern female audience will be at the core of this chapter's analysis.[18]

At the center of "the place where all media converge," readers as fans build affective relationships to magazines, stories, and stars. These can be expressed in their loyalty as customers, and by the practices of religiously collecting each issue (like Amelio's mother) or cutting out photographs (several secondhand cineromances that I collected for this project show evidence of this habit). Movies are turned into objects that fans can *use* to remember a particular scene or stare in awe at a star's close-up, or sing their new favorite song, or read a film's dialogue, reproduced often verbatim from the script in the balloons. Considering the relevance of participatory culture to editorial strategies, stylistic differences between series cineromances can thus be interpreted in continuity with the same practices of engaging readers across media platforms. While I will not analyze fotonovels in depth in this chapter, a few points can be made to exemplify how the format can be molded according to consumers. *Grease* experiments with uneven grids and is "littered with BOOM! TINKLE! sound effects" to appeal to an audience who appreciates the comic art (figure 2.5).[19] In contrast, cineromances usually have regular layouts filled with a much more extensive use of dialogue and captions, a grid that will look familiar to any reader of photoromances (figure 2.6). Also, on the one hand, titles such as *Grease*, *The Invasion of the Body Snatchers*, and *Close Encounters of the Third Kind* suggest that the ideal buyer of fotonovels is not attached to a particular genre (or explicitly feminine labeled film genres such as melodrama), but rather is interested in movies with potential to attract a cult following. The same type of readers also would not mind that only a few titles could be published per year, due to the cost of copyrights and printing. On the other hand, cineromances are produced in high numbers and target a growing mass audience of female readers (and movie-goers) whose hunger for stories must be fed at a much faster pace (and it is already, thanks to photoromances).

Given the variety of magazines available on the market, it is important to not generalize the expectations of cineromance readers, to evade the trap of characterizing female readers according to traditional definitions of femininity. In this light, I disagree with Lucia Cardone's overarching conclusion that in "becoming cineromances, films absorb the dark tones of the feuilleton, because they inherit the same [female] audience, passionate and demanding."[20] In my view, while Cardone correctly highlights the importance of reception in the production process, she homogenizes readers on the basis of the particular case that she is studying, that is, Victory's "Catene amare" (Bitter Chains), which "photoromances" Raffaello Matarazzo's *L'intrusa* (The Intruder, 1955) in a large format of *I vostri film romanzo* (Your Romance Films).[21] "Catene amare" takes the appearance of a feuilleton because of the marketing goals of its publisher, I argue, not because of an established taste of a universal readership of cineromances. This is not a minor detail if we want to undertake a critical study of cineromances that ultimately sheds light on the role they played in Italian culture: (1) as national productions open to a transnational market; and (2) as commercial extensions engaging and exploiting audiences according to their tastes. In an op-ed on the first page of the 1954 issue "Le infedeli" (The Unfaithfuls), based on the 1953 comedy directed by Steno, the editor of *Cineromanzo per tutti* (Everybody's Cineromance) Adelaide Marzullo explicitly addresses preconceived notions about readers' expectations, the same ones that Cardone's analysis takes for granted.[22] Whether to openly challenge the dominant

Figure 2.5

Grease (Los Angeles: Fotonovel Publications, 1978).

LES EGOÏSTES

Avec:

Lucia Bosé

Alberto Closas

Bruna Corra

Carlos Casaravilla

Alicia Romay

Otello Toso

Mise en scène de
JUAN ANTONIO BARDENY

LE CRÉPUSCULE COMMENÇAIT À ENVAHIR LA CAMPAGNE AUTOUR DE MADRID. ↝ LES CHAUVE-SOURIS TRAÇAIENT LEURS PREMIERS VOLS NOCTURNES QUI SEMBLAIENT SANS BUT ET LE SILENCE ÉTAIT TOTAL. ↝
RIEN NE DÉNOTAIT LE VOISINAGE D'UNE GRANDE VILLE, ET SANS LES CHAMPS CULTIVÉS, ON AURAIT PU SE CROIRE DANS UNE RÉGION ABSOLUMENT DÉSERTE OÙ NE RÉGNAIENT QUE LE SILENCE ET LES CHAUVE-SOURIS. BRUSQUEMENT UN FORT CRISSEMENT DE FREINS VINT ROMPRE CE SILENCE, ET UNE AUTOMOBILE S'ARRÊTA.

LA FEMME QUI ÉTAIT AU VOLANT TOURNA LA TÊTE VERS L'ARRIÈRE. ↝ L'ÉTRANGE PÂLEUR DE SON VISAGE LA RENDAIT PLUS BELLE ENCORE.

IL Y AVAIT UN HOMME À SON CÔTÉ DONT LE VISAGE ÉTAIT AUSSI PÂLE QUE LE SIEN. ↝ CETTE PÂLEUR ACCENTUAIT LES PROFONDES RIDES CREUSÉES SUR SON FRONT.

SANS UN MOT, COMME OBÉISSANT À UN MÊME APPEL, ILS DESCENDIRENT DE LA VOITURE NOIRE. ↝ ET CE FUT L'HOMME QUI COURUT LE PREMIER VERS... UNE FORME ALLONGÉE SUR LE TERRAIN.

C'ÉTAIT UN ÊTRE HUMAIN QUI GISAIT À CÔTÉ D'UNE BICYCLETTE TORDUE.

1

Figure 2.6

"Les Égoïstes" (The Egotists), *Hebdo Roman* 2, no. 51 (1957): 1. Based on *Death of a Cyclist* (dir. Juan Antonio Bardem, 1955).

model of photoromance readers or to attempt to maximize the magazine's profits, Marzullo announces that customers requested in their letters that more titles "other than romances" be selected for publication. In response, she claims, *Cineromanzo per tutti* promises to fulfill these requests and to continue to offer "photoromances of mixed genres" whose only constant feature will be the presence of "interpreti eccezionali" (exceptional movie stars). In support of this position, the article mentions other films "che non sono certo d'amore" (that are not really love stories) and have already been published by Edizioni Lanterna Magica: "Riso amaro" (Bitter Rice), "Don Camillo," and "Pane amore e fantasia (Bread, Love, and Dreams)."[23] To be fair, *Cineromanzo per tutti* and *Cineromanzo gigante* (Giant Cineromance) also publish numerous romantic plots and even turn films of a different genre into romances—for example, Alberto Lattuada's *Il bandito* (The Bandit, 1946), printed with the title "Amore proibito" (Forbidden Love).[24] However, the point here is not to deny that love relationships are a lucrative source of narrative materials for Lanterna Magica or to reject that many of its readers are indeed into romances. The question is that cineromances are *not only* (and not necessarily) about romances, both from the business point of view and from that of scholarship: their scope in content depends on their target audience and their place in Italian and global media cultures varies according to editorial strategies.[25]

A distant reading of magazines' formats and titles could only get us a snapshot of an idiosyncratic business for a seemingly multifaced readership. In order to rigorously address the question of fanship, I argue that we must analyze in depth how specific series engaged readers' participation and how each magazine exploited migrating stars and stardom. In this light, the rest of this chapter will focus on Edizioni Lanterna Magica and its *Cineromanzo per tutti* (*Cpt*) and *Cineromanzo gigante* (*Cg*) as media apparatuses of Italian entrepreneur Dino De Laurentiis. Building on the connection with the film industry, Lanterna Magica's publications privileged star-driven movies across the blockbuster/art boundaries, from *Senso* (literally "Sensation," but known in the United States by its original Italian title; dir. Luchino Visconti, 1954) with Alida Valli and Farley Granger to *From Here to Eternity* (dir. Fred Zinnemann, 1953) with Burt Lancaster and Debora Kerr, and provided readers with unique prints of still photographs from the set, both in medium and large sizes (figure 2.7).

De Laurentiis, who worked as agent for Lux throughout the 1950s on films such as *Riso Amaro* (Bitter Rice, dir. Giuseppe De Santis, 1949), was a typical figure in the context of the Italian film industry of the period, hired on a film-by-film basis

Figure 2.7
Cover of "Senso," *Cineromanzo gigante*, no. 5 (1955).

and responsible for securing private and public financing as well as finding artists, in sum, to "package the unit."[26] As his career developed, his ambitions to become an international producer on the Hollywood model are evident, from the founding of the Ponti-De Laurentiis Cinematografica with its own production studios, in partnership with another Lux manager, Carlo Ponti; to his first big-budget movie *Ulisse* (Ulysses, dir. Mario Camerini, 1954) starring Kirk Douglas and Silvana Mangano; and eventually with the building of "Dinocittà" in 1959, at the same time in which Ponti sold him his part of the company.[27] In addition to many Hollywood titles, *Cg* and *Cpt* published many films produced by De Laurentiis for Lux or by the Ponti-De Laurentiis Cinematografica.[28] "Ulysses" is the first issue of *Cg* and came out on October 1, 1954, a few days before the film itself was released in Italy, on October 6.[29] The announcement about the imminent publication of "Ulysses" appears in "Forbidden Love" together with an ad for *Mambo*, just one month after it was screened for the first time and only three months before the cineromance "Mambo" appeared in *Cg*.[30] The first issue of *Cpt* instead is "Anna," which also stars Mangano and includes the lyrics of "El Negro Zumbon" (also known as "Anna") and "T'ho voluto bene" (I Loved You Very Much), the two songs in the film's soundtrack produced by Edizioni Musicali R.P.D. (Radiofilmmusica Ponti-De Laurentiis).[31] Further, an announcement on last page of the magazines brand all Ponti-De Laurentiis films for their indisputable quality: "There are SUCCESSFUL STARS, then there are SUCCESSFUL DIRECTORS, and therefore there are Production Companies whose success is guaranteed by the experience and excellence of its products. In Italy, this is the brand that labels all successful films PONTI-DE LAURENTIIS."[32]

From the point of view of media convergence, *Cpt* and *Cg* serve the purpose of creating connections with the other products of the De Laurentiis' media franchise. What makes them so interesting with respect to fanship is how they promote celebrity culture. In particular De Laurentiis' main actress and wife, Silvana Mangano, is a constant presence in the pages of the magazines, both in narratives and in columns. Her star persona, I argue, fosters her husband's aspirations as media mogul. Although movie stars in Italy (and in Europe) enjoy the freedom of single film engagements, De Laurentiis' personal ties with Mangano make space for an ambiguous long-term business relationship (longer than a typical five-year Hollywood contract), one that scholars have studied only to a limited degree, even though it was not an exception among Italian producers (as fictionally narrated in Antonioni's film *La signora senza camelie* [The Lady without Camelias]).[33] In my view, *Cpt* and *Cg* (and thus De Laurentiis) uniquely follow—in the Italian context—the Hollywood practice of exploiting publicity to match on- and off-screen images of a star, in this case Mangano, to create a persona that both fits the moral code of the industry (and in the Italian case, of society) and can please the star's fans. Moreover, similar to photoromances, *Cpt* and *Cg* are marked as feminine on the basis of columns and advertisements that fill their pages: from "How You Can Become a Star" to "The Workshop of Ideas" and "The Housewife's Notebook," alongside commercials for beauty products, household necessities, and appliances. In this manner, potential readers of *Cpt* and *Cg* are indirectly represented as women in need of advice on how to be beautiful, fashionable, and efficient inside but also outside the home.[34] Groomed by the agony aunt (aka advice columnist) and supported in her dream to make it in the film industry, this preferred reader has a passion for music and film entertainment, but also hopes to win the dowry offered as a prize to Lanterna Magica's loyal customers. In this light, the still photographs and frame enlargements that compose the cineromances do not just retell a story, they also showcase the attitudes, poses, and expressions of a female star whom the same feminine reader can aspire to imitate. By promoting actresses like Mangano as successful both at home and in their profession, beautiful but also caring, attractive, and even provocative as much as lovable and modest, I claim that *Cpt* and *Cg* "contributed to the slow and difficult redefinition of women's roles in Italy" by reconciling heteronormative gender models with the interconnected processes of modernization and liberalization of sexuality going on throughout Western Europe.[35]

ITALIAN STARDOM AND ITS DISCONTENTS

The physical appeal of Italian stars of the 1950s has been much discussed as well as exploited in both genre and art films, nationally and abroad. In *Stardom Italian Style*, Marcia Landy writes that beauty pageant contestants and film stars such as Gina Lollobrigida and Sophia Loren "were the vital signs of the coming 'restoration' of the erotic female Italian body to the body of film."[36] These bodies with "proper measurements," Mary Wood highlights, were also the source of contradiction within film narratives that on one hand used them as signs of prosperity and, on the other, blamed them (and punished them) as morally corrupted.[37] Stephen Gundle maintains that showing their bodies reduced Italian actresses to the lower category of "starlets," for they would lose the aura of mystery and discretion that was proper to stars.[38] The physical allure of Loren, Lollobrigida, Silvana Mangano, and Silvana Pampanini, among others, is a point of contention in film journals like *Cinema Nuovo*. Both directors and critics (including female journalists) argued that these women were harmful to Italian cinema (and to themselves). "It is sad to admit," said Vittorio De Sica in an interview, "but the Italian film industry today exalts above all legs and prosperous bosoms."[39] According to the Editorial Board of *Cinema Nuovo*, "Our actresses, except for a few and in a few films (Magnani for example) are more beautiful than good."[40] "The Scandal of Body Curves," as *Cinema Nuovo* called it, developed into a full-fledged reportage titled "The problem of actors [sic]: We want to go to school," with contributions from film stars Lucia Bosé and Gino Cervi, among others.[41] In this reportage, Italian actresses responded to the accusation that they lacked in skills (the "problem" mentioned in the title) by expressing their intention to attend school. Indeed, actresses themselves chastised the stars' beauty, which was "more a sin than a gift," according to Anna Garofalo.[42] In fact, De Sica's hypocritical judgment (the actor/director worked with both Lollobrigida and Loren after making that statement) cannot be separated from the director's practice of hiring foreign actresses with the prospect of international coproductions. At the same time he was lamenting Italy's lack of any real talent, De Sica was in London to sign a contract with Hollywood producer David O. Selznick for a film that could only have been made if it starred his wife the legendary Jennifer Jones.[43] At the same time, on the very pages of *Cinema Nuovo*, the images of prosperous Italian actresses were both ridiculed and exploited. Summing up the contradictory position of the leftist journal, a close-up of Sophia Loren with a clear view of her breasts is accompanied by the caption: "Italian actresses, an American newspaper reads, are so beautiful that they do not need any talent to act."[44] The caption also introduces another aspect of the debate: even though the Italian stars are blamed for discrediting Italian cinema abroad, their sex appeal and the explicit display of their bodies constituted the backbone of publicity in the U.S. market.

In the press booklet of the movie *Sensualità* (literally "Sensuality," but released in English as *Barefoot Savage*), for example, Eleonora Rossi Drago is advertised "in the tradition of *Bitter Rice*" as she joins "Italy's top sizzlers."[45] While the booklet's sensational language aims to "sell Drago as screen's most exciting new star," a 1956 episode of the popular television show *What's My Line?* delivers in clear language how the American perception of Italian actresses was inscribed onto their bodies.[46] In the episode, Mangano plays the "mystery celebrity" whom Bennet Cerf, one of the game participants, asks, after he discovers she is Italian: "Are you famous for various measurements?" Mangano and host John Charles Daly laugh at the question, while Arlene Francis comments off screen: "Aren't all Italians actress famous for measurements?"[47] So famous that film critic Edgar Morin, in 1957, would coin the term *Lollobrigidism* to indicate a "renaissance of the star system" in which the "the erotic recovery" plays a capital role.[48]

What is lacking in these discussions on Italian actresses is an inquiry not only into the role they played in the construction of their own images, but also into the influence that feminine audiences may have had in their making by the industry (both publicists and producers) through the course of the 1950s. Besides being sex objects for the male gaze, how did Italian actresses thrive in a market of consumerist culture that was increasingly made by women?[49] In a 1996 study on "female images in Italian cinema and the popular press," Luisa Cicognetti and Lorenza Servetti ask: "Why is it, that female spectators can be as fascinated as men by watching actresses who have no social existence, who are nothing but attractive bodies?"[50] Cicognetti and Servetti argue that "the riddle" can be solved by getting out of the picture houses and looking at "popular film magazines:" "What was lacking on the screen, a social status, an interest in daily problems, child care, clothes and domestic worries, was to be found in magazines."[51] It was in *Tempo*, *Oggi*, and *Epoca* that women could not only see but also recognize themselves as both ordinary and outstanding.[52] Citing the results of a survey published by *Oggi*, the two historians go so far as to argue that women were not that interested in stardom at all, since they did not answer the question in the survey that asked them who their favorite female star was. In a more recent article, Lucia Cardone denies such narrow interpretation of female characters in 1950s films and their appeal to Italian women, challenging the idea that they were simply attractive bodies and arguing that they were also a means to spread modern feminine figures.[53] She also claims that cineromances (dismissed in previous studies) are the place where the images of women presented at the cinema are accessed by a much broader female audience. According to Cardone, cineromances are responsible for adapting female film characters to more traditional models of conduct, while still retaining the same appeal of transgression that the same characters have on the screen.[54] Similarly, Réka Buckley contests the widespread opinion that female stars in the 1950s are only perceived as attractive bodies; rather, she shows that these stars are represented in tabloids as common women, particularly through images of motherhood and family life.[55] Focusing specifically on Loren and Lollobrigida, Buckley convincingly demonstrates that off screen representations de-glamourize the stars, while still being anti-conventional enough to spread new models of womanhood. Whereas Cardone focuses on the images of women, not their physical embodiments in the actresses, Buckley's account concerns only the star's off-screen persona and does not analyze in depth the relevance of a star's characters on screen. For example, Buckley mentions the scandal of 1957, when Loren married by proxy, in Mexico, Carlo Ponti, who already had a wife in Italy and was the father of two children. Loren, who started her career as an actress in photoromances, not only was Ponti's companion but also a star for the Ponti-De Laurentiis company. She was particularly affected by the scandal even though she was not married at the time, and she was pictured in the press as the seductress. Buckley explains that, in order to counter public condemnation, Loren was instructed by publicists to build for herself in tabloids the image of a woman who cared for children and wanted to have some.[56] Surprisingly, she only mentions in passing that the actress, after the scandal, also began to play motherly figures in her films as well. Instead, I see this as an important clue to understand the politics of the Ponti-De Laurentiis couple, who knew how to play the game of the star system.[57]

In sum, Cardone's and Buckley's accounts are important insofar as they make similar arguments that characters/actresses of the fifties presented models of womanhood that combined conservative and transgressive elements. However, their approaches keep the analyses of images and of stars compartmentalized. In the pages that follow, I demonstrate that cineromances in their twofold function of tabloids and storytellers suture the private and public images that hold together the star persona of Mangano on and off the screen. Through a horizontal study of cineromances as transmedia products, I show that the independent and sexually attractive characters that Mangano plays in films are imbued in their "photoromanced versions" by the features of traditional femininity that characterize her image in tabloids. I agree with Buckley that Italian stars in the 1950s generally had to be crafted conservatively in representations of their private-life events (above all motherhood). In addition, these stars had to deal with their own fame as seductress, promoted both nationally and abroad by the films in which they starred. *Cpt* and *Cg* aided publicists to assure that Mangano's on-screen persona was not received at odds with her public face, by *interpreting* the inner feelings and motives of her characters in the captions. In this dynamic, columns in the same magazines are pivotal in building an understanding of stardom as based on hard work and moral integrity. Further, both Buckley and Cardone agree that some transgressive residues remain attached to the stars, despite the magazines' or the films' attempt to normalize their behaviors. In my view, the coexistence of traditional and modern characters is not contradictory or surprising but rather typical of the feminine figures that are prevalent in the current media culture, particularly in photoromances, and thus it is also fit to ensure Mangano's success. Economic independence and physical beauty, dosed with self-policing practices of moral and social conduct, make "Silvana" an appealing model of modern woman that fit the consumer culture of potential customers of the magazines.

LANTERNA MAGICA AND ITS STAR: SILVANA MANGANO THE SIZZLING HOUSEWIFE

In the 1954 *Cg* issue "Riso Amaro" (Bitter Rice), the "Corriere di Cinelandia" (News from Movieland) announces Mangano as winner of the "celluloid championship" also called "the chart of film stars."[58] She is ahead of Loren and Lollobrigida, according to the author, thanks to the huge success of *Ulysses* and even greater success of *Mambo*. The announcement should not be taken as proof that Mangano was indeed among everyone's favorite stars. According to a recently published oral history project on moviegoers in the 1950s, for example, Mangano is rated number six, after Magnani, Loren, Lollobrigida, Yvonne Sanson, and Elizabeth Taylor.[59] Whether we should trust more the memory of a sample group of film goers in Rome (both men and women) engaged in the project over the word of *Cg* is beside the point. More relevant is that the announcement "lies" in order to contribute to promote Mangano's stardom, at the time of important De Laurentiis' productions (either with Ponti or with Lux). In 1954, *Ulysses* was number one at the Italian box office, *L'oro di Napoli* (The Gold of Naples, also starring Mangano, in a minor role) was number five, however, *Mambo* was only number eight, negatively reviewed by critics, and definitely in need of some help to gain more profit.[60] In fact, the whole issue of *Cpt* can be read as a well-orchestrated package that combines advertisement and storytelling to sell Mangano (and her films) to its readership. A photo accompanying "News from Movieland" shows a scene from *Mambo* with a caption that explains how Mangano's films often feature "modern" dances: boogie-woogie in *Bitter Rice*, bajon in *Anna*, and now the mambo, whose choreography is directed by Katherine Dunham, a black dancer, choreographer, and anthropologist whose company had been touring in Europe since 1946.[61] Meanwhile, the cineromance retells *Bitter Rice* with an emphasis on Silvana's (the main character played by Mangano) act of repentance and faith in God, both of which are completely absent in the film. None of these details are coincidences, I argue, but rather fit in the industrial project of refashioning Mangano's image throughout the 1950s. It was "una trasformazione programmata, studiata a tavolino" (a planned transformation, constructed on the drawing board), according to Giovanni Cimmino and Stefano Masi in their recent biography of the star.[62] Not only did Mangano's "planned transformation" concern the roles she played in film; rather, from a reading of the fan magazine *Hollywood* and Lanterna Magica's cineromances, it appears to be a concerted publicity effort. In the pages that follow, I attempt to unravel the connections between Mangano's private, public, and screen images, to those of the preferred feminine readers of Lanterna Magica.

Like other so-called *maggiorate fisiche* (busty women), also known for participating in beauty pageants, Silvana Mangano initially was promoted both nationally and abroad for her shapely figure and sex appeal; her body reflects, according to Landy and others, the ambiguities that characterized the country at a time of both restoration and modernization of society (similarly to how Richard Dyer interprets Marilyn Monroe's in 1950s America, "in the flux of ideas about morality and sexuality").[63] The film that made Mangano into an international sensation was *Bitter Rice*, whose purported moralistic message clashed with the publicity that promoted Mangano's voluptuous image. A moral tale embedded in Marxist ideology, the film casts Mangano as a rice worker by the same name, whose hard labor is exploited while, barely dressed when working in the fields, her shockingly beautiful body symbolizes the corrupting effects of mass culture (particularly American) and consumerism.[64] But while most readings of the film highlight the contrast between the ideology of the narrative and the means of advertising (or the appearance of the female star), I am interested in the uneasy fit between Mangano's image in this film and her image promoted in tabloids. After *Lure of the Sila*'s lukewarm reception, and at the time *Il brigante Musolino* (Outlaw Girl, 1950) was released, *Hollywood* published an article supposedly authored by Mangano herself, in which she opens up to explain how "three contracts" have fundamentally changed her life: the two film agreements signed with Lux and the private one that she ratified (the same year)—her marriage.[65] Mangano speaks about herself with irony and candor, revealing her modest origins and her desire to work hard, her dream to marry, her fondness for a dog on the set, and her love and respect for both her father and husband. While to national and foreign audiences she was "l'atomica" (the Atom Bomb) and compared to Rita Hayworth, in the letter, the actress describes the hardship of working while battling with mosquitos in the rice valley during the shooting of *Bitter Rice* or the pain of wearing heavy boots in the wild Calabrian mountains on the set of *Lure of the Sila*. Soon after the publication of the *Hollywood* article, Mangano gave birth to her first child and, simultaneously, announced her decision to retire from acting. The news made a big splash in the press, across the European market of cineromances, and her claim that motherhood and family were more important to her than acting defined her off-screen persona throughout the fifties. In the words of Daria Argentieri, Mangano became "an actress despite herself, a star despite herself, admired despite herself."[66] According to a journalist in the French edition of "Anna," a few years later, Mangano (who spoke French but not English) herself declared: "I have a vocation for motherhood, not for being a star."[67]

Mangano did not abandon the profession, in fact, only her past image on screen. The act that seemed to denounce a fundamental gap between a professional life in the film industry and a private life in a traditional family was in fact just a turning (not an end) point in the star's career.[68] Several other articles from *Hollywood* after 1950 speak of Mangano's new film roles as testimony to her professional skills as well as her moral stamina. In "Silvana's Long Road from *Riso amaro* [Bitter Rice] to the Convent," Giorgio Gaglieri argues that Mangano "did not want to convince critics and audiences by her beauty, but by her intelligence and perfect harmony with the character."[69] In *Anna,* the reporter adds, "Silvana Mangano will fully demonstrate her performance skills and her new image of femininity to everyone who remembers her sensuous and perverse in *Riso amaro.*"[70] These features of strength and empowerment in the professional field are not opposed but complementary to her role as mother, as depicted in the press. Moreover, they are a model for aspiring female artists who want to harmonize their traditional views of gender roles with a successful career in the film industry. In "The Miss and the Trojan Horse," Eligio Gualdoni presents the example of the changing image of Mangano into a lesson for her fans, who also dream about becoming stars by participating in beauty pageants.[71] After the birth of her first child and her "scialba" (modest) performance in *Lure of the Sila*, according to Gualdoni, the "ex-miss" Mangano was now a different kind of role model: "her following two interpretations [*Outlaw Girl* and *Anna*] showed us a Mangano who has substantially changed: her beauty is not sexy and impudent anymore, but chaste, quiet, calming."[72] In the context of the ongoing debate about the lack of talent in Italian actresses, Gualdoni's statements about Mangano are also a warning for fans who aspired to follow in her footsteps.[73] The redeeming appraisal of Mangano for reinventing herself by showing her dedication to both the acting profession and family life is also an international advertising strategy. In a dedicated Spanish edition of "Colección Idolos del Cine," the image of Mangano with short hair and in a turtle neck sweater attending to her small child on the cover is in line with her national picture, as well as the announcement, on the following page, that Silvana did not refuse to shave her head to play Jovanka in *Jovanka e le altre* (Five Branded Women, 1960), a role that Lollobrigida had rejected precisely for that reason.[74] "Silvana did not waver," says the article, "[she] showed up at Cinecittà studios the day after and handed herself over to the hairstylist."[75]

In agreement with her newly gained maturity, Mangano's film roles also change. A seductive and vindictive peasant in *Lure of the Sila* and a devoted partner and unwed mother in *Outlaw Girl*, Mangano in *Anna* and *Mambo* turns into an independent woman who ultimately decides to give up on romance and to devote herself entirely to a profession (nursing in the first case, dancing in the second), but not without a sacrifice. While in the first two films her character is morally ambiguous, in the last two she is literally split in two: a past and a present self. In both *Anna* and *Mambo*, Mangano is torn between two different life-styles, corresponding to different stages in the character's narrative trajectory. In both cases, she eventually decides for a life spent in moral integrity and hard work. In *Anna*, she plays a nun and a nurse who was once a singer in a night club; in *Mambo*, a saleswoman infatuated with a small crook who becomes a successful performer in a dance company. Finally, Camerini's *Ulysses* is the first film that fulfils Mangano's other "vocation" on screen: to have children and care for them. In the film, she plays two characters: Circe the seductress and Penelope the mother. "Rare case for an actress," one reads in *CpT* (1954), "[Silvana Mangano] will give birth to two characters who appear very different: as Penelope she will have to emphasize the virtues, the sweetness of a faithful spouse and as Circe she will be instead the sorceress who enchants men with her unsettling sensual charm, with her superhuman skills."[76] Strikingly, Mangano's double performance in *Ulysses* is a reproduction of her twofold persona: the fantasy of Mangano on screen that is only in apparent contradiction with her image of perfect housewife in fan magazines.

Furthermore, in her roles Mangano transitions from "sex object to sexual subject," to use Rosalind Gill's expression, an idea that can best be exemplified by the different dance acts happening in *Bitter Rice*, *Anna*, and *Mambo*.[77] From the boogie-woogie to the mambo, these dances have in common elements of transgression and exoticism, in Western countries, and they are attached to ideas of liberated sexual conduct. In the sexually repressive era of the 1950s, according to Jane Desmond, "[mambo] gave sexual expression and release in the culturally ritualized and accepted Euro-American context of ballroom dancing" and allowed "middle- and upper-class whites to move in what are deemed slightly risqué ways, to perform, in a sense, a measure of 'blackness' without paying the social penalty of 'being' black."[78] Dance scenes are signature moments in Mangano's films and speak of her childhood dream, according to biographers, of becoming a professional dancer. They are also some of the most iconic images of her that still persist today in the cultural memory of moviegoers: Anna's dance to the tune of "El Negro Zumbon" is featured in both *Cinema Paradiso* (dir. Giuseppe Tornatore, 1988) and *Caro Diario* (Dear Diary, dir. Nanni Moretti, 1994). The dance scenes in *Bitter Rice*, which take place in front of an improvised audience, feature Silvana "making a spectacle out of herself:" negatively connoted vis-à-vis both a leftist ideology and Catholic morals (she dances the American boogie-woogie and, in one of them, wears a stolen necklace), they can be ambiguously interpreted as an act of self-assertion or objectification, or both. In the words of Mary Russo, on the one hand, making a spectacle out of oneself can be perceived as a specifically feminine danger, risking exposure and ridicule. On the other hand, "the bold affirmations of feminine performance . . . have suggested cultural politics for women."[79] There is no room for ambiguity in *Anna*, instead, in which professional dancing is attached to a sinful relationship. In contrast, *Mambo* depicts Giovanna's decision to enter Katherine Dunham's dance company as a gesture of liberation from her sinful past; narrates the process of learning how to dance as an extremely strenuous process that requires incredible strength and dedication; and conveys the final commitment to dance as a long-term occupation through an act of selfless sacrifice that ultimately defines the character's gained independence.

As the episode from *What's My Line?* that I quoted earlier suggests, it may very well be that De Laurentiis and his company's strenuous efforts to establish for Mangano the image of the perfect housewife and the exemplary professional did not work effectively in clearing her past of her sex symbol status. My point, however, is that by the time "Bitter Rice" is published, in 1954, the image of Silvana Mangano as the "hot sizzler" is clearly outdated with respect to her film roles and her public persona, as much as the attack on mass culture conveyed through her character in the same film is anachronistic. Modern dance is not a sin but a popular pastime (or as such is sold). And Lanterna Magica not only facilitated the spread of celebrity culture but also fostered readers' aspirations for stardom: in each *Cpt* issue the column that hosted celebrities talking about their perspectives on "how to become a star" is always followed by a full-page announcement titled "our advice," a contest for aspiring actors and actresses. Mangano thus functions as living proof that such aspirations are not in conflict but in continuity with traditional gender roles in the family. It is not surprising then that in the cineromance, three full pages are taken by the sequence in which Silvana dances the boogie-woogie in front of her coworkers and their male companions, each photo following her moves in slow motion, almost as if in a dance lesson. Over the photos, the captions strive to explain that while still provocative her dance is also a sign of "juvenile exuberance" and even "a voluptuous challenge to the misery that oppress[es] her fresh youth."[80] The message is the same as in favorable readings of photoromances, which aim to justify pure entertainment as social purpose. Further, the cineromance forgives Silvana for the murder and betrayal she committed in *Bitter Rice*, through a reading of the film's ending that does not leave space for ambiguities (figure 2.8). Over a close-up of her face as she stares at the empty space in front of her, at the top of the tower from which she will jump, a caption states with compassion that "her face is scored with tears, tears of repentance, tears of pain; supreme offer to the compassionate God who forgives so much."[81] In the same close-up, Silvana asks God for forgiveness, an important addition to the film script that precedes the tragic ending only two photos ahead.[82] As she lies dead in the field, another caption over a crane-shot declares: "She lies on the ground, immobile and her eyes open look again towards the sky as if she wanted to ask for help and pity."[83]

Similar to "Bitter Rice," "Mambo" heightens the moral dilemma faced by the main protagonist, played by Mangano, who must rely on her skills as a dancer to overcome the loss of her husband, and the betrayal of her ex-lover. *Mambo* was a critical flop, its melodramatic language criticized in reviews that considered the film no more than an "upscale photoromance."[84] Focused on blaming director Robert Rossen for a trite weepie, critics did not pay attention to the fact that, unlike current Italian melodramas, the female protagonist (Giovanna) eventually chooses her career over her lover. In making this choice, Giovanna also explicitly endows her female mentor

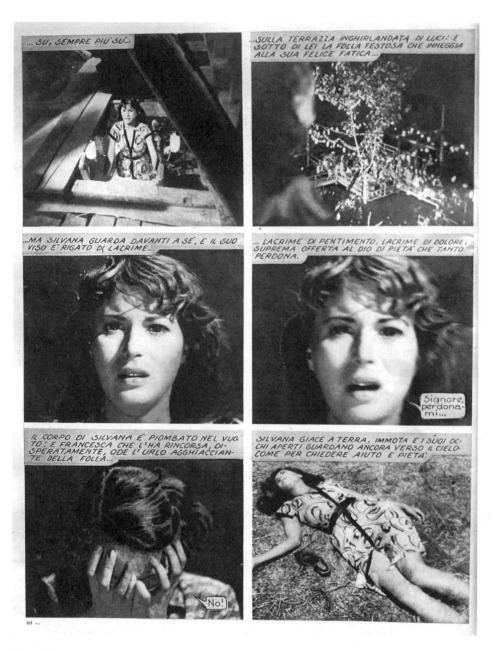

Figure 2.8

"Bitter Rice," *Cineromanzo gigante* 2 (1954): 60.

and Pygmalion Toni with her success, rejecting her past in which she was completely dependent on men. Interestingly, the initial evaluation by the government office that supervised film productions had negatively judged Toni's interest in Giovanna as interpretable as a lesbian relationship, and requested that the script be modified to clarify any confusion.[85] I do not argue for a queer reading of the cineromance, however, I think that the emphasis on female mentorship is an important addition to the film that further completes the picture of the projected reader in the model of femininity constructed in the narrative. A one-page still photograph concludes the cineromance; in the film it appears more subdued, with a fade-out in black over the theater in which Giovanna performs, the caption stating: "Toni was right. It's useless to look for our reality in others, outside ourselves. Nothing can be conquered with a strike of fortune and Giovanna is left with what cost her labor and sufferance. And, above all, love for her own skill" (figure 2.9).[86] In the context of the magazine, these declarations are more than just an educational message of moral conduct; they are an advertisement for the profession, against notions of fame that come easily to attractive women. In the same issue, in the column "How You Can Become a Star," Robert Taylor explains that the key ingredients to success are a positive attitude and, most of all, hard work.

As anticipated in the previously mentioned photo published in "Bitter Rice," "Mambo" is also a way for Lanterna Magica to advertise the songs, and thus the dances, performed by Mangano together with Dunham, amid an already international cast of performers. Dunham was known for integrating her studies in anthropology into Caribbean and Brazilian choreographies and was the first to introduce Italian audiences to a company of mixed ethnic and racial groups. A comparison between the theatrical versions of the film in Italy and in the United States and the cineromance shows the extent to which the magazine aided the film's promotion, nationally, while exploiting the global fame of Dunham and her choreographies.[87] According to Dorotea Fischer-Hornung, American critics received the film negatively precisely because the dance scenes were "photographed so artily."[88] Comparison of the American and Italian versions of the film reveals that dance scenes are in fact considerably cut in the former and one, "La danza delle lavandaie" (The Dance of Washerwomen) is completely missing. In the cineromance, similar to "Bitter Rice," photos of Mangano and Dunham dancing instead fill several pages in the story, including an entire grid dedicated to the practice session in the dance studio.[89] In a way, the cineromance is faithful to the original script, which contains a special note regarding the editing of

Figure 2.9

"Mambo," *Cineromanzo gigante* 4 (1955): 59.

the scene at the dance school. "It must be clearly understood," the note reads, "that this is not a montage in the ordinary sense of the word; pieces of it are, but more or less it is a series of vignettes which serve to illuminate the relationships of Giovanna to Toni, to Dunham and to the rest of the troupe." Indeed, the technical means of the cineromance realizes precisely the very effect suggested in the script's note: each still representing a pose and their sequence creating a grid that has no indication of temporal order. It is not clear from the script who would be the author of this note, but Dunham's own vision of a "film di danza" (dance film) should be mentioned. In an interview with Glauco Viazzi in 1950, Dunham claims that her work in film did not yet satisfy her, since the director's needs in the editing of dance scenes do not match with her vision.[90] She also argues that she would like to direct her own film and that editing, above all, would be of great importance. Whether Dunham was also the author of the note in the script is not possible to say. However, it is evident that the cineromance as a form of storytelling is not simply a slavish copy of a film, but rather, an original text that interprets the expectations of readers (who are interested in the story but also in the dance moves) and, perhaps, the intentions of an artist as well.

THE QUESTION OF THE CINEROMANCE

If the cineromance is indeed an original text, with its own style and content, it should also maintain its own *rights* as a creative work. In other words, the cineromance is not only an important tool for the industry, vis-à-vis other products, but also the fruit of artistic and intellectual labor, both individual and collective. On the one hand, the lack of declared authors and the fact that, as Baetens suggests, the cineromance depends on its audience seemingly make this idea quite absurd or even preposterous. On the other hand, given the strict correlation between the cineromance and the film, it seems legitimate to ask whether directors, writers, and stars were at all involved in the business and its profits. In fact, in the context of 1950s Europe, cineromances appear as hybrid objects in between commercial extensions and grassroots productions: another way to exploit films, in the hands of film producers; a means to make profit at the fringes of legality, for semi-industrial enterprises. With the exception of Del Duca's Edizioni Mondiali, Italian companies involved in the business were not otherwise known in the publishing industry and it is possible that, in some cases, they even worked using pirated film positives. Ultimately, those who benefited from the unregulated commercial exploitation of films on paper were the fans, who had access to considerable resources of films that they could "read" from beginning to end—at least, as long as no one in the legal realm really paid attention.[91] In the mid-1950s, the cineromance appears as a case under discussion in legal literature, more broadly concerned with the reform of the Italian copyright law of 1941, from which the photoromance was excluded. As I will discuss in the next chapter, Italian courts specifically began to question the role of film producers, writers, and directors with regard to authorship and the rights of economic exploitation of films. As both a derivative product of film exploitation and an original creative work, the cineromance constituted an aporia that needed to be addressed through legislation not only for economic reasons, but also to ultimately define the legal basis of film authorship, at the time of the "Golden Age" of Italian Cinema and of the French theories of the "politique des auteurs."

3 PIRATES OF THE FILM INDUSTRY

"How did they get permission to make this stuff?," asks Virna Lisi in *Sfogliare un film* (Browsing a Film), a documentary made in conjunction with an exhibition on cineromances held at the State Archives in Turin in 2007.[1] The exhibition featured about two hundred issues, most of them from the private collection of Italian director Gianni Amelio, in addition to materials belonging to the National Museum of Cinema in Turin.[2] "And how could we know? Do you think that they gave us something in return for these things? They didn't even ask!," says Lucia Bosè bitterly, a few cuts later.[3] Taken aback or fascinated by a whole world of which they claim to be unaware, actresses Lisi and Bosè, and others (such as directors Mario Monicelli, Ettore Scola, and Dino Risi, and screenwriter Suso Cecchi D'Amico) realize that the makers of cineromances have tampered with their work, appropriated their lines, and used their images for commercial purposes. "I don't know whether they could do that," says Monicelli in reference to the producers of *The Unfaithfuls* (1953), which he co-directed with Steno.[4] "What I do know," he adds, "is that they made Steno and I, and all the *cinematografari* [directors] sign contracts at the time, in which we sold all copyrights for an infinite number of years, and for any kind of exploitation."[5]

In the context of convergence, the issue of copyright is a relevant topic. Participatory culture can be exploited by the industry but also can backfire when fans appropriate products to the point of making them their own. Fan fictions and fan films are works inspired by other works whose copyright holders or creators may or may not welcome them, respectively, as the ultimate form of publicity or as intellectual property infringement. The low budget and rudimentary technology needed to make photoromances can foster these kinds of homemade products, as shown in Ennio

Jacobelli's practical guide for the production of a photoromance (*Istruzioni pratiche per la realizzazione del fotoromanzo,* published by Politecnica Italiana in 1956) and in Michelangelo Antonioni's documentary film *L'amorosa menzogna* (Lies of Love, 1949). Ennio Jacobelli's manual indicates that homemade products were at least envisioned if not realized in practice, although there is a gap between models and advice given in the book and the actual production process at work in the industry.[6] At the same time, Jacobelli's book supports an understanding of the medium as open to appropriation from below. Readers could take the opportunity given by the easily accessible means of production to create their own photo-stories, which possibly could then be sold to publishers. The handicraft quality of earlier semi-industrial enterprises defied the idea of standardization common to mass culture when fully developed. As shown in Antonioni's *Lies of Love*, studios could be improvised in a working-class neighborhood. In one sequence, we see that a set could be built in the basement of any apartment building. In another sequence, we discover that when props are lacking, crew ingenuity remedies the problem: if there the champagne glasses needed for a scene are not available on set, they will be manually drawn on the photograph once it is printed. But while the example of artisanal enterprises of photoromances simply challenges the established world of corporate publishing, the making of cineromances pushes the legal boundaries by recycling images from existing copyrighted works. Only a few cineromance publishers have clear economic ties with producers (such as Lanterna Magica), and among the main players in the publishing industry only Edizioni Mondiali had its own series (*Cine-intimità* [Cine-Intimacy]). The other names in the business are small, unknown, and specialized companies that will last only a decade, until the early sixties, when the genre also disappeared from the market.

Browsing a Film indulges in conversations with stars, screenwriters, and directors without really inquiring into what seems a dubious industry at the fringes of legality. As I showed in chapter 2, films could be radically modified in their narratives when turned into photo-textual stories. The latter cannot be properly called fan fictions, however; as Leonardo Quaresima explains, they are the outcome of a process of negotiation between the "institution of cinema" and the "voice of viewers."[7] Further, whereas fan-made works in the digital age are increasingly under strict control of the industry at a global scale, cineromances in postwar Europe could take advantage of the ambiguities in place in the existing legislation in film copyright and the so-called *legge per il diritto d'autore* (literally "law for author's rights" [lda]). Unlike the American system, film copyright laws in Europe take into consideration both the economic rights of producers and the moral rights of the "authors," but without an agreement on whether the director should be the exclusive holder of the latter. In 1956, well-known legal expert Mario Fabiani argued that the cineromance constituted "a financially important phenomenon" that was "sometimes in violation of third parties."[8] Cineromances were not covered by the current lda, which was ratified in 1941, that is, a few years before the first photoromance came out in 1947.[9] Therefore, the judicial challenge was to identify who are such "third parties" that could claim rights on cineromances, with regard to authorship or commercial exploitation. While film novelization in general is a well-established practice and complementary to the viewing experience, documents pertaining to the legal debate and lawsuits problematize historical accounts that treat cineromances simply as a means of publicity. As Lorenzo Gangarossa explains, "the judicial has supported the orientation in film criticism that recognized an almost exclusive ownership to the director in response to his [sic] predominant role, while in jurisprudence, the most accepted theories do recognize some prominence to the 'Artistic Director' but do not define him [sic] as author."[10]

My claim is that an inquiry into the legal "question of the cineromance" is relevant to the study of European film history, in general, and of the Italian film industry, in particular. The expression *questione del cineromanzo* (question of the cineromance) is used by Amedeo Giannini in *Il diritto dello spettacolo* (Show Business Law, 1959), where he recommends that the lda be modified to include photoromances among the protected *opere dell'ingegno* (works of intellectual substance), in other words, because they qualify as intellectual property.[11] According to Giannini, as well as to all legal cases, cineromances are not means of advertisement but rather works "of creative character, autonomous, and distinct from the film."[12] The discussion around the originality of cineromances is thus pertinent to the debate on film adaptation and authorship, in the context of European cinema cultures that are heavily based on the cult of directors and on the idea of cinema as an art, but are not homogenous with regard to legislation.[13] The Berlin Convention of 1908 established that films are protected by copyrights, both when they are adaptations of literary texts and when they are original and creative works of fiction (documentaries are excluded).[14] In Italy, the first official recognition along the same lines as the Berlin Convention was in 1925; however, the Royal Law number 1950 recognizes intellectual property but not the creative value of films. The lda of 1941 thus introduces for the first time, together with literary texts and music, *le opere cinematografiche* (cinematographic works) as creative works, but remains ambiguous with regard to ownership. To put it another way, the law does nothing but exacerbate the duality of films as both artistic endeavors and industrial products. Creativity is the basic element in a work that signifies the existence of an author, and the lda establishes the collectively creative nature of films whose coauthorship must be attributed to four individuals: the director, the *soggettista* (author of the story), the author of the music, and the screenwriter (in case of adaptation from a literary text, the novelist is considered the author of the story). Coauthors only hold moral rights, while producers have complete control over commercial exploitation.[15] In particular, directors are excluded from any decisions made in the name of potential profit (including cuts made to the released version).

Including the photoromance under the lda would raise two questions: first, who can claim economic and moral rights to these photo-textual stories that, like films, are creative works but also mechanically reproduced and commercial products? And second, if modeled on the example of films, could the screenwriter and the director claim any rights to cineromances as "adaptations" of their own work? In the words of Monicelli, directors (as much as any other artists involved in film production) actually sold their rights at the contractual level and thus, they are like any other dependent employee.[16] The claim that cineromances are independent and original works could reverse this statement to be used in favor of the artists. Directors could have sued publishers for not involving them in the making of cineromances because the work whose rights they sold in their contracts was limited to exploitation in the context of film-related publicity, not in a separate realm and market.

When looking at the specialized literature, there are no discussions about cases of lawsuits initiated by directors in Italy (Gangarossa's only reference is a 1950 trial in Paris). Instead, I found a few instances in which actresses sued publishers for using their images in cineromances, which are specifically based on the claim of originality. Notably, the lda does not take film stars into consideration at all, even though in the early years of narrative cinema they are considered fundamental to the making of a film, and their performances constitutive of the work of art.[17] Actors and actresses are the main commercial drive of the entire business of both cinema and cineromances, and yet, they are legally just like any other employed worker. In his account of the "safeguarding of the image of the film actor in the rendition of the film in the form of a photoromance," Vittorio Sgroi explains that "actors do not create, they execute."[18] An Italian judge and legal expert, Sgroi refers in this quote to a case from 1955, when actress Benedetta Rutili filed at the Rome Court a lawsuit against Gino Rippo, director and producer of *Ho pianto per te* (I Cried for You, 1954). According to Sgroi, Rippo made an agreement with the publisher of *Le grandi firme dello schermo* (Signature Films) for a cineromance by the same title, featuring thirteen photos of Rutili as supporting actress. Rutili challenged Rippo on two related fronts: first, whether the producer had the right to use the actress's image without her consent; and second, whether this particular use of her photos (i.e., in a photoromance) was also detrimental to her image and career. The Rome Court acquitted Rippo on the basis that the cineromance is not "a rendition of the film" since it has additional and original elements, "qualitative and quantitative." Because the actress is not considered a creative contributor of the film, Sgroi explains, she cannot claim any rights over the use of film materials for another work.[19] In other words, the argument of originality is used *against* the actress, who would only be reimbursed if indeed the cineromance were a commercial extension of the film, not a unique adaptation. Further, the ruling agrees that "by acting in photoromances, [Rutili] could be stopped on her path toward fame."[20] However, the cineromance is too close to the film to really constitute such threat.[21] Finally, Sgroi argues that whereas there are norms that discipline the use of personal images, film stars constitute the exception to the rule because of their notoriety, which justifies the audience's demand to see their "effigie" (likeness): celebrity implies a silent agreement between stars and their fans on the use of their photos for publicity. In Sgroi's words, "The film star cannot invoke a right to privacy like any other individual."[22]

Ultimately, Sgroi's report and interpretation of Rutili's case reiterate discourses to which I referred throughout this book: photoromances are products of low culture, stardom is a profitable condition that comes at a personal price. Comparing this case to that of Lucia Pasini in 1962, however, we can see fluctuations throughout the decade in the articulation of the same discourses, despite the fact that the lda was never modified during this time. According to the daily newspaper *Corriere d'informazione*, Pasini (mother of actress Luisa Ferida) sued and won a case against publisher Victory for the illegal publication of two cineromances based on two films in which her daughter performed the leading female role, *La bella addormentata* (Sleeping Beauty, dir. Luigi Chiarini, 1942) and *L'ultimo addio* (The Last Goodbye, dir. Ferruccio Cerio, 1942).[23] Giovanni Ponzoni, Victory's legal representative, sustained that the publisher bought rights from producers Cines and Alan Film, in agreement with the lda, which did not presume any additional compensation for the stars. Ponzoni also argued that Ferida's mother did not submit her daughter's contracts, so that it could not be proven on paper that there were any limitations to the economic exploitation of the films. By comparison to other current contracts of the period, it would be fair to agree with Ponzoni, since most likely producers had reserved for themselves all rights of use of the star's image. These circumstances notwithstanding, the Rome Court ruled in favor of Pasini. As opposed to Rutili's case, the same consideration that cineromances are separate works, not commercial extensions of the films, is used to argue that to publish them without the actresses' consent and compensation was illegal. Given that the lda. was not modified between the Rutili case and the Pasini case, why would the court rule differently? It is noteworthy that cineromances disappeared from the market around the same time Victory was found guilty. Whether the events are connected is impossible to claim for sure. However, the case of Pasini testifies that changes in place in cinema culture may have affected judicial interpretations of the star's rights of ownership of her image and work.

THE ILLEGITIMATE GIRLS OF SANFREDIANO

Before Pasini and Ferida's case, the most advertised legal battle against a publisher of cineromances involved a well-known novelist, Vasco Pratolini, whose book *Le ragazze di Sanfrediano* (The Girls of Sanfrediano, 1949) was adapted into a film in 1955, directed by Valerio Zurlini and produced by Lux.[24] In 1956, the Florentine newspaper *La Nazione* announced that Pratolini won a lawsuit against Lanterna Magica over the use of his novel to make a photoromance.[25] The cineromance titled "The Girls of Sanfrediano" was issued in May 1955 in *Cineromanzo gigante*, a few months after the release of the film. The first page of the cineromance quotes both the film and the novel as sources: a list of the film's cast is introduced by the sentence "loosely based on the story by Vasco Pratolini of the same name—Edizioni Vallecchi" and the name of the author of the "photoromanced version" (Maria Baldeva) is placed at the end, after the sentence "A Lux Film," printed in a larger font.[26] Lanterna Magica's common practice to include the name of Baldeva as the author seems to sustain Pratolini's claim that the cineromance is "a work of creative character, autonomous, and distinct from the film" and thus, as the novelist whose work was adapted in the illustrated magazine, he had right to be informed (and paid) prior to its publication.[27] Incidentally, the name of the Florentine neighborhood in the novel's title (*Sanfrediano*) is spelled the same in the cineromance ("The Girl of Sanfrediano") and differently in the film's title (*The Girls of San Frediano*).[28] The publisher's lawyer argued the opposite, that the cineromance "was taken not from Pratolini's story, but from Lux's film, which had authorized the publication as means of publicity for the film itself."[29] In addition, according to Lanterna Magica, "publishing a photoromance with content analogous to its film version, utilizing the frames and dialogues of the cinematic work, falls within the power of economic utilization of the film and constitutes, in a way, a natural form of exploitation of the film itself."[30] The production company then provided witnesses to prove that "it is custom for film producers to distribute photoromances, obtained using the frames and dialogues of the film, without asking for authorization from the author of the literary work from which the film is taken."[31]

A habit that did not, in any case, justify the crime, since the Rome Court eventually agreed with Pratolini and stated that the publication was "illegittima e abusiva" (illegitimate and unlawful), additionally asking that the verdict be published in the newspaper *Il Messaggero* at Lanterna Magica's expenses.[32] It is worth quoting the report at length:

> The law regarding the author's right does not consider, within the protected works, the photoromance. Now, the cineromance, whose diffusion, especially in Italy, is resurging in recent times, constitutes a fictional creative work [creazione della fantasia] and has a form of representation all its own, even though it lacks artistic intentions and targets a *certain* social strata. The cineromance results, in fact, from the combination of photographic and literary elements and represents factual content through the succession of photographs, reproducing characters and environments of fables. [These photographs are] connected by a literary element and vivified through reproduction, in written word, of the dialogues between the characters represented. Because of the elements of which they are composed and the unique form of representation, the photoromance clearly distinguishes itself from the literary works and from the cinematographic works and qualifies without a doubt as a category of work all its own. On these premises, it appears evident the groundlessness of the thesis according to which the photoromance would not constitute as anything other than a form of representation of the cinematic work. This [a film], indeed, has as a proper form of representation only that of the projection on the screen and not also that of its printed publication, which is, instead, properly of literary work and, as is seen, also of the photoromance.[33]

The verdict uses the term *photoromance*, bypassing the fact that photographs are captured from an existing film reel. It also expresses the idea that, because of the support material (paper), photoromances have more in common with literary texts than with film, even though they cannot be called works of art. As I explained, artistry or creativity are not necessary elements of intellectual property; most relevantly, the point made about the target audience confirms, similarly to the case of Rutili, that the Rome Court agrees with an understanding of photoromances as low culture. In this sense, the sentence in favor of Pratolini does not aim at the inclusion of photoromance in the Ida but rather conservatively at protecting the novelist against the cultural industries, which exploit and popularize his work. Competition is tough, explains the article, "especially in the social category addressed by photoromances, having the possibility to choose between the original work and the photoromance, many people evidently would give preference to the latter, with indisputable prejudice for the author of the original work."[34]

In addition to making the verdict an exemplary case to be published in national newspapers, the Rome Court ordered that all copies be destroyed. Clearly, the court's order was only partially successful, since some copies still exist. As I write, I have in front of me the brightly colored cover page of "The Girls of Sanfrediano," showing the faces of its protagonists: Antonio Cifariello, Rossana Podestà, Giovanna Ralli, Marcella Mariani, Giulia Rubini, and Corinne Calvet (figure 3.1). From a close reading, it seems clear that the Rome Court's decision to eliminate all copies respected Pratolini's desire to maintain the authenticity of his novel when confronted with a product that substantially modified the original. Similar to the film, the cineromance's distinctive entertaining quality is in opposition to the book's educational message and goal of social investigation. In its representation of female characters, Lanterna Magica's publication is also closer to the commercial world of photoromances than to the leftist culture of Pratolini's novel. "The Girls of Sanfrediano" opens with a dedication to the girls who live in the working-class Florentine district of Sanfrediano: a "mondo a sè" (world of their own) where they "work and love, are sweet and noisy, tender and feisty, shameless and faithful."[35] The back cover further emphasizes the centrality of female characters in the plot, by presenting a drawing in which five young women (vaguely resembling the five actresses who play the protagonists of the film) are standing together at the top of a green hill, while a young man looks at them from far away, hiding behind a tree (figure 3.2). The drawing is reminiscent in style of *Grand Hotel*'s graphic artist Walter

Figure 3.1

Cover of "Le ragazze di Sanfrediano" (The Girls of Sanfrediano), *Cineromanzo gigante*, no. 9 (1955).

Figure 3.2
Back cover of "Le ragazze de Sanfrediano" (The Girls of Sanfrediano), *Cineromanzo gigante*, no. 9 (1955).

Molino. Text at the top of the page reads "Spring winds!" and at the bottom: "They [the girls] bring the springtime with their dreams of love."[36] In its design and captions, this page encapsulates the feminine gender model that I have discussed at length in this book, each "girl" embodying in her individual characterization an idea of femininity as both traditional (branding feminine beauty as a tool for success) and liberated (seemingly embracing sexual attractiveness as empowering rather than objectifying). Tight skirts and blouses, high-heeled shoes, and bright makeup enhance their bodies as they fearlessly gaze straight at the reader. The "spring wind" lifts one girl's dress, revealing her knees and underskirt, as she smiles untouched by the event (while a man hiding behind a tree widen his eyes at the scene). In this sketch, exposed on the back cover of a popular magazine, readers may find an enticing model of female emancipation, carefree and full of pleasure.

On the contrary, Lux's film focuses on the male character as protagonist and begins with an overlay text superimposed on the images of a young man on a motorbike. The text explains that, since Robert Taylor appeared on the screen, all attractive young men in Florence are now called "Bob" and that the film is dedicated to these "poor boys, innocent victims of their charm."[37] Bob is the nickname name of the protagonist, Andrea Sernesi, a modern Casanova who has sentimental relationships with different girls at the same time, until one of them discovers his ploy and eventually leads him to his demise. A typical masculine figure of Italian comedies of the fifties, Bob speaks to a postwar masculine audience who could relate to the projected image of ineptitude of the main protagonist whose multiple attempts to catch a girl are never portrayed as predatory behavior. Screenwriters Piero De Bernardi and Leonardo Benvenuti are more or less faithful in their rendition of the novel's plot, but make an important modification to its ending, which reflects the overall lighthearted look at Bob's "weaknesses." According to a reviewer in *L'Unità*, by comparison to the novel, the film lacks the critical view that is expressed in the book's finale.[38] In the novel, the six girls eventually play a terrible prank on Bob to vindicate their honor and dignity. Afterward, Bob repays his debts by doing what was expected of him as a man in a patriarchal society, that is, he marries one of the girls (Mafalda). On the contrary, in the film, no revenge takes place and Mafalda leaves to work as a dancer. Bob's multiple love affairs, presented uncritically as comic plot devices, are not punished but rather are forgiven, and the possibility that the same story will continue remains open. Cineromance and film are in this respect similar not only because they literally close in the same way, but also because they lack any moral judgement. Neither forces Bob (or the girls) to comply with traditional gender models and start a family. Once his unfaithfulness and ploys are uncovered, Bob is left alone and, in both the film's and the cineromance's final scene, chased by his big brother who will beat him up "until the end of the world," in the words of the voice-over narrator (and of the caption): a closing scene that resembles those in the *commedia dell'arte*, in which the story frequently ends with a never-ending brawl at the expense of Harlequin.

What is remarkable here is how the finale challenges the suggestions made in the documents of the Commissione di revisione cinematografica (Film Revision Committee), later a section of the Ministry of Tourism and Culture.[39] The Law Decree ratified in 1947 (Legge Cappa, no. 379) created this committee to evaluate proposals seeking government funds and to control their national and foreign distribution. In order to receive financial support, producers were obliged to present (in pre-production) a synopsis to the committee, as well as the list of cast and crew. The committee then decided whether to grant approval for the film's release (*nullaosta*) and export. A document dated May 22, 1954, reveals that *The Girls of San Frediano* was supposed to end with the girls' prank on Bob, which the committee criticized for its dubious moral message. Its report invited the film's director to reinterpret the screenplay in a "moral" way.[40] On July 7, 1954, when the film is already in its final version, a second report makes no mention of the ending but only requests elimination of colloquial language considered vulgar.[41] However, a new ending appears in the duplicate of the *nullaosta* (authorization of screening) issued by the Undersecretary of State and approved on December 23, 1954—five days before the film's theatrical release. According to the authorization, "In the end, we see Bob married and dealing with the serious issues of family life."[42] How did Lux manage to release a film with a far less conservative statement about Bob's love escapades, even though the authorization clearly states that no modifications should be made to the storyline? The film's ending is more in line with the kind of comedies to which most viewers were accustomed, and potentially more successful. Also, the cineromance's similar ending should have raised the same moral concerns. The case of "The Girls of Sanfrediano" thus goes beyond the juridical debate on the legal status of the genre, and into the realm of governmentality.

What if at the core of legal opinions on the cineromance was not the validation of the artists as copyright holders, but rather, the need for normative rules that could extend the disciplining power of government apparatuses on mass culture? The moral concerns regarding the film *occasionally* slipped through the net of the Film Revision Committee while cineromances were *regularly* unsupervised in their adaptation of movies for the popular press. To be fair, publishing was also under the scrutiny of government censorship in matters of moral content, however, not in the same capillary manner as cinema.[43] And yet, photoromances are potentially as "dangerous" as films because of their wide popular audience, their visual language, and the narrative treatments of topics concerning social and sexual behaviors. To go back to Quaresima's point on the grassroots basis of fan magazines, the "institution of cinema" is a complex system involving audiences, artists, the industry, and the government; therefore, cineromances are the products not only of compromises between perspectives inherent to the films and those of viewers (their expectations, lifestyles, social rules, and literary preferences), but also of the private and public bodies involved in their making and distribution.

Indeed, a second aspect that is relevant to the "question of the cineromance" is the extent to which the "archontic" process of remaking film narratives in the murky waters of Italian copyright legislation also had the positive outcome of eschewing government censorship, as well as the control of producers, to the benefits of consumers.[44] By the attribute "archontic," I mean that we can understand the relationship between films and cineromances as a form of retelling that expands the textual archive. In particular, close readings of contested films reveal that sequences or images removed at the behest of the Film Revision Committee, or cut by the producer for commercial reasons, or as a practice of preemptive self-censorship, can be found in cineromances, albeit decontextualized or overwritten by captions. These "rescued" images are perhaps not necessarily supporting radical positions; yet, they challenge the moral boundaries set by the government and the industry, as well as give us access to lost frames of film history.

AT THE MARGINS

In 1952, Vittorio De Sica corresponded extensively with the General Command of *Carabinieri* corps to ask permission to shoot "as a background, barely seen through the glass doors, the arrival of the head of State with the honorable security detail of Cuirassiers Regiment" (*Carabinieri* are the national police of Italy and a corps of the Italian army; the "cuirasser" is a type of armor).[45] The scene is part of the film

Stazione Termini (Terminal Station, 1954) and the so-called "background" is in fact a main feature of De Sica's style (and of Cesare Zavattini, the screenwriter): a look at the everyday life of travelers that socially grounds the story of two lovers meeting, for the last time, in Rome's main train station. In fact, in order to make the scene look real down to the smallest detail, De Sica wrote directly to the Ministry of Defense (via lawyer Randolfo Pacciardi) to ask for a set of original cuirassier uniforms promising that "the film is inspired by decorous and aesthetic principle and the cursory use of this shot cannot in any way damage the righteous fierceness and utmost dignity of the Cuirassiers Regiment."[46]

The extremely pompous statements that De Sica signed for the sake of creating this sequence cannot be understood outside the context of postwar Italy, where cinema was under tight government control, particularly concerning representations of the Italian army. The most clamorous case took place in 1953, when director Renzo Renzi published in *Cinema Nuovo* in collaboration with its editor Guido Aristarco a film project titled *L'armata s'agapò* (The Love Troops, from the Greek verb *agapò*—love) about the Italian Fascist occupation of Greece. Renzi and Aristarco spent forty days in a cell and were then punished to a few months in prison for the crime of contempt of the armed forces (the so-called *vilipendio*). Carefully measuring his words, De Sica's goal is to get hold of official uniforms without compromising the film itself. Indeed, *Terminal Station* does not in any way comment directly on the carabinieri or any other corps, neither in this scene nor in others. The same could not be said about the cineromance "Stazione Termini" (Terminal Station), published by La Torraccia's *Cinefoto romanzo gigante* in 1957 (figure 3.3). The magazine not only makes dubious remarks about a group of soldiers, but also uses them to create a risqué expansion of the narrative. At some point in the film, the main male protagonist Giovanni slaps his love interest Mary, a married American woman who would become his lover that very day, in an abandoned cart on a dead railway track. Frustrated by his ineffective attempts at convincing Mary to stay in Rome with him, rather than going back to her husband in Philadelphia, the Italian lover unexpectedly hits the woman in the main lobby. Nobody really pays attention to the couple besides Mary's nephew, who is there to bring his aunt her suitcase and who acts as a sort of surrogate husband throughout the movie.[47] The group of coscripts that happens to be "in the background," exactly like the parade of Curaissers in the previously mentioned letter, witnesses the dramatic event without showing any interest, in a typical Zavattini-De Sica style of everyday

Figure 3.3
Cover of "Stazione Termini" (Terminal Station), *Cinefoto romanzo gigante*, no. 28 (1957).

settings. In *Cinefoto*, instead, the soldiers engage with the characters by means of added dialogue and a caption. The latter states that the soldiers find the scene "interesting" and thus gather around Mary, after Giovanni has left, "commentando salacemente l'accaduto" (commenting on the fact salaciously). One of them says in a balloon: "Sweet brunette, your boyfriend is jealous, isn't he? I would have happily given you a kiss, not a slap!" (figure 3.4).[48]

The case of "Terminal Station" is relevant to exemplify two important points: (1) modifications to the film's plot and dialogue do not take into consideration the screenwriter's and the director's intent but rather an ideal reader modeled on current successful products; and (2) cineromances are not under the same level of government control as cinema. The chauvinist attitude paraded by the soldiers could either please or antagonize the audience (especially women), but with certainty fits the discourse of gender that is pervasive in popular Italian comedies of the period. Given that the American actor Montgomery Clift played Giovanni, the clash between the machismo of the soldiers and the ineptitude of the male character could also be interpreted in the name of national pride. This aspect is of particular interest considering that *Terminal Station* is at the center of a battle between the two co-producers, De Sica (who is also the director) and the American David O. Selznick, precisely in reference to the film's possible commercial success or failure. It is known that Selznick heavily modified De Sica's version of the film on the basis of poor reviews from viewers at preview screenings in California; in fact, *Terminal Station* was released in a much shorter version in the United States (where Selznick held all rights and with a different title, *Indiscretion of an American Wife*.[49] The crass rewriting of the previously mentioned scene is similar to Selznick's intervention in trimming the film with a certain target audience in mind, whose perspectives on masculinity differ from what is embodied by the main character in the film.

Being outside the lda had its disadvantages as much as its perks: discrepancies between the printed and audiovisual texts (in both versions) speak about the greater freedom granted to publishers who were at the margins of the cultural economy. The film industry and the national government were bound to each other in many postwar European countries, including Italy, and the lda enforced this connection. Under Fascism, Article 47 of the lda established that, in cases of dispute between producers and coauthors, the Ministry of Popular Culture (MinCulPop) was called in as an arbiter. After the fall of the regime, the Presidency of the Council of Ministers simply

Figure 3.4
Cover of "Stazione Termini" (Terminal Station), *Cinefoto romanzo gigante*, no. 28 (1957): 11.

replaced the MinCulPop, thus continuing to allow political meddling in the judicial system.[50] Since several laws also went unchanged in the transition from Fascism to Democracy, such continuity in the lda would not surprise if it did not clash with an opposite rush to change film legislation, in the name of artistic freedom. Immediately after the Liberation of Rome and as early as October 5, 1945, during Nazi occupation in Northern Italy, the Italian Parliament approved a new law on cinema with the immediate consequence of liberalizing the market.[51] Nobody bothered to change the lda as well, and to actually give more power (of authorship) to the artists. Meanwhile, the flaunted freedom of expression was soon contained in the name of social order. In 1954, following a discussion at the Presidency of the Council of Ministers, in which the Christian Democratic government explicitly announced that funding would not be available to film productions that were deemed to have been under the influence of the Communist Party, a "McCarthy-style" campaign spread in the press, culminating with publication of a list of directors openly or allegedly Communist. While "the silent acceptance of governmental instructions" had always defined the attitude of producers vis-à-vis the Italian government, in this case the Associazione Nazionale Industrie Cinematografiche Audiovisive, Anica (the National Association of Film and Audiovisual Industry) went as far as to establish a *commissione di autocensura* (self-censorship committee).[52] This committee had the goal to preemptively examine those films that might be subject to government censorship. De Sica was among the directors under scrutiny as openly Communist or sympathizers, together with Antonioni, Luchino Visconti, Carlo Lizzani, Alberto Lattuada, and Giuseppe De Santis, who were also among the subscribers to the "Manifesto" of the "Circolo romano del cinema" that, in 1955, publicly denounced the Italian government and its policies. According to the Manifesto, "the recent declarations and initiatives of the current Undersecretary of the Presidency of the Council of Ministers [Giulio Andreotti] are about to collapse the already dead freedom of expression under a gravestone."[53]

This discussion of film legislation and censorship should not be taken as a digression. In the broader context of the power struggle between artists, the Italian government, and the industry, the uniqueness of cineromances consists of marginal yet deconstructive narratives in the established media system. Not by chance, Amedeo Giannini, whom I previously quoted in this chapter, is in favor of including photoromances under the protected works in the lda; at the same time, he is a member of Anica's self-censorship committee, a promoter of more rigorous controls on films to "protect" viewers from their psychological effects, and in support of recognizing producers as film authors. A thorough comparative analysis of photoromances of controversial films in the history of Italian cinema may be fruitful to discover the extent to which the inclusion of cineromances under a revised Ida that granted authorship to producers could ultimately aim at controlling how magazines popularized them to a mass audience. If recognized as "works of intellectual substance," cineromances would also have to go through a rigorous policing that would protect but also inspect their content. Space here does not permit an extensive examination in these terms, but I would like to conclude this chapter by looking closely at one particular instance: a 1955 issue of *Cineromanzo gigante* based on *Senso*, directed by Luchino Visconti in 1954 and produced by Lux. For this film, Lux borrowed warfare materials from the Ministry of Defense that were necessary for the film's realistic representation of the famous 1866 battle of Custoza, between the armies of the Austrian-Hungarian Empire and of the Kingdom of Sardinia.[54] The same ministry asked Lux to cut some scenes and dialogues from the film that allegedly undermined the honor of the Italian army. The accusation was, once again, of *vilipendio*. The contested scenes are one that represents Austrian soldiers drunk and engaging with prostitutes in the streets of Verona (considered an attack on the moral integrity of the military) and one with dialogue between patriot Count Ussoni and Captain Meucci of the Kingdom of Sardinia that the Ministry of Defense alleged conveyed incomprehension and animosity between independent fighters and the official army. In addition, the Film Revision Committee requested some cuts of love scenes and related dialogues.[55] *Senso* is, in fact, a story about the Italian Unification told through the love affair between Countess Livia Serpieri (married to a pro-Austrian aristocrat and cousin to the fervent Italian patriot Ussoni) and the Austrian Lieutenant Franz Mahler. Their relationship constitutes the backbone of a political narrative ridden with compromising moral and ideological content: Livia, played by Alida Valli, falls for Franz, played by Farley Granger, and for him she betrays both her husband and her country, using the money that she safeguarded for the cause of Italy's independence to pay for Franz's medical excuses that would cover up his desertion.

The film's intricate plot and the main stars make *Senso* the perfect material for a cineromance. The vicissitudes of the film's production provide an additional layer to the convergence of cinema and the press that is worth further attention. According to official documents, the Film Revision Committee asked Lux to cut a scene from "reel n. 4." The document reads: "Livia is still in bed, after consummation of their love meeting [sic], Franz is near her. Livia combs her hair with a brush, also sitting in bed. (Eliminate the entire scene)."[56] Instead, the cineromance includes not only this scene but also exactly the shot mentioned in the report. Valli is brushing her hair and sits on the bed, looking away from Granger, only covered by a sheet that reveals her naked shoulders; Granger looks at her while lying on the bed, with some distance between them (figure 3.5). The two-image grid is anticipated by a full-page picture of Granger and Valli, side by side in a close-up, with a neutral background that may or may not be the film set (figure 3.6). It is a publicity film still: the two actors are now close to each other, in a switched position, and Granger is looking right at the camera, breaking the illusion of film realism. Valli is instead taken in profile, which according to one biographer is also her best angle.[57]

Senso was meant to mark Valli's great comeback, to regain the attention of her fans and to build positive publicity around her. Extremely popular during the Fascist period, the actress who was once "the most loved by Italians" had just come back from Hollywood, where she moved right after the end of the war amid accusations of being a spy for the Fascist regime. When *Senso* was released in 1953, she was again involved in a scandal that could ruin her image: her boyfriend Piero Piccioni's alleged involvement in Wilma Montesi's murder.[58] *Senso* was a success at the box office, and the cineromance is a testament to Valli's (and Granger's) star power. Further, the character that Valli plays in the film is not in continuity with the wholesome image she held before the war. Rather, her role fits with those she interpreted under contract with Selznick in Hollywood productions such as *The Paradine Case* (dir. Alfred Hitchcock, 1947) and *The Third Man* (dir. Carol Reed, 1949): fatal beauty, a mix of corruption and redemption, extreme passion and irresistible desire. As expected, the Film Revision Committee requested changes to smooth over the explicit reference to the character's moral ambiguities. In particular, the producer was asked to cut the line in which Franz alludes to the fact that Livia is worse than a prostitute, when she gives away the patriots' money for her lover's faked medical excuses.[59] Of course, the line appears in the cineromance more or less in the same form, but with the additional argument that, in fact, she is not like a prostitute but rather like an old client of a gigolo: "What is the difference between the two of you [Livia and the prostitute]?," Franz says. "I

Figure 3.5

"Senso" (Sensation), *Cineromanzo gigante*, no. 7 (1955): 14.

Figure 3.6
"Senso" (Sensation), *Cineromanzo gigante*, no. 7 (1955): 13.

will tell you. You [the prostitute] are young and beautiful . . . and you [Livia] are old. Men pay for her, and you, for an hour of love, you had to pay me."[60] The caption condemns Livia's behavior, and her decision to "forget any duty and any shame" when overwhelmed by her passion, indicating a conservative approach to the story.

And yet, the images of Valli's (and Granger's) attractiveness send a different message, despite their moral perversion, and much more questionable elements than marital unfaithfulness are kept in the story: in particular, the images that represent the Austrian soldiers in promiscuous activities with prostitutes, drunk and uninhibited, which the Ministry of Defense specifically censored. In the film, after the battle of Custoza, Livia arrives in Verona in a carriage to visit Franz. The guards let her in, but the Commander warns that "the city is not safe for a lady." Right after the carriage enters surrounded by a crowd of men in uniform, including a stretcher on which a wounded body lies, a sharp cut introduces the scene inside Franz's apartment (where he is staying with the prostitute). Instead, in the cineromance, the photo showing Livia in her carriage is followed by two contrasting images, representing the Austrian and the King of Sardinia's soldiers, respectively. The first frame shows a street crowded with white uniforms. Its caption explains that an excited mob of drunken soldiers and prostitutes is taking over the city, laughing, singing, and making love, "while the defeat sends back hundreds of broken and bloody men." The latter sentence is the caption on top of the second image, representing a caravan of wounded combatants, including both patriots and the King of Sardinia's army.

The cineromance notably does not in any way support the critical vision of the Unification claimed by Visconti in his own reading of the film; rather, it modifies its content against the moral policing of the Film Revision Committee and in favor of a more enticing reader's experience. A comparison between the representation of the only political event included in the cineromance, the battle of Custoza, to that in the film clearly shows how the former maintained a glorifying image of Italian patriots, albeit in its own popularizing fashion. In the film, Custoza is a chaotic event of extreme violence seen through the eyes of Count Ussoni, who wanders helplessly and wounded across the battlefield, walking over dead bodies and trying to find shelter behind dissolved trenches. The sequence begins with Ussoni as he passes by the army of the Kingdom of Sardinia that is slowly retreating ("it's an order!" some soldier cries in the background). It ends with him looking at a small group of combatants who are firing the cannons. One of them announces that they will continue to fight despite the order, however, laughing coarsely together with his mates, he appears to have lost his mind rather than gained courage for an impossible mission. Ussoni observes them silently, and eventually disappears from the screen (and he will also no longer be seen in the film). In the cineromance, in contrast, the two pages representing the battle not only show Ussoni acting heroically (until his own death), but also joining forces with a group of Italian soldiers who are fiercely resisting the enemy, rather than frantically shooting at nothing as in the film. For those readers who may not have been aware of the historical facts, the battle retold on the pages of *Cineromanzo gigante* appeared more like a Western movie: "Un pugno di uomini deciso a resistere" (A bunch of men resolved to resist), states a caption over a frame enlargement showing Ussoni in the front, and a man on a horse in the background. Lanterna Magica's version of Custoza celebrates the heroism of Italian soldiers, and if the Ministry of Defense had known, it probably would have approved. Its rendition is not really celebratory of the Nation, however, but rather, is appropriately geared to engage a cinema audience, at a time when a character that resembled John Wayne was more palatable than a trite eulogy of the fallen soldier.

The same could be said for what seems the most shocking discrepancy: the final sequence. Riccardo Gualino of Lux asked Visconti to reshoot the scene, at the behest of the Ministry of Defense, to include the execution of Franz by the hands of an Austrian fire squad as the closing image of the film. In an interview published in *Cahiers du Cinéma*, Visconti argued that *Senso* should have ended differently, with a sequence in which Livia walked (again) by a group of drunken soldiers.[61] The last shot was supposed to be that of a young draftee, totally inebriated, who cried while shouting sarcastically "Viva l'Austria!" (Long live Austria!) Similar to the battle of Custoza, this instance should have represented a dark vision of war, emptied of heroic gestures and afflicted by the lack of meaning. According to Visconti, the negative that he shot was burnt and no positives of this sequence could be found. The final pages of the cineromance challenge Visconti's assumption. After the execution of Franz, ten additional photographs (one page and a half) show Livia wandering in an empty street of Verona, eventually passing through a small square where, according to the caption, women and soldiers spend the night together. The first four photographs are taken from a previous sequence, after Livia leaves Franz's apartment to visit the headquarters where she will denounce him to his superiors. The six-photo grid of the last page, however, does not appear anywhere in the film (figure 3.7). In these images, Livia is seen encountering

Figure 3.7
"Senso" (Sensation), *Cineromanzo gigante*, no. 7 (1955): 59.

Austrian soldiers, while the caption states that "nel suo cervello, la follia è esplosa" (in her head, madness has exploded). It is impossible to say with certainty whether these images are in fact taken from the negative that Visconti originally shot for the final sequence. Their focus is different from Visconti's planned critique of war as violent and senseless; the attention is on the female character and her tale of corruption and redemption. At the same time, the shadow that the scene casts on the Austrian army is closer to Visconti's intentions and definitively against the directives of the Ministry of Defense. Lost in her sins and desperation, according to the captions, Livia is soon to be violently taken by an "aroused soldier" ("voglioso") against her will. "She does not even see those outstretched hands and sneering faces," the caption says, "as the circle of soldiers narrows around her."[62]

At the end of *Senso*, the image of justice served to a traitor serves to make a moral statement. The film's "archontic" retelling in *Cineromanzo gigante* is much darker in its reading of the same story from the point of view of the female character, whose symbolic death happens by the violent hands of the men in white uniforms. This ending in fact reconnects the cineromance to the literary text, "Senso" (1883), a short story by Camillo Boito, on which the film is loosely based. Both the cineromance and the story concentrate on Livia's vicissitudes, told from her own perspective, while the film (despite the use of the voice-over commentary by Valli) ultimately gives more prominence to the historical context and thus to an allegorical reading of the romance at its center. Told in a long flashback by means of Livia's diary, recounting her past and sin, Boito's text ends similarly to the cineromance (and differently from the film) with a scene that explains what happened to the woman after the death of Remigio (aka Franz): she is now the lover of a man who left his fiancée the day before their wedding, and whom she embraces while still thinking about her past companion. This is perhaps what awaits Livia beyond the last photo in the cineromance; most relevantly, both in Boito's story and in the film's "photoromanced version," Livia's moral degradation is what seals the whole narrative.

Lucia Cardone has argued that, when turned into cineromances, films "absorb the dark tones of the feuilleton, because they inherit the same [female] audience, passionate and demanding."[63] While I do not think that this is necessarily true for every cineromance, it is at least partially the case in "Senso," which rewrites Visconti's historical drama by drawing from Boito's nineteenth-century short story. At the same time, considering the scenes that I previously analyzed, including that of the Battle of Custoza, the "dark tones" appear to be mixed with the bright ones of heroic gestures typical of other, popular genres. In the end, the hybrid text of the cineromance, rich in intertextual discrepancies and continuities with both the literary story and the film, is a growing "textual archive" that, in its expansions across media platforms and its exclusion from the legal system, challenges established notions of copyrights and intellectual property.

4. COLD WAR PHOTOROMANCES

A short documentary produced by the Catholic educational film producer San Paolo Film on the sixth commandment, titled *Non commettere atti impuri* (Thou shalt not commit adultery) features a scene about the deleterious effects of sinful readings and the threat they pose to the moral and sexual behaviors of youth and women alike.[1] Over the image of Carlo, a young boy who is looking at a postcard picture of Saint Mary, folded in the book that he is studying, a male voice-over comments: "Beware not to get caught by fantasies, let's pray to the Madonna to free us from the suggestion of the mind" (figure 4.1a).[2] A medium shot of two women reading an issue of *Sogno* together is sandwiched in between the image of the boy (figure 4.1b) and the close-up of a man playing Jesus wearing a crown of thorns and with blood on his face (figure 4.1c). In a montage intended to be instructive, the easily interpretable visual analogy is further explained (in a didactic tone) by the commentator: "We must avoid bad readings and bad company," he says, "sins of thought are like so many thorns that we stick in Jesus' head."[3] Behind the women, a man seems to supervise their reading or, perhaps, he is simply there to once again suggest that "bad readings" go hand in hand with promiscuity (figure 4.1b).

The disapproval of photoromances in a Catholic educational reel does not make news. What is worth more attention is the very use of a mass media to preach the Catholic faith. *Thou shalt not commit adultery* is only an episode in a series of shorts based on the Ten Commandments, and typical of the publisher's educational program. San Paolo Film is a branch of Edizioni San Paolo, funded by Father Giacomo Alberione of the religious congregation Società San Paolo in the 1920s. After War World II, San Paolo was developed in line with other firms such as Rizzoli and Mondadori,

Figure 4.1a
Thou shalt not commit adultery (San Paolo Film, n.d.). Courtesy of Istituto Luce Archive.

expanding from publishing to filmmaking, and investing in the rotogravure.[4] Father Giuseppe Zilli, who directed *Famiglia Cristiana* (Christian Family [*FC*]) the widely read illustrated magazine published by Edizioni San Paolo, explicitly promoted the idea of a "catechesi fatta in lingua rotocalco" (cathechesis in the language of tabloid) during his tenure from 1955 to 1981. By the 1970s, Edizioni San Paolo had become a media corporation involved in publishing, film, music (Paoline Editoriali Audiovisivi), radio (Nova Radio), and television (Telenova). Across media platforms, the Catholic media industry responded to the decline in organized religion that, according to Chris Rojek, paralleled the rise of celebrity culture, the democratization of society, and the commodification of everyday life.[5] If mass media representation is key in the formation of celebrity, the case of San Paolo shows how Christianity exploited the same devices of consumer culture "in branding belief and communicating faith."[6]

Figures 4.1b and 4.1c

The innovative role played by Edizioni San Paolo in the direction of media convergence and consumer culture is relevant not only in reference to the political stance of Christian Democracy (waging war against illustrated magazines and other products of the industries) but also across the political spectrum, by comparison to the experiments of the Italian Communist Party (PCI). As Stephen Gundle has shown, the PCI held an ambiguous position in the postwar period: on the one hand, PCI's official line was to resist standardization and consumerism by rejecting mass culture; on the other, members of the same party understood the need to employ popular genres and the mass media in order to attract and maintain voters and membership.[7] It is within this context that, in the late 1950s, different local agencies of the PCI went against the grain by creating and publishing photoromances. Communist photoromances were single issues that narrated stories of troubled sentimental relationships that ended in marriage or with the reconciliation of the married couple, as well as with the political conversion of the female protagonist (usually from an undecided voter to a fervent Communist). Soon after, in the early 1960s, San Paolo's *Famiglia Cristiana* seemed to respond to the Communist initiative by publishing a series of photoromances that narrated the lives of popular female saints, but adopted the successful formula in installments. The goal of Catholic and Communist publishers was one and the same: to win the consensus of Italian women via their vote or their worship.

PCI and *FC* did not simply recycle an established photoromance form according to their own political and moral agendas.[8] The Communist agency and the Catholic publisher engaged with the photoromance medium, both its content and its style. In this chapter, I analyze aspects relating to the host media, the kind of stories, and the type of signs, including the types of photography, in order to understand the degree to which Communist and Catholic photo-textual narratives draw and depart from the commercial model, and from each other. Close reading of texts will highlight differences and continuities in social and cultural discourses, with particular regard to femininity, womanhood, and consumer culture. I will study how the visual-textual narratives embrace (or reject) the behavioral models and the politics of gender that magazines such as *Bolero Film* conveyed to their readership. In this way, I will also explore similarities between Catholic and Communist models of social, sexual, and moral conduct. According to historian Sandro Bellassai, despite the opposite political stands, Catholic and Communist cultures in the postwar period did not differ much in relation to the moral values and behaviors they upheld: "the two cultures effectively tend to be so indistinct from one another as to make one think that analysis should turn towards a third ground with which the osmosis of the Communist and Catholic cultures is not only constant but even fundamental."[9] This "third ground" is, in Bellassai's words, "a deep cultural *humus*, of a traditionalist and chauvinist character."[10] This chapter will examine how, in the practice of making popular culture, the two blocs not only fought the same battle against a common enemy (the cultural industry), but also built upon this shared *humus* in order to win the hearts of Italian women: that is to say, on the very "third ground" that the escapist fantasies of popular romances threatened to destabilize.

The main difference between Catholic and Communist photoromances consisted, rather, in the type of readers. The intention of the Office of Propaganda was to reach out to working-class female audiences in an attempt to politicize them. Wives, fiancées, and daughters of Italian workers were both the privileged readers and protagonists of Communist readings. Instead, the goal of *FC* was to homogenize its readership across the social ladder, in the name of modern culture. With one million copies sold in 1961, the Catholic magazine was mostly successful among middle-class women in the small provincial towns of Northern Italy, but the publisher's objective was to expand the market in larger urban centers also in the South, where both working-class and peasant readers were prevalent.[11] In the words of Mario Marazziti: "*FC* carries out a work of wide cultural dissemination and of the 'modernization' of the masses, thus contributing to the diffusion of a *koinè* of the uses and manners of civil coexistence that are more homogeneous between city and country, between workers and the small middle classes."[12] In addition, both Catholic and Communist photoromances were not available at newsstands and could only be bought in Catholic churches, Communist Party headquarters, or from door-to-door activists (PCI or Catholic Action).[13] Thus, their audience was self-selective, which suggests that the producers' goal was not to find new converts but to make sure that those who were already under their supervision would not stray or let their family members do the same.

GRAND HOTEL, COMMUNIST STYLE

In the early 1950s, in *Quaderno dell'attivista* (Notebook of the Activist), Giuliana Saladino sharply addressed Communist Party members for their lack of understanding in regard to women's attachment to photoromances, particularly those women in the poorest rural areas of Sicily. Saladino acknowledged not only the cultural potential of the media, but also the active role played by young women who, in the poorest conditions, would find time to gather and to read or listen to other women reading.[14] In the PCI, it was mostly women who spoke in favor of photoromances in order to foster literacy and, therefore, political awareness. Already on May 18, 1947, Marisa Musu wrote in PCI's illustrated magazine *Vie Nuove* an article entitled "Young Women Dream," in which she claimed that "if at the National Conference of Communist Youth some delegates have *Grand Hotel* in their purses, . . . we should not be scandalized: even in such a way, the girls are moving towards democracy."[15] Musu's perspective clashed with the general opinion expressed in *Vie Nuove* that photoromances not only spread bourgeois and capitalist "insidious propaganda," but also mortified women, who were sexually objectified in their photographs. Such evaluations were oblivious of women's desires that could be satisfied by these readings, according to Teresa Noce, the secretary of the Textile Union. In a letter published in 1952 in the Socialist newspaper *Il Lavoro*, Noce reminded PCI executives that whether female readers were married or not, they needed a "prince charming" because what "he" meant for them was often "only the aspiration for something better than the present, that is, a nicer and more happy life, less difficult and strenuous, more peaceful and civil, without having to worry about unemployment or an insufficient salary, about a small and noxious house, about an unsafe tomorrow."[16] Despite their similarly positive take on photoromances, Saladino's and Musu's accounts are different from Noce's. While the first two women reevaluate the media for educational purposes, the latter appears to criticize the idea that culture must necessarily be educational. What if the issues of *Grand Hotel* in the handbags of Communist women were there solely to entertain rather than to educate them? And on what basis would PCI decide to publish photoromances: to use them as tools to educate women (building on their existing familiarity with the genre and their love for romances), or to exploit the potential of cultural entertainment as a tool of propaganda? In other words, the question is whether Communist photoromances simply exploited the form to convey a political message (eliminating any escapist elements in the narratives), or instead embraced both content and signs of the commercial model to please their readers while also persuading them.[17]

To address the questions just raised, I will use a sample of seven photoromances collected at the Istituto Gramsci in Rome, the only ones currently available (Gundle and Giovanna Calvenzi mention an earlier experiment in Sicily during the 1953 elections, a photoromance titled "Per chi vota Caterina Pipitone?" [For Whom Does Caterina Pipitone Vote?], but I could not locate any copy it).[18] One of these seven ("Il destino in pugno" [Destiny in Your Hand]) is drawn, while the rest use photographs. "Destiny in Your Hand" (1959) is also the only one to be published by the Regional Committee of the Communist Party in Sicily. The other six were published by the Sezione Stampa e Propaganda of the Central Committee in Rome. "La grande speranza" (The Great Hope) and "Più forte del destino" (Stronger Than Destiny) were published in 1958, "Cuore di emigranti" (Heart of Emigrants) and "Frontiera tra gli sposi" (Border between Spouses) in 1963, and "Diritto di amare" (The Right to Love) in 1964.[19] "La vita cambierà" (Life Will Change) does not have a date, but from the style and content it is most likely from the early 1960s (figure 4.2). Six out of seven narratives end with election days and have an invitation to vote for the Communist Party ("Vote Communist," "Vote PCI," "Vote Like This") on the back page; only "Border between Spouses" ends simply with reconciliation in the family and says "Enlist in P.C.I." on the back cover (figure 4.3).

Most of these photoromances employ a fixed grid of nine (and up to twelve) images per page that rarely make use of close-ups and, most frequently, frame characters in a medium shot. Maintaining the same settings and types of shot for each narrative unit, photographs are usually sequenced with minimal changes from one to another, and these are limited to the position of characters within the frame. There are no emotional pauses on the faces of the protagonists and, with no ellipsis or gaps to be filled in the gutters (the white lines between photographs), readers are rarely forced to interpret. In sum, the focus is mostly on dialogues and captions, on the story more than on the visual quality of the text. Two exceptions are "Life Will Change" and "The Right to Love," which show some craft in page composition and in the use of photographs and captions. Rather than repetitively using a fixed grid, these texts creatively play with different sizes of photographs and caption boxes. In both cases, the romantic plot revolves around unmarried couples. These couples are also featured on the back or front cover, or both, a move that places more emphasis on their relationships than in any other case in which the family is central in the plot and also featured on the cover. Thus, it seems that the latest photoromances are also the closest to the commercial example both in their stylistic elements and in their content. In particular, in both "Life Will Change" and "The Right to Love," visual narratives develop by syntagmatic rather than paradigmatic sequences of photographs. These sequences do not represent

Figure 4.2

"La vita cambierà" (Life Will Change) (PCI Sezione Stampa e Propaganda, n.d.). Courtesy of Fondazione Istituto Gramsci.

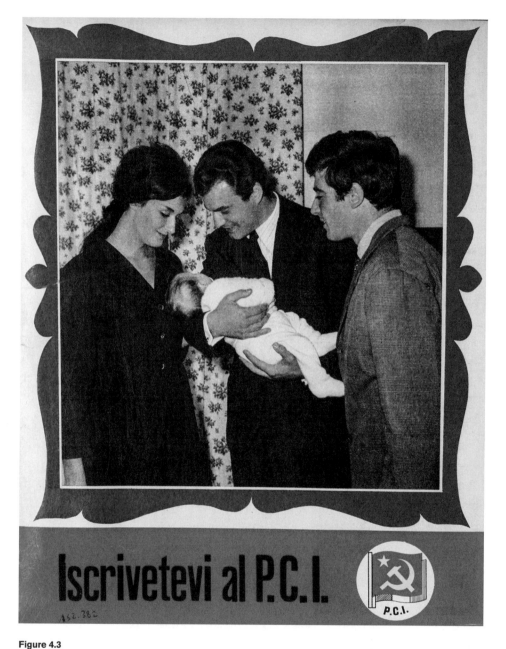

Figure 4.3
Back cover of "Frontiera tra gli sposi" (Border between Spouses) (PCI Sezione Stampa e Propaganda, 1964). Courtesy of Fondazione Istituto Gramsci.

different moments of an action but rather the same situation from different angles (figure 4.4). Consequently, the customary representation of time as chronological development seems to be replaced in these instances by a static field of vision that rotates from left to right, from top to bottom, around the couple in conversation.

These stylistic elements are relevant to a main aspect in Communist photoromances. All of them take place in the historical time of the readers, never in what Serge Saint-Michel describes as "the a-historical, mythical, time of the eternal feminine."[20] They are bound to historical contingency instead of being collocated in the atemporal space of fantasy. Furthermore, their stories project readers into the future while also addressing their present. "Life Will Change," "The Great Hope," "Destiny in Your Hand," "Stronger Than Destiny": these titles do not refer to an unknown future, but to a future that readers can control should they join the Communist cause. Most PCI photoromances are set in Southern Italy, where the message of faith in historical progress directly addresses cultural and social issues dependent on a logic of fatalism, that is, the belief that nothing can be done to change one's fate. Layered through centuries of exploitation by local, national, and foreign colonizing forces, fatalism was a detriment to the working classes because it nurtured hopelessness and distrust toward any kind of authority. In the Communist photoromances, the resolution of romantic and familial vicissitudes constitutes the material proof that change is possible. These private matters are inextricable from economic and political factors, particularly unemployment and the Christian Democratic politics on emigration. Couples are separated because of unemployment, which forced Italian men (husbands or fiancées) to emigrate to Germany or Switzerland. In "Border between Spouses," for example, the husband works abroad (in this case, in Switzerland) under difficult circumstances—and so does his brother-in-law—while his pregnant wife must stay in Italy because she could not otherwise receive free medical assistance. The story eventually ends with the family reunited in their small southern Italian village and with a message of hope for the future: the male protagonist declares to his wife his certainty regarding their chances of finding a better life in their hometown, especially should they sustain the activities of the Communist Party. Several other photoromances deal with the issue of emigration and the horrible pains and injustices that emigrants endure in order to support their families. "Heart of Emigrants" more generally describes oppression and exploitation in the workplace in Germany, as well as the poor living conditions of workers, who must share a room and cannot have a place of their own. Also, "Heart of Emigrants"

Figure 4.4

"Diritto di amare" (The Right to Love) (PCI Sezione Stampa e Propaganda, 1964): 6. Courtesy of Fondazione Istituto Gramsci.

describes the isolation of workers and their lack of any contact with local people (not even women, to engage in love affairs!). Furthermore, these workers are frequently victims of racist comments or discrimination. In "The Great Hope," workers tell their stories as they return to Italy in order to vote. As the Christian Democrats are blamed for abandoning the emigrants to their fate, emigration is presented simultaneously as a curse and a necessity.

As Evelyne Sullerot points out, emigration is also a main trope in commercial photoromances, and is portrayed as the cause of love troubles.[21] Although the French scholar suggests that the photoromance exploits emigration exclusively as a narrative device impeding the realization of the love fantasy, in the Communist narratives romance is the means to acquire awareness of both economic and emotional exploitation, and, thus, to trigger women's support. The commentary placed at the end of "Heart of Emigrants" concludes: "From the story of Giovanna and Carlo appears the true, real, human condition of hundreds of thousands of Italian families that have been divided by the migrant politics followed by the governments that until now have had a turn in guiding the country. . . . It is necessary therefore to deny votes to the D.C. [Christian Democracy] and to all the other governmental parties responsible for mass emigration and division of hundreds of thousands of Italian families."[22] Also similar to the commercial examples surveyed by Sullerot, Communist photoromances exercise, vis-à-vis their readers, "a compensation of profound frustration on the affective level."[23] These photoromances did not envision the fantasy of a Socialist revolution. Ultimately, they represented the verisimilar reality of the personal conversion of workers' wives and fiancées from undecided or apolitical to Communists. The emotional toll that the men's departure provokes in the female protagonists, as well as the greatest satisfaction triggered by the men's return to the motherland (and to the wife/fiancées), takes a central role in relation to the struggle against capitalists and the Christian Democratic government.

Similar to other cases of Marxist-inspired narratives of the period, an aesthetic of realism is not the only explanation for this narrative solution.[24] Rather, I see the decision to focus on individual stories as a way to relate personally to female readers. The effects of such stories are still relevant politically, since they may produce micro-social change precisely by compensating frustrations at the affective level. Through the resolution of conflicts within couples (married or engaged) or between family members (usually between daughters and fathers), romantic stories among working-class characters are politically charged with converting women to Communism by raising awareness about the workers' (i.e., their husbands') condition of exploitation. Earthly justice is then transferred from the hands of the exploited to the greater entity of the PCI and projected into the future. In the meantime, women can vote righteously at the next election or enlist in the local branch of the party.

As my brief summaries already highlighted, gender roles are traditionally assigned in Communist photoromances: women are entrusted with the care of the family and children, and, although young women may sometimes study, they do not work and all wish to get married. Women's suffering is only consequent to that of their husbands and fiancés, and their role in the domestic sphere is taken for granted, just as is their devotion to male characters. Indeed, women acquire political awareness by accepting their husband's or father's values and point of view. Female characters also do not have leading roles, but instead act as companions of male workers, whose stories remain at the core of each narrative regardless of whether it takes place in Italy or abroad. Even in "Life Will Change," in which the main female character Maria is a constant presence throughout the story, the male characters (her suitor Franco and her father Pasquale) are the ones who lead the action and move the plot forward. Pasquale refuses to submit to a "psycho-technical" test that is required to get a job at the new factory, which he helped to build, claiming that anyone in need should be employed, not—as the company's doctor replies to him—according to a scientific evaluation. Unemployed, Pasquale must emigrate and leave Maria and the family behind. Consequently, Maria decides to join PCI and to lead a protest against the corrupt Christian Democratic local government, which is behind the decision of the factory owner to eventually reject all Communist workers' applications, overriding the initial plan to hire according to the results of the test. Blackmailed by the politician who helped him receive the subcontract, the corrupted industrialist agrees that the factory needed politically aligned workers rather than the best workers for the jobs. Franco, however, disavows the PCI so that he can find employment at the same factory. For this reason, Maria rejects Franco, even though she has fallen in love with him. After an accident at work, in which he loses his hand, Franco reverts to his initial political position and joins the comrades by announcing that he will vote Communist in the next election. With Maria's father finally having returned home, she is now ready to marry Franco. On the last page of the photoromance, Maria suggests that political commitment is the main drive behind her decision to marry Franco, rejecting physical attraction as a reason for being together (she does not mind that he lost his hand). On the very day in which they will both vote Communist, Maria asks Franco to promise "to never leave her again" so that the same day will be for them "the celebration of feelings."[25]

This story is particularly emblematic because it charges the female protagonist with increasing power in the social context, yet without any radical change in gender hierarchies and identities. In fact, Maria's leadership aims at fulfilling the demands of male workers: all employees in the factory are men and her political efforts are generally concentrated on fighting male unemployment.[26] Maria does not consider any specific women's issues either at work or in the private sphere. Instead, she replaces her mother (a housewife), who appears to be unable to deal with the loss of her husband, and then is ready to return to her previous role of devoted companion once her fiancée returns to her and to the Communist Party. "Judge the past, look at the future: Vote Communist:" the propaganda motto on the back cover synthesizes narrative time in "Life Will Change," wherein the female protagonist is inspired by her father to take the lead in fighting for workers' rights in her southern village, but also to consider her future, that is, the male worker whom she wishes to marry. Perhaps due to her leading role in the story, Maria is an exception, as she looks straight at readers in the headshot on the cover of "Life Will Change." All the other actresses not only are modestly dressed, but also never gaze directly toward the camera and rarely look directly into another character's eyes—including those of their partner, even when they are married. Baetens argues that this type of composition is typical in photoromances, in which characters appear to be isolated in the space where they act, a fact that excludes intimacy with their viewers.[27] In addition, from a gendered perspective, rather than looking into their partner's eyes, the women in these photoromances are looked *at*; they are submissive and docile bodies, even when they act as political subjects (who exhibit their support of the Communist Party).

Ultimately, Communist photoromances failed to speak to women for two reasons. First, by conforming to a patriarchal logic, they did not investigate issues relevant to the female subject (such as sexuality). Second, even though they cast women in traditional roles of mother and spouse, they never really addressed problems specifically relevant to gender (such as motherhood). Rather, conforming to the same patriarchal logic, they treated only those problems that were dependent on men's troubles (in the economic or political sphere). In this respect, the Catholic Edizioni San Paolo demonstrated a deeper interest in the psychology of female readers, albeit in the name of their moral education. In *FC*, the illustrated magazine for "family and women," most photoromances star female saints, explore female subjectivities, and address the issue of governing women's desires.[28] These photo-hagiographies convey Catholic rules of conduct, especially with regard to sexuality and the family, through the means of popular culture. In a fast-changing society, where sexual liberties are potentially dangerous to the traditional family and thus to the regulation of people's conduct, *FC* exploits the photoromance in order to speak to women's hearts and teach them how to behave.

MARIA GORETTI SUPERSTAR

Of the twelve photoromances published between 1959 and 1966 in *FC*, only four have male protagonists.[29] Moreover, several features in the hagiographies of these men correspond to those of women: martyrdom, chastity, conversion, and poverty.[30] Furthermore, all protagonists are laywomen and laymen, with the exception only of Saint Anthony, who was not a member of an official order, but a Franciscan Friar. Beginning in the early 1950s, the stories of these so-called "saints dressed in pants and jackets" were published in *FC*, as a "novella" (short fiction) in a series of installments in a section with the same title.[31] The column was meant to provide examples of everyday sainthood. According to Marazziti, holding the "internal front" of the battle against secularization, it displayed "heroic and silent individuals," whose role was juxtaposed to that of saints on the "external front"—missionaries working toward individual and mass conversion. The magazine perceived the global job of missionaries as dependent on male virtues even though both men and women starred in the column. My research shows that a specific interest in female saints only becomes evident when the column is replaced by the photoromance, a feminine-labeled media. At this point, the saints who are meant to put forward "accessible ideals to common believers in their everyday life" are mostly women.[32] At home, where the Catholic war against modern society's secularization takes place "in front of the TV," *FC* preaches Catholicism "in tabloid language," specifically by addressing female audiences via visual narratives that sanctified virgins and faithful wives.

Even though *FC* was quite open to consumerism, photoromances confirm Niahm Cullen's opinion that the magazine was not open to changes in matters of sexual conduct and gender relations.[33] Other columns such as *Talking to the Father* sustain this assumption. In a letter published in 1955 and titled "Uomini bestiali" (Beastlike Husbands), Father Atanasio preached to his readers "the virtues of a female soul": "The priest will reproach a beastlike husband, but good mothers and faithful wives must continue to offer up their daily martyrdom with faith in the Lord."[34] The same preaching articulates the narrative of Saint Rita's life in "La rosa rossa (Santa Rita)" (The Red Rose [Saint Rita]) (figure 4.5).[35] Although Father Atanasio did not foresee this outcome in his counseling about "everyday martyrdom," it is an effect that aptly represents the excess that characterizes the hagiographies of photoromances with respect to the other columns in the magazine. In the last episodes of the photoromance, Rita becomes a nun after her husband's violent death, and moments of ecstasy fully visualize her inner desires. Projected into the afterlife, while on her deathbed calling out for Jesus, Rita's passionate inner feelings are idealized and spiritualized, and her past carnal relationship is said to have been a duty she fulfilled for the sake of her parents and her children. The photoromance narrates Rita's experiences as the wife of an abusive and alcoholic husband, whom she never left and never stopped serving, and whom she never even wanted to marry (her desire was to become a nun, but her parents forced her to marry the rich man). Eventually, Rita succeeded in converting her husband to the point that he was killed for his faith.

The case of Maria Goretti is also exemplary. In the words of Cullen, "The cult of Maria Goretti, a young girl who, at the turn of the twentieth century had been brutally murdered for resisting an attempt at rape to preserve her virginity and was canonized in 1950 was symptomatic of [the Church's] desperate attempt to turn back the tides of modernity."[36] Her story appeared in *FC* in the form of a serial novel, in six issues, from April to May 1952, and then as a photoromance in seventeen issues, from October, 16, 1960, to February 5, 1961, titled "Sangue sulla palude: La storia di Maria Goretti" ("Blood on the Swamp: The Story of Maria Goretti").[37] Maria's story in *FC* is not only popularized via pulp fiction and photoromance, but also through tabloid news. The first episode of the photoromance appeared in the same issue as an interview with Sandro Serenelli, the girl's murderer, who was then seventy-six years old and living in a convent. According to both "Blood on the Swamp" and the interview, Maria forgave Serenelli before she died; later, he claimed that she miraculously appeared to him several times when he was in prison. Having repented, Serenelli was released from

---

Figure 4.5
"La rosa rossa (Santa Rita)" (The Red Rose [Saint Rita]), *Famiglia Cristiana*, no. 22 (1960): 35. Courtesy of Edizioni San Paolo.

la Rosa rossa
(Santa Rita)

PERSONAGGI E INTERPRETI: RITA - Marina MEDICI - PAOLO - Orazio SABATINI
MADRE SUPERIORA - Lidia MANCANI - MADRE di RITA - Paolina MAGRELLI
PADRE di RITA - Giulio NARDI - LA CUGINA - Anita TERMINI
I due figli di RITA - Luigi e Livio RIBECCA - NANDONE - Agostino MARINI
I tre BRAVI - M. GIACOMINI e A. TERMINI - FALEGNAME - Nazzareno

regia di Eduardo Falletti
fotografia di Adolfo Guerrieri
Soggetto: S.C. Fuzier - Sceneggiatura: Giorgio FASCETTI

POCHI CRISTIANI SEPPERO UBBIDIRE TANTO UMILMENTE ALLA VOLONTÀ DI DIO COME SANTA RITA CHE TUTTO DETTE DI SÈ, MERAVIGLIOSAMENTE, FINO ALL'ESTREMO SACRIFICIO. L'AMORE È LA LEGGE ETERNA ALLA QUALE RITA MAI TRASGREDI': E L'AMORE E LA FEDE LE ACCESERO IL CUORE, FIN DALLA FANCIULLEZZA, FACENDO DI LEI UNA SANTA.

ERA NATA A ROCCA PORENA, UNO SPERDUTO PAESINO DELL'UMBRIA, E FU BATTEZZATA IL 22 MAGGIO 1363 NELLA CHIESA DI SANTA MARIA DELLA PLEBE A CASCIA... GIOVINETTA, SI DEDICAVA AI PIÙ UMILI LAVORI.

ERA ALTA, SNELLA, BELLA, MODESTISSIMA... TUTTI I GIOVANI DEL VILLAGGIO LA DESIDERAVANO...

Non ci degna di uno sguardo!

Rita! Perchè non parli?

I SUOI GENITORI, AMATA E ANTONIO MANCINI, ERANO MODESTI AGRICOLTORI; MA SPERAVANO CHE RITA FACESSE UN BUON MATRIMONIO... QUEL GIORNO VI ERA UN OSPITE DI RIGUARDO IN CASA MANCINI...

Ho da farvi una proposta, caro Antonio!

Di che affare si tratta, Nandone?

jail after twenty-seven years and went on to become one of the greatest promoters of Maria's canonization. He reconciled with the Goretti family, and, in the article on *FC*, he is portrayed in a picture with Assunta, Maria's mother.

"Blood on the Swamp" is written by Sara Fuzier du Cayla (aka Zia Betta, author of a popular advice column in the same magazine), also the author of Assunta's biography (1956), in which Maria's story is told from her mother's perspective.[38] The opening caption in the first episode of "Blood on the Swamp" includes a quotation from the Gospel (Matthew 6:10; Luke 11:12): "Do not fear those who kill your body: they cannot kill your soul; fear instead him who can damn your soul and send your body to Hell."[39] For those who knew the story of Maria Goretti (and in 1960, these were many, especially among readers of *FC*), the citation clearly summarized the moral content of the events: teenager Sandro Serenelli could kill nine-year-old Maria's body, but he could not conquer her soul and, most important, could not taint her purity, meaning her virginity. In this light, I disagree with Marazziti who claims that, since the 1930s and 1940s, *FC* "presents itself with all the traits of the popular-Catholic 'sub-culture' that is primarily interested not in information or politics, but in education, in the evident sense of a clear and articulate continuation of Sunday's preaching."[40] Rather than opposing "education" to "politics," photoromances recounting the lives of female saints can be examined for their political relevance, both for what they avoid addressing in narratives (thus maintaining certain social structures), and because of how they fashion their protagonists, for example, by exalting the natural predisposition of women to sacrifice and martyrdom. These traditionally feminine qualities make women preferred political subjects (in this sense, they empower them), for women are seemingly naturally accepting in their conduct and defer ultimate decisions to God's will. In this perspective, women's will to power is one of self-denial and masochism, and, in the eyes of God, it is as such that they excel against male villains.

David Forgacs and Stephen Gundle have already argued how the Vatican used Maria Goretti's case for political purposes. They write: "The Church repressed not only the violence of the episode but also the other possible reading: that such acts of sexual coercion might be influenced by social conditions of extreme poverty and forced cohabitation; that Maria's refusal may have been prompted not by her religiosity but simply by fear; that acts of sexual violence such as Serenelli's were sustained by a culture of male supremacy that the Church not only did not condemn but, with its advocacy of female submissiveness and obedience and its tacit acceptance of coercive customs such as the "deflowering" of virgin brides on their wedding night, helped to sustain."[41] A reading of "Blood on the Swamp" both supports and problematizes Forgacs and Gundle's assessment. First of all, "Blood on the Swamp" emphasizes that Serenelli's sexual attraction to Maria, his attempted assaults, and his final murderous act were due to the bad influence of popular culture, more specifically, illustrated magazines. Just before assaulting Maria for the first time, Sandro is lying on his bed and reading a magazine that, according to the caption, did not have any "moral content." The same caption reads: "For some time, the boy has desperately indulged in unhealthy readings" (figure 4.6).[42] In the subsequent photograph in the same page, Sandro appears in a medium shot, with his gaze fixated on an invisible object and his hand on his chest, underneath his open shirt. Here the caption comments: "Readings that excite him and leave him distraught. While a murky thought, steady like a nail, has not left him for some time."[43] Immediately after, Sandro turns his thoughts into action and we see him standing in front of the window looking outside and downward. Between photographs, the gutter does not connect an action to another action. Rather, each photograph represents Sandro's reaction to his inner emotions and desire: (1) he reads and, because of what he reads; (2) he touches his body and looks distraught, and, because of what he feels; and (3) he goes and looks outside the window. While these photographs visualize the invisible narrative of Sandro's psychology, the following photograph shows readers, via the filmic style of a subjective take, what Sandro sees outside the window: Maria walking down the street. The caption comments on Maria's photograph that "the girl in that moment is passing by and does not suspect that impure eyes are scrutinizing her from a window."[44] Again, in perfect cinematic style, Maria is made into a sexual object by Sandro's act of looking and by the photograph that embodies his gaze. Her body, however, is not exposed but rather excessively covered so that moral temptation depends, once more, on the gazing subject himself and the effects that previous readings had on him: Sandro's gaze is "impuro" (impure) and "si anima di una luce sinistra" (comes alive with an evil light).

In the last photograph, Sandro's face, shown in a close-up, conveys his distress and anticipates the action that will follow. A balloon indicates what he is thinking ("Right away . . . no more waiting . . . Now! Here she is, she's coming."), and creates expectations of violence for the next page.[45] In fact, very little will happen, and the reader will be able to see even less: Maria's assault is reduced to a single shot in which Sandro touches her hand. The setting suddenly moves to the cemetery where Maria goes to

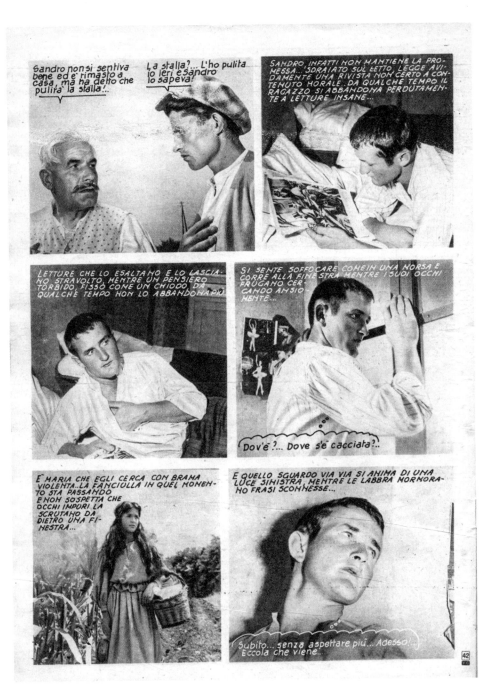

Figure 4.6

"Sangue sulla palude" (Blood on the Swamp), *Famiglia Cristiana*, no. 50 (1960): 42. Courtesy of Edizioni San Paolo.

visit her father's grave and prays that he take her to him, so that she would not have to see Sandro again (figure 4.7).

Throughout the photoromance, sex is synonymous to violence. Maria's father is the only positive male figure (if we exclude the priest), and, in fact, his relationship with Assunta is not romantic; his paternal role identifies him as a seemingly asexual individual. The men's relationship to women takes place through oppression and exploitation, with the goal to possess them both psychologically and physically. In this sense, there is an attempt in "Blood on the Swamp" to criticize what Forgacs and Gundle refer to as the "culture of male supremacy." Sandro is not the only man to have obsessive thoughts toward women and to sexually assault one of them: his father also harassed Maria's mother, an aspect of the story that was not included in the official account of the saint's life. Ultimately, "Blood on the Swamp" does not show much violence, yet it is structurally permeated by the constant fear of male violence, a fear perpetrated against all women in the story. Assunta must withstand Sandro's father Giovanni's requests twice. On the second occasion, her refusal triggers the man's abusive behavior toward the entire Goretti family: "After Assunta's refusal that time, life at the ironworks becomes impossible," the captions recounts.[46] It also prompts Sandro's second attempt to possess Maria, who appears to catalyze all of her family's misery. We read in the same page that "her sad face clearly communicates all the suffering, all the fears, all the deprivation to which *the family has always been submitted*."[47] Maria embodies her family's oppression, creating a link between the social condition of the peasant family and the condition of the female subject, both of whom are violated by male abusive power.

The two main female figures in the photoromance (Maria and her mother Assunta) are not only the embodiment of oppression, but also champions of religious faith as they consistently remind everyone of the necessity to believe in Providence. They also exemplify modesty in their behaviors and clothing. Assunta rejects having another relationship after her husband's death; Maria, who is a child, completely ignores the existence of sex (she does not understand what Sandro wants from her, and thinks he is simply upset), and, when she is eventually murdered, she does not seem to consciously reject Sandro to protect her virginal purity, but rather—as the caption I previously mentioned indicates—does so out of fear, the fear in which she and her family have always lived. In other words, her killing is the ultimate gesture of abuse, the most brutal because it is against an innocent child. By no means does the photoromance appear

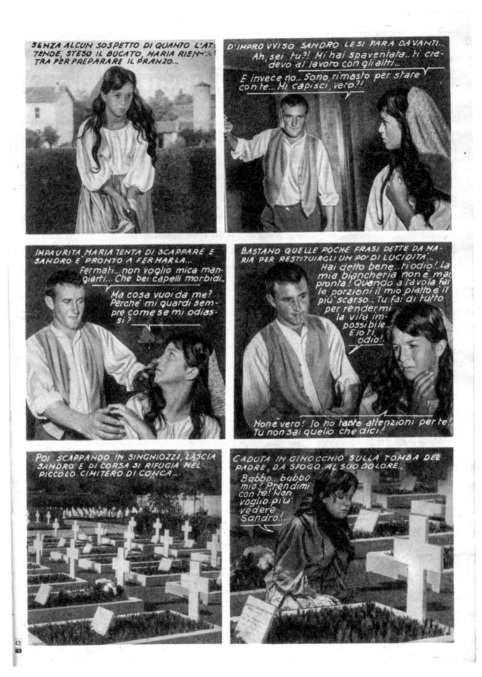

Figure 4.7

"Sangue sulla palude" (Blood on the Swamp), *Famiglia Cristiana*, no. 50 (1960): 43. Courtesy of Edizioni San Paolo.

to make a radical statement regarding the social and political conditions in which Maria and her family lived, for justice still remains in the hands of God and not in those of the oppressed. At the same time, however, "Blood on the Swamp" does speak of Maria's story as something more than solely an example of chastity. The social relevance of her murder is not denied, but exploited in order to address both middle-class and lower-class audiences, particularly women.

This double targeting of middle- and lower-class audiences is also demonstrated in the stylistic choices that are modeled on current commercial productions of photoromances. First, by using the traditional format of installments, which often end episodes with a cliff-hanger, Catholic photoromances attempt to create suspense, to excite readers' expectations, and to attract loyal customers. "Beware of monotony!" declared Father Alberione, founder of San Paolo Edizioni.[48] Also, Catholic photoromances dealt with readers that most likely already knew the stories being presented, and thus exploited the same mechanism of expectation that one can find, as Umberto Eco points out, in popular fiction such as *Love Story*: "Cautioning the reader, from the beginning, that s/he will follow the apparently cheerful loves stories of two young people already marked by a tragic destiny, promotes the acceptance of the final shock, places it under the sign of necessity, empties it of any provocative power, and furthermore helps the reader to anticipate the expected implications page by page."[49] Eco's comment highlights how popular fictions could both entertain readers and enact conservative politics of social containment. In the case of hagiographies, the necessity of the saints' lives, in which any action is meant ultimately to fulfill a prophecy of sainthood, perfectly agrees with the form of *Love Story*. Most readers of *FC* in the late 1950s knew Goretti's story and thus also how "Blood on the Swamp" would end; the pleasure of reading derived from retracing the sequence of events and celebrating the necessity of Maria's sacrifice. In this sense, "Blood on the Swamp" both engages the reader and empties any possible subversive value from the saint's final act of rebellion against male violence.

Not unlike other illustrated magazines' displays of film stars, *FC* photoromances created the myth of exceptional, but relatable, female saints interpreted by modestly dressed but physically attractive actresses. The type of photography used appears to be closer to the popular model that, according to Baetens, responded to both "the glamourized eroticism of the face" and the "payout principles of the new magazines."[50] Here, the paradox of a Catholic magazine aiming to preach the Gospel and, at the same time, to entertain the modern reader becomes evident. Although film stars were banned from the magazine, the prevalence of close-ups (rather than medium shots, as used in the Communist magazines) in its photoromances fashion female actresses quite similarly, as their faces are often portrayed with expressions of longing and anguish, while their make-up and hairdos give them a stylish appearance (figure 4.8).[51]

Furthermore, close-ups emphasize the emotional and moral struggle that are at stake in the narratives and that take place internally with the characters. Thus, photography responds to the magazine's need to market sexual morality via emotional, as much as rational, means of communication. In other words, female saints not only speak well, as they follow Catholic rules of conduct, but they also look good, according to the same principles of beauty and modernity that defined the mothers who dominated (together with their children) the front covers of *FC*: "always beautiful, but it is worth highlighting that they are often blond and somewhat American-looking, with slim waists and stylish dresses" (figure 4.9).[52] Considering that readers were predominantly middle-class, from northern and provincial Italy, these images corresponded to the same model of bourgeois propriety and well-mannered femininity that therefore allowed for the process of identification needed in order to promote the status quo. Emphasizing desire, as opposed to conformism, photoromances instead represented the excess of these models both in the sexual appetite and violent acts of male characters, and in the gestures of devotion and love for God of female protagonists.

THE STRUGGLE FOR WOMEN'S MINDS

The Communist Party's decision to publish photoromances was not about lowering expectations or giving the popular audience some debased form of entertainment: the goal was to fashion the PCI itself in a new light, one that put it closer to the people and their preferred forms of entertainment. In the context of a Catholic magazine such as *FC*, photoromances played the role of educational tools as well as entertaining materials, aiming at popularizing hagiographies while engaging female believers with the same and latest technologies of the cultural industries. Communist and Catholic photoromances both attempted to educate Italian women by mobilizing their emotions rather than by indoctrination. This aspect was particularly relevant at the time when the Christian Democratic Office of Propaganda produced several short films that exploited fictional narratives and generic conventions in order to attract people's

Figure 4.8

"La rosa rossa (Santa Rita)" (The Red Rose [Saint Rita]), *Famiglia Cristiana*, no. 22 (1960): 37. Courtesy of Edizioni San Paolo.

Figure 4.9
Cover of *Famiglia Cristiana*, no. 49 (1960). Courtesy of Edizioni San Paolo.

attention and their emotional reactions toward the government's initiatives, such as the Agrarian Reform or urban planning.[53] Even if PCI did not participate in the same kind of film productions, however, the decision to publish photoromances can be seen in the same context of innovation and transformation of propaganda practices that were initiated by the government. In the same vein, San Paolo was interested in the emotional effects that reading had on believers (especially young women), and used films to stir their fears for punishment when indulging in magazines that were deemed too risqué.

At the same time, the patriarchal and sexist logic based on which both Catholic and Communist sponsors fashioned female subjectivities in the photoromances, prevented the agencies from truly addressing their readers' expectations and concerns. The stories of Communist families do not tackle issues of sexual conduct, and while *FC* photoromances consistently allude to sex, they do so exclusively as violence, abuse, or moral deviance. In this way, *FC* photo-hagiographies chastise sexual desire but also shed light on the actual threat that these products of mass culture posed to Italian society. The challenge was not that *Bolero Film* distracted Italian women from politics, worship, or urgent matters; the danger was that photoromances could affect sexual conduct. A few years later, in the mid-1970s, the Italian Association for Demographic Education (AIED) would turn this logic upside down by engendering the migration of celebrities into the realm of sexual rights activism. As I will show in chapter 5, the 1975 AIED campaign to promote birth control methods revolutionized the political use of photoromances because it employed, for the first time, notorious public figures. Actress Paola Pitagora and TV contestant Mario Valdemarin, among others, anticipated Leonardo Di Caprio and the like in their testimonials for social causes, by appearing in photo-stories that popularized sexual liberation while voicing their support for the contraceptive pill in the press.

5 BIRTH CONTROL IN COMICS

In 1976, on the pages of *Corriere della Sera*, Umberto Eco praised an experiment that took place in a middle school of the popular Roman neighborhood "Torre Spaccata:" a group of students had created a photoromance about one of their favorite celebrities, swimmer Novella Calligaris. "Knowing to read these new myths and discovering the teaching hidden beneath forms of entertainment is a new approach to schooling that prepares one for life," claimed Eco.[1] Written about ten years after the publication of his seminal essay on mass culture *Apocalittici e integrati* (Apocalypse Postponed, 1964), Eco's short contribution sustained a positive attitude toward mass media, arguing that the form itself could be used to criticize the ideas that were purportedly imposed on its users. Speaking of photoromances, Eco's friendly words were at odds with the widespread contempt or condescension that most scholars and journalists usually employed at the time when they talked about these magazines. In a sharp and typical critique, Luigi Compagnone in the same *Corriere* had only two years earlier declared that, the photoromance "does not give people to read, only to look; thus it eludes language and accustoms them not to think."[2] Writing in a column titled *Risponde Compagnone* (Compagnone Responds), the well-known fiction writer and journalist received many letters from readers who were offended by his words, which he quoted in a follow-up article in the same column (a few weeks later). In a highly ironic tone, Compagnone replied by dismissing resentment and complaints, and insisted that "the reader of photoromances is a passive subject because he [sic] is deprived of language."[3]

However, Eco was not alone in believing that the photoromance could contribute to people's education. Initiatives like the one in Torre Spaccata were not unique in the seventies, especially in educational contexts such as schools and activist organizations, both in Italy and abroad.[4] In 1972, for example, a group of Italian architects and designers named Gruppo Strum participated in the exhibition *Italy: The New Domestic Landscape* at the Museum of Modern Art in New York with three photoromances that, according to an officially released document, depicted "the present conditions of urban decay," described "the methods which may be adopted to change the present situation," and catalogued "all forms of urban utopias presently envisioned by designers."[5] The architects and designers used the area assigned to them as a space where the illustrated stories were distributed free of charge to visitors because, in their words, no "physical forms" were capable of communicating their thought. Between 1973 and 1976 in Ecuador, the Peace Corps also experimented with the use of "photonovels" (instead of films) to educate Ecuadorian peasants on "subjects as diverse as environmental sanitation, prenatal and postnatal nutrition, malaria control, and family planning."[6] According to a Peace Corps publication titled *The Photonovel: A Tool for Development*: "Filmstrips, posters, and flipcharts were abandoned, after trials, in favor of the photonovel, because of its ability to communicate a detailed message through words and vision, while entertaining at the same time."[7]

Among the letters that Compagnone received against his tirade, the one written by Sergio Montesi advertised a "fotoromanzo anticoncezionale" (contraceptive photoromance).[8] Montesi wrote on behalf of the Italian Association for Demographic Education (AIED), which sponsored the publication of three photoromances as part of a larger campaign to educate Italians on the benefits of birth control and the low risks of the contraceptive pill. Against the idea that romances could only be apolitical and escapist, the stories of relationships narrated in AIED photoromances aimed at spreading behavioral models that were deemed appropriate by its sponsor's policy of public health. In doing so, AIED addressed not only the issue of unwanted pregnancies but also that of sexual rights for both men and women in a country still predominantly patriarchal, despite women's increasing liberties in both the private and public spheres. The extremely low number of contraceptives users and the high number of illegal abortions made the AIED's romantic stories a timely effort, supported by the extraordinary success of the photoromance itself among mass audiences.[9]

Published by the Institute for Demographic Research and Initiative (IRIDE), the AIED's research arm, "Il segreto" (The Secret), "Noi giovani" (We the Youth), and "La trappola" (The Trap) used the technique of the *foto-racconto-lampo* (flash photo-story) a type of photoromance first invented by the Roman firm Lancio in the late 1960s.[10] The AIED flash photo-story consisted of a brief narrative that delivered a clear message: contraceptives were the secret weapon for a happy sexual, romantic, and social life. As I will show in the following paragraphs, this message was embedded in stories that pushed the previous boundaries set by the Italian birth control movement with regard to sexual conduct. Following the tradition of American educational media, however, AIED's rhetorical strategies were not as new and original as Montesi claimed; at the same time, they departed from this tradition by uniquely engaging with Italian celebrity culture.[11] In this way, the 1970s AIED campaign not only was innovative in Europe in the use of photoromances for propaganda purposes, but also demonstrated a deep understanding of what made the medium so successful among the masses.

THE CAMPAIGN: CROSSING BOUNDARIES

"Birth Control in Comics": with this title, in 1974, the national newspaper *La Stampa* announced in the imminent publication by AIED of the three photoromances mentioned earlier—"The Secret," "We the Youth," and "The Trap"—to advertise and promote the use of contraceptives.[12] Celebrities such as actress Paola Pitagora, TV celebrity Mario Valdemarin, and singer Gianni Morandi provided testimonials for the campaign. Morandi eventually did not take part in the project, with Ugo Pagliai replacing him in the leading male role of "We the Youth." The three photoromances initially were distributed for free, 60,000 copies in three pilot cities: Novara, Arezzo, and Salerno.[13] In the following years, other cities were targeted as well as smaller groups for more specific survey purposes. For example, the photoromances were given to a focus group of two hundred male factory workers to test their attitudes toward birth control via an anonymous survey.[14] The back cover of each issue featured the AIED as sponsor, followed by a list of different birth control methods and products, and addresses of local "consultori" (i.e., free clinics where women could receive medical attention, psychological support, and access to birth control methods). Ugo Fornari is indicated as author of both the story and the script of "The Trap" and "We the Youth" while Marco De Luigi is indicated as the same for "The Secret"; both names, however, were pseudonyms of Luigi De Marchi (figure 5.1).

The 1975 AIED contraception campaign was announced in the press as both the evidence of progress in the sexual education of Italian citizens and as the ultimate success of "the tireless" De Marchi, president of the AIED and sexual rights activist,

who had just a few years earlier appeared in Italian newspapers for the groundbreaking court ruling that legalized the making and distribution of birth control propaganda in Italy.[15] In the mid-seventies, Italy was still behind in comparison with other nations, such as the United Kingdom or the Netherlands, with regard to sexual rights legislation as well as sexual education. According to Gianfranco Porta, in a recent history of the AIED titled *Amore e libertà*, "founding norms of fascist natalism" that considered neo-Malthusian theories of population planning "a crime against the integrity and health of race" were still in place in the new Republic.[16] In fact, Fascist laws against the use of contraceptives were not dismantled but converted into prescriptive rules that regulated sexual behaviors according to Catholic moral values.[17] Until 1971, Italian law prohibited fabricating, importing, buying, distributing, and possessing writings, drawings, and images to propagate birth control methods. Article 553 stated that "anyone who publicly incites use of birth control methods and makes use of propaganda in their favor can be punished to up to one year in prison and to a fine up to four hundred thousand lira."[18] In 1975, contraceptives were still officially accepted only for married couples: the official commentator of a newsreel portraying a parliamentary discussion on contraception stated that "it is necessary to inform pervasively, starting from the idea that planned parenthood has nothing to do with free love."[19] Finally, while in the 1960s and 1970s new laws were passed in many European countries to introduce sexual education in school, in Italy the topic was never seriously debated in the Parliament (see for example, the law proposal by Communist deputies Giorgio Bini, Adriana Seroni, and others in 1975).[20]

According to Dagmar Herzog, "scholars ten[d] to oscillate between presuming either that the growth of a culture of consumerism and the medical-technological invention of the birth control pill in the early 1960s sparked the sexual revolution or that this revolution was the logical result of courageous social movement activism on behalf of sexual liberties, legalization of abortion, and gay and lesbian rights."[21] De Marchi's photoromances, and their reception in the press, convey the idea that the use of contraceptives was both a trigger and an effect of the sexual revolution in Italy.[22] In this context, the AIED's photoromances constituted the first nationwide

---

Figure 5.1
Cover of "Il segreto" (The Secret, 1975).

campaign for the birth control pill that detached the sexual act from both procreation and marriage. In anticipation of their publication, De Marchi declared to the press, in open confrontation with both the Vatican and the current political establishment, that Italian doctors who were not in favor of contraceptives contributed to a widespread demonization of sexuality in Italian society. Furthermore, birth control was strictly related to modifications in the ways in which sex was perceived, represented, and repressed. He reportedly said, "Historically, sexuality has been based on a neurotic balance—a sin that leads to a guilty conscience one must overcome through penance. Until now, such penance has been presented under scientific terms."[23]

De Marchi's statements were clearly influenced by Wilhelm Reich's theories (of which he was a translator), which he programmatically embedded in his book *Sesso e civiltà* (1960). There, De Marchi basically asserted that sexual taboos prevented the healthy functioning of societies. In many ways, dialogues and captions in "We the Youth" and "The Secret" reflect De Marchi's perspective and present the pill as the tool to liberate sexuality, while also communicating that the commercialization of contraceptives depended on the spread of radical thinking about sexual conduct. In "We the Youth," the youth talk about the pill as the means to free love but also as "a form of revolution against the fathers' civilization."[24] In the closing photograph of "We the Youth," the young couple of the story is caught in a close-up as they look obliquely at the future, sealed by a caption that says, "Once upon a time, people made little love and many children. We that are young, we want less children and more love!!" (figure 5.2).[25] In "The Secret," the female protagonist Lia explicitly argues for the use of the pill in order to liberate sexual intercourse from the burden of reproduction. A culture of pleasure substitutes for an imperative of fertility as a sign of virility, for men, and of faithfulness, for women. In the story, Lia contemplates being unfaithful because she is not satisfied with her partner, Franco, but is plagued by "l'angoscia di restare inguaiata" (the anxiety of getting in trouble).[26] Franco, on the other hand, wonders whether it would be better to go with a prostitute since "at least she doesn't make a fuss and doesn't have any fear."[27] Eventually "the secret of [their] new happiness" is the pill, thanks to which Lia can finally let herself go and, in her words, "taste ultimate bliss for the first time" (figure 5.3).[28]

Figure 5.2

Last page of "Noi giovani" (We the Youth), starring Ugo Pagliai and Paola Gassman (1975).

E GIANNI, DICE FRANCAMENTE AL PROFESSORE COME LA PENSANO I RAGAZZI.

Vede, professore, noi non vogliamo ripetere l'errore delle generazioni passate, che ci hanno lasciato questo mondo sovraffollato, pieno di guerre, di fame e d'inquinamento.

Una volta, la gente faceva poco amore e molti figli. Noi giovani, invece, vogliamo pochi figli e molto amore!!

Sei stata splendida, questa volta:
così appassionata, così vibrante.
Non sembravi più la stessa...

MA QUALCHE SETTIMANA DOPO, IL SOLE BRILLA DI NUOVO SULL'AMORE DI FRANCO E LIA...

Sì, amore, non è mai stato così bello: un delirio meraviglioso...

5

Però ti eri talmente avvinghiata che non ho potuto lasciarti nel momento supremo: speriamo che non succedano guai...

Non preoccuparti, tesoro. Le nostre ansie sono finite. Sto prendendo la pillola: questo è il segreto della nuova felicità. Per questo ho potuto finalmente abbandonarmi a te senza timore e gustare per la prima volta il piacere supremo...

6

7

In a country where, in 1978, women's pleasure was still "marginal and accessory" and "accepted only as [a] component of the procreational purpose," to quote Fabris and Davis's survey on the sexual behaviors of Italians, "The Secret" was truly ground-breaking.[29] At the same time, "The Secret" fit perfectly in the historical context of 1970s Italy where, while conservative positions were still predominant at the level of legislation and government, mass culture was increasingly more risqué in representations of sexuality and the press suffered from a "polling fever"[30] that—like in other European countries before—resulted in sex being "talked to death."[31] In addition to academic research, surveys were published in popular Italian news magazines such as *Panorama* (1977) and *L'Espresso* (1978) to discuss the knowledge and habits of Italians in matters of sexuality.[32] As Lucia Purisol writes in *Corriere della Sera*, "Women's weeklies tried to fill the gap in sexual education via 'R-Rated' surveys, reports and inserts."[33] Other articles published in *Corriere della Sera* and *La Stampa* celebrated the AIED for its contribution to the sexual education of Italian citizens. Such publicity for the AIED aligned with other journalistic reports on sexuality insofar as it redefined the public discourse by "a marked medicalization and scientification."[34] An example can be found in *La Stampa*, which in 1974 published in three subsequent articles the results of a sexual education survey conducted at the Istituto Superiore Einaudi.[35] On the same page of the second report, in which students freely discuss their sexuality, another article advertises a press conference titled "Fate l'amore, non i figli" (Make Love Not Children) during which "a new contraceptive method" was presented: the photoromances.[36] While the article's intention to turn this cultural product into a scientific method in itself may be farfetched, it is fair to say that medicine and scientific innovation play a significant role in the stories. In addition, each story ends with an advertisement of contraceptives including brand products such as Rendell, Lorofin, and Taro Cap. While the "inserto informativo" (informative insert) was clearly meant to provide scientific knowledge with regard to these products, their branding added commercial value to a publication whose goal was supposed to be exclusively social (and not for profit).

Despite the fact that public information campaigns promoting birth control were illegal, other contraceptive methods had already been advertised in magazines in the

Figure 5.3
"Il segreto" (The Secret, 1975), 7.

late 1960s. In *Bolero Film*, a commercial for CDI, "il nuovissimo Sistema Combinato" (the very new Combined System) promoted a "natural method" of contraception that was supported by the Catholic Church and recommended by doctors (according to the ad).[37] There are no documents that prove the AIED was in any way behind this initiative; however, the slogan for the product was strikingly similar to Vittoria Olivetti Berla's motto in the essay she wrote in defense of family planning in 1954. "CHILDREN, YES (but at the right moment)," said the CDI commercial; "all and only wanted children, at the right time," wrote Berla, who was at the time vice president of the AIED.[38] What is relevant in the similarities between *Bolero Film*'s ad and Berla's statement (as well as Planned Parenthood's, for that matter) is the focus on the institution of marriage as the appropriate space to speak of "responsible procreation."[39] Indeed, in its founding principle, the AIED did not aim at freeing society from sexual taboos, as De Marchi argued in his books and interviews; moreover, the organization did not at all consider contraceptives to support the sexual revolution. Founded in 1953 by a mixed group of bourgeois intellectuals, industrialists (such as Adriano Olivetti), radicals, and Socialists (including De Marchi), the AIED promoted birth control as "an economic intervention"—to solve the world's overpopulation problem—and "the means to allow an individual to be free and aware of his [sic] own life and of his offspring."[40] In this sense, the AIED resumed the activities of Socialists and radicals who, since the early twentieth century, considered birth control in response to the effects of industrialization, and embraced the Neo-Malthusian ideas with the goal of fighting poverty as well as with the purpose of regenerating Italian society.[41]

In both "We the Youth" and "The Trap," the radicalization of these principles conveyed De Marchi's unique perspective rather than that of the Italian birth control movement as a whole. In "Noi giovani," the young activists aim to solve worldwide issues of overpopulation, hunger, war, and environmental damages, like the birth control movement did; at the same time, their leader Gianni announces that free love is the tool to achieve such a goal (as claimed by De Marchi in his conversation with Guido Credazzi).[42] In "The Trap," the main character Marco is an unskilled worker employed by a greedy contractor who struggles to make ends meet when his fourth son is born. At the end of the story, Marco warns a young fellow worker not to have more than two children (as De Marchi did in the previously noted interview) and explains that "priests and bosses" want workers "full of children and crammed like ants to better dominate and exploit [them]" (figure 5.4).[43]

Non cadere anche tu nella trappola! Non fare più d'un figlio o due! Preti e padroni ci vogliono pieni di figli e fitti come formiche per meglio dominarci e sfruttarci.

FINE

Figure 5.4
Last page of "La trappola" (The Trap, 1975).

In sum, AIED photoromances draw from both mass culture and the tradition of the Italian birth control movement while pushing their own political and moral agenda. In "We the Youth" and "The Trap," anti-capitalist and anti-clerical ideas infuse the middle-class concerns for the world's overpopulation and the poor, while free love is claimed to be effective in solving the issue of the "population bomb" and its deleterious effects on humans and the environment. Furthermore, while photoromances on the market were mostly conservative in their visual representations of sexuality, "The Secret" was far more explicit in both words and images. According to a Lancio spokesperson, "There was never a nude scene, never pornography. In bed, she wears a high-necked shirt with long sleeves and he wears a sailor shirt."[44] The scene in the bedroom in "The Secret" shows precisely the "nudo" so much feared by Lancio. Several pictures represent in medium shots and close-ups a couple lying in bed, undressed albeit under the covers; the woman reveals her bare shoulders, the man sits upright with his chest naked. The couple not only shows that they had been intimate, but they both talk about sexual intercourse and about the pleasure that they may (or may not) have gained from the act. Furthermore, neither Lia nor Franco refers to each other as husband and wife. Some critics take for granted that the couple represented in "Il segreto" is married; however, this is not at all made explicit in the narrative. Such detail, in addition to the characters' conversation, shapes the message in support of contraception delivered by "The Secret" with the purpose of liberating sexuality from both the act of procreation and from the institution of marriage.

These claims were not only radical vis-à-vis the AIED's founding principles, but also with regard to the position held by the association in current contributions to illustrated magazines. In 1974, one year before the publication of "The Secret," two reports on women's "intimate lives" sponsored by the AIED were published in *Grand Hotel*.[45] Each report featured an advertisement for the AIED that stated: "A center where they teach you how to make love without the woman getting pregnant."[46] The first report discussed the topic of virginity "with candor and without prejudices" while the second explained "how to avoid unwanted pregnancies."[47] In both issues, *Grand Hotel* sent a clear message to its female readership: sexual intercourse was both natural and acceptable—however, "in una cornice di sentimento" (in a love setting) that could only be legitimated by marriage. As written in the second report, "The main goal of marriage is no longer to have children, but the couple's happiness and harmony. . . . However, we must learn how to have children only when both desire them. It is necessary that everyone knows how to do that."[48]

CLARENCE J. GAMBLE AND DE MARCHI'S RISE TO CELEBRITY

"Every child a wanted child" not only is the message conveyed in illustrated magazines and in Berla's essay, but also the title of Doctor Clarence J. Gamble's biography, which Doon Williams and Greer Williams wrote in 1978 to celebrate the life of this American millionaire who devoted his fortune to the cause of birth control in the world, particularly in developing countries. Gamble was initially associated with Margaret Sanger and Robert Latou Dickinson, and the American birth control movement more generally; "every child a wanted child" was also the slogan of Planned Parenthood, previously known as the American Birth Control League and founded by Sanger. In 1957, Gamble created his own organization, Pathfinder Fund, to continue promoting education and funding distribution of birth control supplies, especially outside the United States (in 1991, it was renamed Pathfinder International). Both Gamble and Sanger considered eugenics an acceptable method to control overpopulation. Retrospectively, their position is controversial; however, at the time, forced sterilization was part of the broader effort to fight the so-called "population bomb." Similarly, the AIED's intention was to "reduce illegitimate births, infanticides, voluntary abortion, teen mother suicides, *genetically retarded offspring*").[49]

In the mid-fifties, Berla was Gamble's initial contact in Italy, but soon he became close to De Marchi and his wife, Maria Luisa Zardini De Marchi (from now on, Zardini).[50] The relationship between Gamble and the De Marchis has not been investigated much; however, I maintain that it considerably affected the history of AIED and its campaigning efforts.[51] As an official publication of Pathfinder International states, "support from Clarence Gamble and Pathfinder enabled AIED to flourish and the De Marchis turned their mission to legalize birth control into their permanent employment."[52] Beyond the celebratory goal of this booklet, my goal is to understand the influence of such a partnership on the politics of the AIED in general, and on the making of the 1975 campaign more specifically.

De Marchi had been at odds with Berla since the publication of *Sesso e civiltà*. In Berla's view, De Marchi advocated free love and therefore was a menace to the Italian birth control movement.[53] De Marchi, on the other hand, claimed that his "personal" opinions should not matter to the AIED, since he deemed his engagement as the secretary of the Roman branch separate from his work as social psychologist and sexual rights activist. Berla never made peace with De Marchi, left the AIED in 1963, and with her departure the association lost the support of the International Planned Parenthood Federation (IPPF).[54] This seemingly marginal incident is relevant to my discussion because it sheds light on how De Marchi's rise to a prominent role in the AIED (he became its president in 1961), and thus his ability to single-handedly manage the 1974–1975 campaign, happened at the expense of its more moderate faction, represented by Berla. Furthermore, Berla's departure from the AIED, together with the IPPF sponsorship, corresponded to the increasing involvement of Gamble and his organization, the Pathfinder Fund, in support of the De Marchis' personal and political battle for birth control *and* sexual rights.

Gamble and Pathfinder Fund financially supported De Marchi consistently so that, despite the opposition he faced inside the AIED, he could rise to national and international attention for the historic ruling of the Italian Supreme Court in favor of birth control. Indeed, Zardini and De Marchi distinguished themselves from other activists at the AIED not only because of their radical ideas but also by openly and aggressively defying the Italian law. As Anna Treves explains, De Marchi (together with Guido Tassinari) was at the head of the AIED's "radical wing," employing strategies of civil disobedience in order to repeal Article 553 and liberalize the use of contraceptives. In her words, "they wanted to be charged, moreover, they demanded it; and then, systematically, they rejected the judiciary's tendency to dismiss charges."[55] Treves does not acknowledge, however, that this "radical wing" could not have engaged in unruly behavior without Gamble's help. Pathfinder Fund regularly paid De Marchi a consultation fee, which allowed him to concentrate on his legal battle almost full time. In addition, he provided free vaginal diaphragms and contraceptive jelly (from the United States) to the free clinic that De Marchi and Zardini opened in Rome in 1956, and which resulted in De Marchi being charged for violation of Article 553, but did not lead to trial. In 1969, De Marchi was again charged in violation of the same article for opening a free birth clinic in Rome. By that time, Gamble had passed away, but Pathfinder Fund continued to help the AIED with funding, and while the American organization did not provide financial support for the court case, it publicly supported the couple throughout it. Eventually, when the Supreme Court ruled in favor of De Marchi in 1971, the AIED was finally free to promote birth control and to open more clinics (the so-called *consultori*); a few years later, in 1974, Pathfinder Fund financed the first major campaign that included the publication of photoromances.[56]

Beyond financial support, Gamble also invested in both De Marchi and Zardini to foster his own agenda. In this context, Zardini was especially important in promoting Gamble's project of spreading the use of contraceptives among the poor. Gamble visited the couple for the first time in 1958, right after he split from the IPPF, when he created the Pathfinder Fund. The IPPF criticized Gamble's work ethic, specifically, his trial in Punjab, India, where he pushed a "simple" birth control method (the so-called salt-and-sponge method), which was proven to be very uncomfortable for women and not very effective. Gamble and his fieldworkers were criticized for their colonial approach toward their clients (who received contraceptives without much control over their own well-being). In addition, the IPPF did not approve of Gamble selecting nonmedical personnel (particularly women over age fifty) as fieldworkers. During his first visit, Gamble came up with the idea of a contraceptive field trial to be conducted in extremely poor Roman neighborhoods.[57] Soon after, Zardini was appointed to lead the trial and began door-to-door visits to families in the tenements and shacks to deliver vaginal suppositories, which were provided free of charge by a manufacturer in England. For a while, Zardini also promoted the salt-and-sponge method, at the behest of Gamble; however, the method was not successful among Italian women and was quickly abandoned.[58] Zardini's endeavor, which she undertook with only one other female colleague, was impressive: working against current laws that prohibited the distribution of contraceptives and under the strong opposition of the Vatican (whose emissaries spied on her movements), she had 588 clients and made about forty thousand visits.[59] Zardini reported on these visits in the book *Inumane Vite* (1969), and yet we know very little about her attitudes toward the women she encountered. An episode in the documentary *I misteri di Roma* (Rome's Mysteries, 1966), titled "Maternità" (Maternity), uniquely represents Zardini at work as she talks to a woman who had been receiving her assistance for a few years.[60] In a scene, Zardini hastily engages with the woman, asking how many packages she would need during the summer (saying she might be gone for the entire month of July); then, she scolds her client for not taking good care of the products that are "so expensive" and makes her promise that she will be more careful in the future. The woman looks both grateful and intimidated, and when she speaks to the cameraman (who is also present in the scene), the client fiercely declares that she does not want any more children and does not care whether the Catholic Church disapproves of her actions, as the interviewer suggests is the case.

Clearly, this scene does not reveal the "truth" regarding Zardini's role as an educator, especially given that the film was intentionally shot in a *verité* style, questioning all claims of the ontological truth of cinema. At the same time, by connecting these images to the commentaries on Gamble's colonial approach in his trials, I aim to broaden the picture of their relationship and better understand its impact on the Italian birth control movement. In particular, I think that this background information is useful to explain the strong criticism expressed by feminist groups against the AIED in the mid-1970s, that is, right around the time of the campaign.[61] For example, the Associazione per l'Educazione Democratica (Association for Democratic Education, AED) argued that the AIED neglected women's rights to control their own health and reproductive power. In the preface to *Manuale di contraccezione* (Manual of Contraception, 1975), AED's National Secretary Nerina Negrello claims that the process of "population planning" was incentivized in Italy thanks to American funding agencies that financially supported associations that focused on decreasing pregnancy numbers rather than promoting free choice. In her words: "Power does not care about individual self-management with regard to contraception. To acquire freedom means to frustrate the monopoly of the fertility tap."[62] Negrello does not refer to Gamble or Pathfinder, but the manual nominally attacks the AIED for experimenting with contraceptive methods on Italian women while being aware that they were not effective.[63]

Negrello's commentary and De Marchi and Zardini's association with Gamble, a conservative Republican, problematize readings of the AIED's photoromances that claim their evident support of the feminist cause—for example, that of Elisabetta Remondi in *Genesis*, the journal of the Italian Association of Women Historians. At the very least, Negrello addressed a gap in the discourse of sexuality and reproduction conveyed via their narratives: on the one hand, plot and characters support women's emancipation by claiming their right to sexual pleasure; on the other hand, they do not address what was also in women's rights, that is, their freedom to decide whether or not to be mothers. Pathfinder Fund's influence on the photoromances, beyond its financial support, can thus be approached from the point of view of the ways in which the American funding agency may have limited the political message that De Marchi promoted in his own claims to the press. According to Remondi, AIED photoromances radically rejected patriarchy by promoting birth control: "The goal was to have a couple in which individuals were connected to each other, neither according to a model of women's subjugation to men typical of patriarchal societies, nor by the fear of loneliness that characterized so many women's lives, but rather on the basis of mutual growth and knowledge."[64] In fact, as I previously mentioned, these narratives are certainly radical in the way they address sexuality but do, however, maintain male partners in a position of leadership, and female characters as subordinate companions. Indeed, in "The Secret," Lia does make the revolutionary gesture (and openly tells her partner) to fully enjoy sex; at the same time, she concludes that her satisfaction has the ultimate effect of gratifying her man. In her words: "Now other men don't interest me anymore because you give me everything."[65]

"The Trap," "We the Youth," and "The Secret" did not undermine the system in which men ruled over women; instead, they motivated men to allow their female partners to take the pill. In Dagmar's words, De Marchi "developed a brilliant strategy for promoting contraceptive use which also implicitly revealed men's discomfort."[66] As both "The Trap," with its male leading character, and the focus group of male workers in a factory further testify, if women were considered by default the target audience of the campaign—"Accetteranno questa lezione le lettrici dei fumetti?" (Will women readers of photoromances accept the lesson?) states a journalist most explicitly—a careful reading of the project reveals that men were equally addressed as an interested party.[67] Furthermore, in order to be persuasive, women's sexual freedom had to be presented in a way that was not threatening to traditional notions of masculinity. As reported by Aida Ribero in *La Stampa*, Italian women hid from their husbands that they were using the pill. "Lui non vuole" (he does not want me to), Ribero states in *La Stampa*, quoting unnamed sources; "if he knows he gets mad" and "he keeps my pills locked in a drawer."[68] Similarly, Zardini reported that husbands of women in her trial were often suspicious, made her visits difficult, and many "felt that contraceptives were an affront to their manhood. They worried that without the fear of pregnancy, their wives would 'be free to go with someone else.'"[69]

Rather than trying to convince women and their male companions that contraception was needed to prevent a global crisis, or to rid them of guilt (for having more children than they could possibly care for), these photo-stories were meant to engage them on the basis of positive incentives such as sexual satisfaction, happiness, and freedom.[70] In other words, instead of basing the information campaign for contraceptives on the repressive logic of top-down instruction, the photoromance exploited the popularity of the media and the entertaining function of photography and narrative to productively involve readers in their education, and thus promote self-policing practices. This kind of "motivational propaganda," nevertheless, was not De Marchi's "brilliant idea," as Remondi and Dagmar suggest. His technique followed a model already experimented with by American organizations and corporations, since the 1940s, to educate and train workers, soldiers, and the youth.[71] More relevantly, as I previously mentioned, the Peace Corps experimented with the use of photoromances to educate Ecuadorian peasants. The project was funded by the U.S. Agency for International Development (USAID), the same agency that in 1973 had provided Pathfinder Fund with a worldwide family planning grant of $11 million over three years, part of which was used to support the AIED's campaign. Could it have been just serendipitous that De Marchi had exactly the same idea in 1974, when trying to figure out a more effective way to spread the use of contraceptives in a country where only 5 percent of the population made use of them?[72] Was the AIED's initiative a unique initiative, or, rather, was the Italian organization inspired by the work of the Peace Corps in Latin America (or instructed by Pathfinder)?

The Italian and Ecuadorian projects had many aspects in common. In both countries, photoromances were widely popular, a cheap form of entertainment, and particularly liked by sectors of the population of low income and little education. What was really new in De Marchi's experiment was the engagement with the media system and with the world of celebrities. The imminent publication of the AIED photoromances was advertised in major newspapers. "Paola Pitagora teaches how to use the pill through comics," titled a full-page report on the initiative in *Corriere della Sera*, which included interviews with Pitagora, Gianni Morandi, and Mario Valdemarin.[73] Pitagora revealed that she herself took the pill, while Morandi expressed his opinion in favor of contraceptives to fight illegal abortion. "Volunteer and unpaid," these celebrities were said to be taking part of the initiative for "social reasons."[74] Morandi stated, "I promised to collaborate in AIED's initiative also because I think that workers will be able to better fight their cause when they are not worried about a large family."[75] Even though Morandi did not act in "Noi giovani," the main character (also named Gianni) appears to be modeled on his star persona in the Italian musicals of the time. Gianni not only urges Maria (the female protagonist) to go to the lecture, but he also voices the youths' concerns toward their parents, and their wish to not "make the same mistakes" by postponing parenthood and enjoying free love. In his behavior, Gianni may recall the rebellious and charismatic protagonist of *In ginocchio da te* (On My Knees For You, 1964), interpreted by Morandi, and even though "Gianni" is not Morandi, such cross-references seem intentional to make the character (i.e., the user of contraceptives) a more likeable and positive model to young readers.[76]

Eventually, Gianni was portrayed instead by Ugo Pagliai. The casting of Pagliai is again very significant, since he was in a romantic relationship with Paola Gassman, who played Maria. Pagliai and Gassman had been together since 1967 and often in the spotlight for their steady and passionate relationship.[77] Considering that they were both in their thirties, the couple did not seem appropriate to interpret the role of college students. However, their private life together may have been more relevant here in order to bridge the fiction of the photoromance and the reality of readers. Their modern relationship was not institutionalized (they were not legally married) but lasted a long time; they had a child together, and lived as a family with Gassman's daughter from a previous relationship as well.[78] Pagliai publicly declared that he did not know whether he would marry Gassman but that he valued his family's happiness more than "la carta bollata" (a piece of paper).

Morandi and Pitagora were also known for their sentimental affairs, even though in a very different way. Pitagora's celebrity persona was built on being both sexually attractive and a feminist. As explained in an interview with *Corriere della Sera* in 1975, titled "Alle femministe piacciono molto gli uomini" (Feminists Like Men Very Much), Pitagora was known for being frivolous and exhibitionist, on the one hand, and politically engaged, on the other. In her responses, Pitagora argues that from her perspective, taking part in the AIED campaign was "something civil" however negatively viewed by many.[79] She calls herself a feminist, and explains that her feminism is a new kind of womanhood: "freer and more informed."[80] In this sense, Pitagora's role in "Il segreto" played on her existing star persona that, in turn, may have influenced a feminist reading of the photoromances. Her initial pairing with Morandi in the announcement of the campaign could have further influenced similar expectations. In 1973, Morandi allegedly had an affair with Pitagora, when the two of them starred in the musical *Jacopone*.[81] On the cover of *Grand Hotel* from July 1974, the three of them are portrayed together; the title reads: "There is still the shadow of Pitagora . . . between Morandi and Laura."[82] The news of the affair had increased both Pitagora's and *Jacopone*'s popularity (the show had failed at the box office), but had also made Pitagora and Morandi's joint participation in the AIED project more intriguing from the point of view of their fans.

In this light, the use of celebrities mirrors the project's mixed position with regard to gender roles and sexuality. On the one hand, the AIED's photoromances promoted traditional ideas of true love and fidelity; on the other, they openly supported modern types of relationships (i.e., not institutionalized). Furthermore, both female and male stars appear to have been chosen for their looks, thus paying attention to the affective rather than the intellectual engagement of both male and female readers. Pagliai was certainly a favorite "divo" among women, as stated in 1971 in "Il mondo della donna" (A Woman's World), a special section in *Corriere della Sera*. An acclaimed theater performer, but popular for his roles on television (he played among others Casanova, "the irresistible Latin lover"), Pagliai allegedly received even more letters from fans than Mastroianni ever had, and was one of the celebrities most photographed by paparazzi.[83] Mario Valdemarin, who plays the protagonist in "The Trap," was hailed "il Montgomery Clift italiano" (the Italian Montgomery Clift) by his young female fans who followed him on the show *Lascia o raddoppia,* where he was a contestant in 1957.[84] A theater actor, Valdemarin earned a living as an employee of the national railways when he entered the contest as an expert of Westerns; at the end, he won five million lira and a film contract, as well as the attention of fans enamored with his looks.[85] When he participated in the AIED initiative, Valdemarin's fame as an actor in films, television serials, and photoromances was established (he was also a spokesman for Alka Seltzer) but many probably remembered him as the handsome man who rose to stardom from an office desk thanks to a quiz. Symbolically, on his first day after the victory, Valdemarin was immortalized as he descended from a train wagon (on which he had not really traveled) in a newsreel produced by the Ministry of Transportation.[86] His past certainly gave more validity to Valdemarin's claims regarding the need for the government to take care of birth control for the sake of the working class to which, once upon a time, he had also belonged.

In conclusion, the case of the AIED campaign is not only relevant because it sheds light on competing social discourses regarding birth control and contraception (especially in relation to sexuality). In addition, the way in which such a campaign was conceived and conducted anticipates what is now a growing trend of celebrities' involvement in social causes. This trend sheds light on "the societal and cultural embedding of celebrity" in 1970s Italy.[87] In other words, the case of the AIED campaign shows how "a long-term term structural development" of "celebritization" took place in those years, in continuity with the ongoing process of modernization (of both society and the media system) taking place since the aftermath of World War II.[88] As I showed in the previous chapters, photoromances had been innovating media strategies of production and consumption since the late 1940s, fostering participatory culture and absorbing conventions as much as human capital from other media industries. Collaborating with the AIED in the campaign for birth control, celebrities like Pitagora and Morandi who had already migrated across media platforms by diversifying their activities in the film, television, music, and photoromance industries, also migrated into an area that was not previously associated with fame. Regardless of whether this decision helped boost their popularity or (as in the case of Pitagora) actually damaged their images, the migration of celebrities at work in the AIED campaign signaled an important moment in the history of Italian culture and society, at the forefront of change.

6 REVENGE OF THE FANS

"Waiting for a TV star in the street for hours to get an autograph is not only stupid, even worse . . . it is *something that maids do*."[1] With these words, Edoardo Albinati in the 2016 novel *La scuola cattolica* (The Catholic School) interprets his mother's perspective when she forbade his sister to join her friends outside the hotel where "the actor playing Sandokan in a TV series" resided.[2] The Italian mini-series in six episodes based on Emilio Salgari's novels about a Malaysian pirate named Sandokan was broadcast on RAI's number 1 channel in 1976. By that time, according to Anna Bravo, the photoromance (like other forms of mass culture) was considered "merce per plebe arretrate" (commodities for backward hicks) because the medium goes against any norms of social and cultural respectability. But the situation in which Albinati's sister found herself is not only a case in point with regard to the class shaming that reading photoromances or being a fan of TV celebrities could bring to a middle-class girl (and her mother). It is also an example of how fandom could signify a generational rather than a class conflict. In this concluding chapter, I will discuss this question in the particular historical context of 1970s Italy to provide a nuanced understanding of the political and social relevance of reading photoromances during and after the sexual revolution and the second wave of feminist movements. Following Janice Radway's advice, I will consider fans' own theories about what they read and who they worship. Thanks to the World Wide Web, I explore photoromance fandom in the past through its collective and individual memories in the digital present.

THE RISE OF LANCIO

Starting in 1961 with the publication of *Letizia*, Rome-based publisher Lancio began its successful path to become the major figure in the Italian press du cœur. By 1972, Lancio owned eleven titles in Italy alone and sold millions of copies per week. *Bolero Film* officially closed in 1984, while Lancio acquired *Sogno* in 1974 and its series were distributed globally and were the first to hit the U.S. market in the late 1970s. In 1979, as I mentioned in the introduction, Lancio's *Darling* and *Kiss* invaded the world of American pulp fiction with "TV soap operas in magazine format." *Grand Hotel* continued to be relatively successful through the decade but did not attract the same young readership of its Roman competitor. In an interview with media scholar Ulrike Schimming, photoromance director Paolo Brunetti argued that, in the seventies: "50% of Italians were reading our [i.e., Lancio's] photoromances. But nobody has the courage to confess it—stupidly."[3] In fact, many more people read the same Lancio stories in both North and South America. According to Carlos Roberto de Souza, there were 130 issues of Lancio's *Kiling* published between 1972 and 1984, fifty-nine of which were reprints of Italian stories; the rest were Argentinean-produced adventures.[4]

Contrary to common assumptions, Lancio's publications were not technically unsophisticated. The quality of photographs in their black-and-white editions was unbeatable, compared to others, and they were the first to publish entirely in color.[5] Furthermore, the in-house celebrities were incredibly successful in Europe: "beautiful, skilled, magnetic" actors and actresses who exclusively played in Lancio's photoromances. Above all, Franco Gasparri, "the most handsome man in the universe," especially paired with Claudia Rivelli, as well as Franco Dani, Katiuscia, Michela Roc, Max Delys, and many others. Their physical beauty attracted loyal buyers and convinced casual readers to purchase every episode of the saga *Le avventure di Jacques Douglas* (The Adventures of Jack Douglas, starring Gasparri and Rivelli), or the latest issue of the other crime series, *Le avventure di Lucky Martin* (The Adventures of Lucky Martin, with Dani, Katiuscia, and Roc), as well as any other magazine featuring their favorite actor/actress as protagonists or side characters. Fans stood in awe of their favorite celebrities, imitated their clothing fashions and hair styles, and dreamed of becoming like them (perhaps not as famous but similarly adored and sought after). Some fans even hoped and planned to meet their photoromance idols in person, at Lancio's headquarters in Via Tiburtina. Further, the convenient publication of complete stories in single issues encouraged readers to buy Lancio photoromances exclusively and to religiously store the copies in order to read them (in their words) anytime they wanted, as many times they wanted, alone or in groups.

Lancio readers are not bothered by the fact that Lancio celebrities' fame is limited to the world of photoromances, because readers rather value the affective relationships they have with these stars and the collective experience of discussing photoromances with others who share their passion. Also, these fans are no longer ashamed of whom they like and what they read, because they find in the Lancio fandom an outlet for their innermost feelings as well as a common, constructed identity.

These assumptions are not my own description of a hypothetical readership, but rather summarize my observations on contemporary digital platforms and social media where Lancio fans are today actively sharing opinions and personal stories of past consumption. To my knowledge, there are currently at least twelve different Facebook groups dedicated to Lancio magazines and celebrities ("Lancio Facebook Groups" [LFGs]); many members subscribe to multiple groups and administrators know each other, at least online. The transnational scope of the Lancio fandom is demonstrated by the fact that profiles of group members reveal they are not only located Italy, but also in other countries, in particular, in France, Argentina, and Brazil. However, most of them can post in Italian and the most active members are usually either foreign nationals living in Italy or having some connections to Italy. In addition to the various forms of narration and self-expression present on these platforms, my account draws from data collected through an ongoing research project sponsored by the University of Texas at Austin since January 2018. In the fall of 2017, I became a member of several LFGs in order to immerse myself in their cultures and understand the extent of the social phenomenon that they represented. My intention was to undertake the project from a combined cultural studies and ethnographic approach. In September 2017, I introduced myself to the largest of these LFGs, named "Noi, i lettori dei fotoromanzi . . . Lancio!!!" (We the Readers of Photoromances . . . Lancio; from now on, "We the Readers"), sharing my academic interest on the world of Lancio reader-ship.[6] Their enthusiasm was overwhelming. I also created an online anonymous survey, which I posted on my Facebook page titled "Fotoromanzi: Chi, Come, Quando, Perchè" (Who, How, When, Why) and on LFGs' timelines, in order to collect qualitative data regarding readers' past experiences (asking, for example, when they started reading; what did they like about the magazines; what stories did they remember and which photos; did they prefer to read photoromances or to go to the movies/watch TV and why, etc.) and current habits (do they still read photoromances; what do they like about them now; are they members of any LFGs and what are the motives for their choices).[7] I also gathered information about gender identities, occupation, and level of education; however, this was not for statistical purposes but rather to add background information to the answers that I received. According to the survey's report from February to June 2018, forty-five out of sixty-six respondents read photoromances in the past, while nineteen read them today *and* in the past (nobody identifies only as current reader); twenty out of fifty-nine responded affirmatively to the question of whether they are a member of LFGs; most respondents read Lancio exclusively and these respondents also took more time in writing detailed answers to my questions. Numbers are useful to understand that the responses I will quote in this chapter are broadly from Lancio readers, however, not necessarily from users who identify as members of online communities. In addition to the survey, I engaged in individual conversations with members of LFGs via Facebook Messenger and observed their interactions on the web. This data will also be included in the discussion that follows. I do not claim that the materials I collected in these months of research provide an exhaustive or objective picture of Lancio readership in universal terms. Rather, my goal is to understand the dynamics and structure of a contemporary culture (i.e., Lancio fandom) "through 'thick,' detailed, nuanced, historically-curious and culturally-grounded interpretation and deep description" of the world of online fans and communities.[8]

My goal is to demonstrate that the rise of Lancio in the 1970s signaled an important shift in the structure of Italian cultural industries toward media convergence, which was defined by the increased relevance of fandom and of participatory culture. According to Anna Bravo, Lancio publishing was a marginal event in the transition from the 1960s to the 1970s, one of the many stimuli for increasingly demanding Italian mass audiences. On the contrary, I argue in this chapter that the company's editorial strategies resulted (intentionally or not) in a distinct realm of celebrity culture and an object-specific fandom, which ensured the longevity of the brand (as demonstrated by the dominant presence of LFGs). In Bravo's words, Lancio cast "unknown beauties" as regular cast members and turned them into celebrities, making their role in the industry less relevant than that of other publishers, which instead employed film stars, television personalities, or singers. On the one hand, one can argue that Lancio did not capitalize on the established fame of performers and that made their magazines less appealing to a broader audience. On the other hand, by inventing "the professional photoromance actor," as director Brunetti claimed in the previously mentioned interview, the publisher ensured the lasting loyalty of readers and their attachment to the Lancio's "lovemark." Beyond the brand, the success of these magazines is based on a kind of loyalty beyond all reason, exploiting both the emotional investment of fans and their reverence toward the performers.[9] More specifically, as an LFG member who signed her comment via Facebook Messenger "Lancio nell'anima" (I am Lancio in my heart) explains, Lancio is perceived, engaged with, and represented as a *family* rather than a company, both by the industry and in the various forms of self-expression of employees and consumers. These dynamics of personal investments, and how they speak of Lancio fandom and fanship, on the one hand, and the publisher's editorial strategies, on the other, will be the object of this study.

The vast majority of users who were and are Lancio readers claim (either in the present or in the past) "a common identity and a shared culture with other fans"; that is, in the words of Henry Jenkins, a *fandom.* Noticeably, users call themselves *lancetti* (male Lancio fans) and *lancette* (female Lancio fans), or *ragazze Lancio* (Lancio girls). Lancio's editorial strategies that nurtured its fandom are immediately evident in surveying a sample of their series published between 1970 and 1979, such as *Charme, Kolossal, The Adventures of Jack Douglas, The Adventures of Lucky Martin, Idilio* (Idyll), and *Sogno.*[10] All issues have in common the specific attention toward readers not as aspiring celebrities, as in *Bolero Film,* but as loyal customers, with both an emotional and an exclusive attachment to the Lancio "family." Katiuscia's response to a fan who had sent a few pictures hoping to get an audition helps to exemplify this point. In her words, "Lancio does not hire its performers this way. It's a joke, at the very least, while we have for readers the utmost respect."[11] Rather than the usual contest for aspiring artists, typical of *Bolero Film, Kolossal* announced one to win "a day with your favorite star" (to participate, readers must also buy the soap bar "Panigal," advertised by Lancio actress Claudia Rivelli).[12] The relationships between fans and celebrity and fans and industry are thus built, in the words of both Lancio management and its employees, on the basis of affection and reciprocal understanding, while evidently embedded in consumerist culture. In the words of Rivelli, in her response to a fan's letter: "Lancio can sense your desires and tries to support them, even to beat you to them."[13] Fanship is represented in narratives: in "Il ragazzo venuto dal Texas" (The Boy from Texas, *The Adventures of Lucky Martin*), for example, Katiuscia is caught by her distant boyfriend (Franco Dani) as she sighs while reading a story starring Franco Gasparri.[14] Moreover, fans are used as characters, for example, in "Fotoromanzo dedicato a Lia" (Photoromance Dedicated to Lia, *Kolossal*, September 1979), which tells the story of a terminally ill admirer of Max Delys who finally manages to make him fall in love with her, after tirelessly waiting outside the Lancio headquarters where she stood every day, waiting be noticed. In the photoromance, Delys addresses readers directly and introduces them to his life as a Lancio celebrity. "The most pleasing and most difficult obstacle . . . ," he comments in a caption, is "overcoming the most faithful fans, who never get tired" (figure 6.1). The cover of the issue also features the typewriter Lia used to write a story that was meant to star Delys (figure 6.2). As the photoromance develops, Lia eventually becomes the protagonist of a photoromance in the photoromance, with the leading man also played by Delys.

In contrast to Mondadori and Universo, Lancio magazines did not prioritize educational goals, but instead invested in commercial strategies that enticed casual readers to become loyal fans. Even though publishing stories in complete monthly or biweekly issues (rather than installments) was a Lancio innovation, the Roman publisher exploited seriality too, perhaps even more than the two "majors," since each issue of a series like *The Adventures of Lucky Martin* was in fact an episode in an open-ended saga. Actors and actresses played the same characters, often in couples, such as Gasparri and Rivelli in the *Jack Douglas* series and Katiuscia and Dani in the *Lucky Martin* series. Furthermore, Lancio's stories did not try to elevate the supposedly low culture of the photoromance, by using nineteenth-century novels as inspiration for the photo-textual narratives. According to Barbara Mercurio, Lancio's stories were in this respect more "modern" than those of competitors because they used fiction to talk about contemporary issues in real-life settings. In fact, Lancio did more than just modernize photoromance plots in order to broaden its readership, as I mentioned earlier; some Lancio magazines also exploited recent and successful film genres, particularly the *giallo* (Italian horror subgenre) and the *poliziottesco* (cop movies), introducing comic characters along with suspense to the plotlines, and alongside the usual romance.

Figure 6.1

Max Delys in "Fotoromanzo dedicato a Lia" (Photoromance Dedicated to Lia), *Kolossal* 6, no. 58 (September 1979): 19.

«SALVE, MI CHIAMO MAX E SONO UNO DEGLI ATTORI DELLA "LANCIO". LA MIA VITA? SIETE CURIOSI DI CONOSCERLA? NIENTE DI PIU' FACILE...»

«ACCODATEVI E SEGUITEMI, MA SENZA DARE NELL'OCCHIO, MI RACCOMANDO. CON UN PO' DI DISCREZIONE, QUASI IN PUNTA DI PIEDI. PER NON DISTURBARE IL LAVORO.»

«IL PRIMO OSTACOLO. IL PIU' SIMPATICO E IL PIU' DURO DA SUPERARE. LE FEDELISSIME, QUELLE CHE NON SI STANCANO MAI.»

Calma, ragazze, sono qui. Non spingete, lasciatemi entrare. Come al solito sono in ritardo.

Una foto...

Firma qui, sul diario di scuola!

19

Figure 6.2

Cover of "Fotoromanzo dedicato a Lia" (Photoromance Dedicated to Lia), *Kolossal* 6, no. 58 (September 1979).

Fans' recollections and current personal accounts support the idea that Lancio nurtured a new kind of reader-industry relationship and a new type of fan, who was so loyal that her fandom survived the company's closure in 2011. This is not to say that Lancio fans are all the same or that, like in any other family, there are no signs of discord. On the contrary, the goal of this book is to review the cultural significance of Lancio's success from the viewpoint of historical audiences, in order to highlight nuances and contradictions in previous accounts that understood readers as universal subjects. My communication with fans took place exclusively via the Internet, which is in fact the only space where a Lancio fandom exists today, since the publisher discontinued new productions in the late 1990s and officially closed in 2011. The term *netnography* is therefore more appropriate to signal "not only the presence but the gravity of the online component" in the ethnographic part of my research.[15] This component does not limit but rather opens up new opportunities for researchers interested in studying how readers today respond to these photoromances, or in gathering readers' memories of past experiences of this form of cultural consumption—or both. Since most online fans of Lancio publications started to read the magazines in the 1970s, they can help build the cultural memory of that period. In addition, online communities can give researchers access to data regarding the habits and preferences of current audiences. In sum, social media and other digital platforms allowed me to collect memories, observe fans' interactions and self-narratives, and examine various forms of fan-made extensions (for example: photomontages, renarrations, digitized issues). These extensions of the original stories are a rich source of information about the photoromance fandom in general, and are telling of the unique status of Lancio magazines, vis-à-vis other publications of the same genre.

Even though *Grand Hotel* is still sold in newsstands and Lancio's *Letizia* or *Lucky Martin* series are not, readers of the latter are predominant on the web, particularly on Facebook, making their performances visible (and readable) to other users. In fact, most Facebook pages created by Lancio fans are closed groups and members consistently express in their posts not only their devotion and fidelity to the brand (above all, to its celebrities), but also their thankfulness toward other members and page administrators. LFGs thus perform different functions. They are (1) safe spaces where lancette can talk about their own identity as fans; (2) open platforms where they can discuss topics related to the objects or subjects of Lancio fandom (other fans, narratives, celebrities, the industry . . .); (3) marketplaces where members can sell and buy issues; and (4) "rogue" archives, where fans can store digitized copies of their favorite issues and collect creative examples of "archontic" literature (re-narration of stories, remaking of layouts, cutting and pasting of single photo-text, and so on). In the following sections, I will discuss these functions in more detail in order to understand the social, psychological, and industrial dimensions of Lancio fandom.

COMING OUT

By communicating exclusively through digital media and focusing solely on online communities, I took advantage of what Robert Kozinets highlights as four specific factors of the electronic language: anonymity, alterity, accessibility, and the possibility of archiving.[16] The first two factors are important with regard to how fans exchange information and expressed themselves with me as well as with other members—the second factor particularly so in defining the space of the community in which such communication takes place. Most LFG users (as well as my survey's respondents) were teenagers in the 1970s, which often means that they have little familiarity with digital tools and language. In many occasions, though, the lack of skills becomes a topic of conversation as well as a way for more seasoned members of the community to engage with newcomers, and for the latter to express their own insecurities and feelings. Eventually, the second nature of electronic language use becomes for fans the only way to be in contact with "la vera Lancio" (the true Lancio) or, in the words of a woman in the LFG, "We the Readers," to "meet people whom I unfortunately do not know in person, but who have been close to me on many occasions."[17]

The fundamental role played by digital media is thus the emancipation of readers that the Internet facilitates, allowing users to finally come out as fans. According to Jenkins, to speak as a fan is "to forge an alliance with a community of others in defense of taste which, as a result, cannot be read as totally aberrant or idiosyncratic."[18] When considering Lancio fans, I agree with Jenkins that readers speak out as fans *because* they can speak from a position of collective identity. Further, as Jenkins also argues, "One of the most often heard comments from new fans is their surprise in discovering how many people share their fascination with a particular series, their pleasure in discovering that they are not 'alone.'"[19] In the words a member of "Noi lettori," the group is a place in which to exchange opinions "in a civil way" with people who share the same interests and, as another member states, to discover that other people have the same passion, "without looking stupid."

In her chapter on the photoromance audience, Bravo argues that female readers have remained underground since the time in which habits of cultural consumption started to matter across the social composition of the Italian population. She describes a trajectory in the degree of readers' awareness of what I would call their *abjection*: from the immediate postwar period when readers only knew about moral judgments against them but ignored cultural discredit of the genre, through the late 1960s when aspirations of social and cultural respectability were expressed by means of (self-)contempt toward "low" products such as TV and tabloids and, above all, photoromances.[20] Her analysis culminates in the example of a series of interviews conducted in the late 1970s by a group of researchers in the popular Roman neighborhood of Trastevere.[21] Published outside academia, the work of these researchers was highly original. Although it did not lead to further inquiries, their findings provide a unique historical background to my analysis of today's fandom. The qualitative interviews that they collected verified that stories were discussed and re-narrated communally with other readers. At the same time, while thirty-two photoromance readers agreed to answer the researchers' questions, many more refused, denying that they ever looked at the magazines, or even attacking its narratives and characters for their "stupidity" (despite the fact that they actually read photoromances regularly). These acts of rejection are meaningful to make a point about the sense of shame that many readers shared. According to Bravo, women read photoromances for entertainment, but knew that they were being shamed for it and eventually came to despise themselves and what they liked.[22]

Today fans of Lancio recall past experiences of prohibition and shaming, and express relief in having found a community that allows them to be part of a community of like-minded fans. Respondents to my survey and members with whom I communicated via online messaging speak of different situations in which their parents or, more specifically, their mothers discovered stacks of magazines and trashed them, or punished them on finding out that their child had read a copy. For example, S.C. remembers that she began to read photoromances when she was seven, in 1973, against the wishes of her mother (S.C. described her as "a bit rigid and severe") who thought that reading was, in general, a waste of time.[23] S.C. writes: "How cute I was when, as a little girl, I would go to the newsstand in the afternoon to buy photoromances! The seller was a bit skeptical, but in the end, he would even keep copies for me aside until I had money to buy them. And at that time there were so many new issues! Luckily, my dear aunt E. would gift me some. Over the years, I did not miss an issue and I had a collection that I always needed to hide because otherwise it would end up in the trash."[24]

In many of the fans' memories that I collected, adults who were against them reading photoromances judged them according to Bravo's twofold description: either as not respectable—photoromances were stuff for maids, affirms B.B.; or morally dangerous—to people of their age, writes A.C.A.[25] However, when recalling these memories, all fans describe themselves not with shame but with pride, because they were transgressing parental rules either for their own enjoyment or to bond with their girlfriends. Social media today, then, becomes a newly found safe space where they can share their opinions freely with people who "understand them." Although numerically less significant, the experiences of masculine fans could be useful to study how gender-labeled readings functioned, and continue to do so, in negotiating masculine identities and how digital platforms may constitute a safe space where they can come out as fans. Nonetheless, most respondents to my survey (sixty-one out of sixty-six) as well as all members who agreed to communicate with me via online messaging identify as women. To remain faithful to my intention of basing my assumptions on fans' narratives and personal accounts, this chapter is dedicated to the lancette or "ragazze Lancio" (Lancio girls), with the hope that future research will bring the experiences of masculine fanship to the fore.[26]

IT'S A FAMILY AFFAIR

In their own recollections, lancette often blame their parents for preventing them from fulfilling their desires, but also use the metaphor of the family to describe their relationship with the industry. In multiple instances throughout the data that I gathered, fans replace the materialistic nature of commercial transactions with imaginary bonds of an affective nature. In the present day, LFG members perform activities that are at the boundaries of legality (digitizing entire stories and making them available to users, for example), but claim consistently that they act for the good of the Lancio *family*, by which they mean both the industry and themselves, as an online community (sometimes, users even mention personal relationships, encounters, or exchanges with the Mercurio family, who owned the business). This behavior is self-described in the posts of LFGs and in survey responses in continuity with a tradition of reciprocal trust and care set up by the publisher in an undefined past.[27] In a relatively recent interview (1997), Barbara Mercurio stated, "We call ourselves somehow a family Lancio and we have a somewhat close relationship with everyone. There's a chance to be constantly in contact with everyone. And so, this sensation, this relationship is transferred onto the audience as well."[28] Her testimony is in continuity with her declarations of sentimental attachment to both employees and customers. When she announced to readers the end of the series *The Adventures of Jack Douglas* (no. 180, 1980), after the motorcycle accident that forced main protagonist Franco Gasparri into a wheelchair for the rest of his life, Mercurio stated that her decision was meant as "a gesture of sincere affection" but also "to safeguard a patrimony of experience and popularity" that was based on ties with the audience "beyond the simple economic aspect."[29] The article, posted on the LFG "Noi lettori," triggered a series of members' responses that were overwhelmingly in support of Mercurio's decision and her statement, described as moving, respectful, and intelligent, and reminiscent of old times.[30]

In this respect, the metaphor of "family reunion" used by C. Lee Harrington and Denise Bielby to define the American soap opera fandom's relationship with the daytime television industry likewise applies to LFGs, specifically, the return of Lancio in the lives of members.[31] Similar to the soap opera fandom, Lancio fans do not have a contentious relationship with the industry, as happens in most cases of fandoms. Unlike Harrington and Bielby's case example, however, Lancio had left its fans orphans *before* the opening of LFGs. This situation bestowed on lancette, from their perspectives, the status of inheritors of the brand and of "la vera" (the true) Lancio. S.C., whom I previously quoted, remarks: "Unfortunately, at some point, you would get to the newsstand and the seller, full of sorrow, would give you those few issues that he had found and kept aside for me, until I lost track. Nothing. Not even one more page. I was in mourning. Then, in 2013, I opened my fb [sic] account and with great surprise I found several groups of Lancio enthusiasts. Luckily, I signed up for this. I believe that the *true* Lancio is now here, thanks to the administrators and to many members, in particular, those who publish so many stories here with so much effort and passion, so that this way they will never die."[32]

In other words, lancette consider it fair use to digitize and publish Lancio stories because they see themselves as part of a Lancio family and, moreover, they believe they are simply continuing a tradition—really, they're doing the industry a favor. A recent article clipped and posted by A.C.A. on "Noi lettori" illustrates this point. Titled "Teniamoci in contatto" (Let's Keep in Touch), it speaks in the name of the company and is signed by "lancio." The topic is the opening of a website, thanks to which "chances to talk among each other have multiplied and with them also the possibilities offered to female and male readers to . . . visit us, albeit virtually."[33] The announcement acknowledges that the Internet is only improving practices that were already in use: the website is "like always" a place where fans' ideas and suggestions will be taken into great consideration; it provides information about actors and actresses who are "present" at the firm, so that fans can organize a visit to meet them in person; it can help all users to communicate with each other and thus build a long-lasting fandom.[34] In fact, "Teniamoci in contatto" announced what in reality was only a short-term commitment of the industry to technology. In a comment to the post, E.G. claims that Lancio was unable to maintain the blog, which was removed a few years after it was created. Instead, the webpage (still available online) included a link to another blog, which E.G. herself opened once the official one disappeared, before she transferred her time and effort (and content) onto an LFG. Bottom line: fans are actually more skilled and have more time to dedicate online, in order to keep the communication between fans open.

This episode opens up interesting leads with regard to the peculiar case of the Lancio "family reunion" metaphor. As I said, there is something about the particular history of this company that affects the way in which grassroot extensions of Lancio photoromances are freed from control. According to A.C.A., when the company closed for good, it sold its archive to another publisher that later went bankrupt, leaving the issues of preservation and copyrights unsolved. Also, from E.G.'s claims, it seems that Lancio did not mind that fans might be producing commentaries and other kinds of extensions of Lancio stories on online platforms that were not administered by the publisher itself. On these premises, we can understand the shared belief among lancette that "la vera Lancio" is now made of LFGs, and that the work of members is fundamental in order to keep the memory of both the industry (texts, celebrities, and other related products/activities) and its readership alive. In the words of Lancio actress Anna Maria Cozzolino, who commented on the opening of new LFGs: "Lancio does not belong to anyone in particular, and I am only a small piece in the puzzle, but it belongs to everyone—women and men—who loved *her*."[35]

What interests me in the case of the Lancio fandom, then, is that the family (living in the past and reunited in the present) is not a metaphor, but a modern myth. That is, the family is not an image that I use to describe fans' interactions among themselves and with the industry. Rather, it is a "type of speech," in Roland Barthes's terms, used by fans in the specific social setting of their virtual relationships (among themselves and with the imagined industry) in order to give meaning to individual and collective forms of expression and identities. In its origins, the contemporary discourse on Lancio fans–industry relation as family is built on the representation of the same relationship in these terms by the publisher in the past (as we have seen from my previous examples). In these historical instances, and in the contemporary blogs and FB posts of fans/customers and celebrities/employees, Lancio is everyone's rather than only belonging to a seller or employer. To put it another way, the modern myth of the Lancio family muddles affective bonds and commercial transactions in an interesting way. On the one hand, in the fans' point of view, property (in the sense of copyrights) has no place in the world of the fandom, which is also freed from commodification (the profit that comes from such relations): Lancio is not a company, Lancio is everybody's, lancette are constantly sharing messages of love and friendship together with digitized copies of past issues. On the other hand, online communities enable the sale of issues to collectors, and thus nurture these purchases by building on users' attachment to the brand, and on their longing for the youthful past that the magazines and celebrities embody. The accessibility of the Internet, and the possibility to archive the objects that keep the relationship alive (potentially ad infinitum) sustain the myth that there are no boundaries to the way in which users can express their attachment to Lancio as much there are no limits (so far) to fair use and under-the-table transactions.

In the next sections, I will discuss the extent to which fans negotiate the meaning of this social and cultural discourse that is the myth of the Lancio family (and its reunion). In particular, I will focus on two relevant aspects: the question of proximity/distance vis-à-vis the relationship between readers, texts, and celebrities; and the practice of archiving sustained by LFG users. These two aspects also indicate internal differences within the Lancio fandom, in particular, between respondents to my survey who claim not to be part of online communities, and those who are active members of LFGs maintaining the memory of Lancio alive in the present.

MILD RESISTANCE

Most respondents to my survey and most members of LFGs began reading photo-romances in the 1970s, and their recollections of past experiences of consumption are embedded in the rich political context of workers' struggles, radical movements, second-wave feminism, and right- and left-wing terrorism.[36] However, there is usually no mention of this context in their memories, and there are really no instances of political debate among group members in any FB or blog posts that I read, including discussions on gender, race, and class when debating about narratives, celebrities, or the industry. In this respect, there are no differences between the responses I gathered via survey or via Facebook Messenger, and there is no discrepancy between past and current Lancio fans: they all like to remember the time when they dreamt *with* their favorite celebrities when they were young, so as to read, remember, and dream once again.[37] V.D. is the only one to explicitly refer to the political context, and yet only to say how reading made her "dream" nonetheless. In her words, "Photoromances of the 60s and 70s were the most beautiful thing for us girls who dreamt as we read . . . there were love tragedy death accidents but they still made us dream I grew up with them they conquer me with their stories [sic]."[38]

The question here is whether the lack of political content and the t(a)int of nostalgia that colors fans' recollections also indicate the absence of any form of political gesture or political approach to their fandom. Lancio fans were tweens or teenagers at the time of transition from the "hot autumn" to the "post-ideological" era, that is, from the students and workers' struggles of 1969 to the end of radical movements in the late 1970s. With respect to these fans, the so-called *riflusso* (re-flux) of the 1980s can instead be called the coming of age of a generation to whom the shaming practices of leftist critics (with regard to the products of mass culture) did not seem to differ from those of the Catholic Church or the bourgeoisie, as they were both embodied in the strict rulings of their middle-class parents. In fact, on the basis of collected data, the social and educational backgrounds of Lancio fans differ from those of the photo-romance readership in the 1950s or 1960s: rather than working-class women with low education, they are for the most part (today) white-collar workers (or homemakers) with a high-school degree and they were (in the 1970s) daughters of middle-class parents still attending school. This aspect highlights some limitations with regard to the Lancio fandom, which is clearly a middle-class and white phenomenon. At the same time, responses show that inter-class relationships in the 1970s among teenagers allowed for the spread of publications and, consequently, for the use of this kind of pop culture in ways that were transgressive of the social norms of the middle class. For the question "When did you start reading photoromances?" one respondent to the online survey (A.) wrote this answer:

> I was thirteen years old, I was in middle school and I did not know about them. A friend from elementary school, who lived close by, talked to me about them. She had a group of girlfriends who adored Franco Gasparri and parents who were open minded (even though they were the pre-68 generation) and who bought photoromances for her, so that she handed them down to me. Instead, my parents considered them stuff for maids, and so you can imagine that they would never have bought them for me. To tell you the truth, I liked Franco Gasparri, too. To not be "different" I pretended that I liked those stories, but honestly, I thought it was all fake, starting from some actors' faces (for example I could not stand Katiuscia with her fake upset expression, I found ridiculous the way a slap on the face looked in the pictures, etc.).[39]

A. does not correspond to the image of women reading photoromances that media representations constructed in the past and that are held as truthful in many historical accounts. A teacher with a master's degree, A.'s responses are perhaps more articulate than others. At the same time, A. is in many ways similar to most fans, who connect their experience of reading photoromances to a generational conflict. An admirer of Franco Gasparri, A. was, in a sense, a victim of her parents' sense of cultural respectability, but also defied their standards and transgressed their rules by secretly reading Lancio with her girlfriends. Furthermore, A. shows a degree of awareness, rather than passivity, vis-à-vis her relationship with the texts. While attracted to reading photoromances because of Gasparri, A. admits that she was not completely blind to any flaws in the texts themselves. In sum, A. addresses two aspects that recurrently describe readers' first encounter with photoromances: (1) the importance of a common identity and a shared culture with other girls; and (2) the presence of both proximity and distance in featuring the relationship between her, the products of mass culture, and the celebrity (in this case, Gasparri). A. remembers her experience as a reader in a communal environment, which both triggered and nurtured her passion, and constructs an idea of the feminine self as willingly transgressing the boundaries of a traditional, patriarchal society, both in terms of class and gender. In their nostalgic portrayal of their youthful experience, other respondents similarly describe the act of reading photoromances as the way in which they undermined the authority of middle-class parents, and crossed the boundaries of middle-class girls' "appropriate" pastimes. In sum, the fans' act of mild resistance to elite culture does not have the features of radical politics but questions the idea that passions generated by celebrity culture necessarily derive, in Chris Rojek's words, "from staged authenticity rather than genuine forms of recognition and belonging."[40] The act of buying (sharing, discussing) Lancio photoromances was the gesture that we may call political. In their expressions, very much in continuity with their recollections, the "ragazze Lancio" communicate a genuine wish to build a collective identity, albeit isolated from the political turmoil surrounding them.

Furthermore, I wonder if proximity to texts, celebrities, and the industry can only indicate a position of submission and passivity on the part of these users. It's fair to say that Lancio magazines exploited both the usual conventions of romance and those of the Italian cop films, which were very popular at the time, and often narratives ended with the death of the protagonist, her/his departure, or separations. Passionate or thrilling plots, beautiful characters, and dramatic endings suggest the emotional attachment of readers to both narratives and celebrities, especially women who, in the words of Mary Ann Doane, "can only be seen as reinforcing [their] submission."[41] On the other hand, contemporary online platforms reveal the active role played by fans and, as in the above-mentioned case of A., their distance in proximity. Discussion boards deconstruct common notions such as the fact that lancette only liked romances ("I found them comical," says a survey respondent) or happy endings ("the happy ending diminishes the masterpieces, except for some rare cases," claims one LFG member).[42] Even the relationship with celebrities is often worked through a tongue-in-cheek look back at adolescence. In the words of B.C., who argues ironically that Claudia Rivelli was her model: "I was uglier than a toad and I was dreaming to become a beautiful woman like Claudia (and of course, I am now exactly like her!)."[43] In this light, while readers were blamed in public debate for their proximity to the text and the idolatry of celebrities, I argue that that they were, in fact, victims of distance, that is, of the cultural politics of the elites (publishers, authors) who wanted to keep them outside the realm of production.[44] In the same fashion as fans of cult movies, in Umberto Eco's analysis, lancette relate to Lancio as a "complete furnished world" (i.e., the brand is approached as a whole narrative space) and are able to "unhinge [the cult object], to break it up or take it apart," in other words, to make it their own. Ultimately, I claim that by self-fashioning themselves as the heirs of the Lancio "family" and appropriating Lancio photoromances to rewrite their own stories, lancette revenge those readers of the late forties and fifties whose attempt to own the means of production was chastised on every political front. And, while for past readers like A., this process of appropriation takes place in the private space of memory, made public only in her recollections, for active members of LFGs, their participatory culture is displayed on the web by means of two concurrent practices: that of "archiving" and that of "repertoire."[45]

REPERTOIRES AND ROGUE ARCHIVES

In *Rogue Archives*, Abigail De Kosnik argues that digital archiving "has been most enthusiastically embraced by nonprofessionals—by amateurs, fans, hackers, pirates, and volunteers—in other words, by "rogue" memory workers."[46] In her view, digital archives have been built as an alternative to official, institutional ones, thus democratizing cultural memory: "The rogues of digital archiving have effectuated cultural memory's escape from the state; memory will never again be wholly, or even mostly, under the control of the state or of state-controlled capitalists."[47] Finally, Internet fan fiction archives provide another function: in Kosnik's words (quoting Achille Mbembe), they "confer status on their contents, and on the culture and society that produced those contents."[48]

In a way, we can look at Lancio fans as "rogue memory workers." Lancette use FB to preserve the objects and construct the memory of their shared past: by posting clippings and photos from magazines; by speaking of celebrities like Franco Gasparri, Max Delys, Claudia Rivelli, Paola Pitti, Franco Dani, and Michela Roc; by talking about their favorite stories in the past and asking others about their opinions; by bragging about their latest purchase and publishing its cover (or their covers: the more the issues, the better the deal) and, always, asking for comments; by digitizing entire issues and then sharing them with other members. To borrow both De Kosnik's and Diana Taylor's terminology, LFGs like "Noi lettori" serves a twofold function: to build the digital "rogue" (De Kosnik) archive of Lancio and to preserve the "repertoire" (Taylor) of its fandom, the embodied memory of their performances as fans.

E.G. and other members of LFGs replace professional archivists by digitizing and making Lancio stories available. Since the company closed without much concern for preservation, fans take on the responsibility to keep its memory alive, employing their passion and much effort to keep pages updated and enlarge digital collections, to allow other fans to enjoy their findings, and constantly speaking about themselves as readers, about celebrities, about issues, covers, and the like. This is what Taylor calls "repertoire," as different from archive: the physical, bodily acts of repetition and human performance that are needed to maintain actual archives and to feed metaphorical ones. On the one hand, the many personal stories published on FB add to the body of texts that make up the "Lancio archive"; on the other, members can use the same materials to build their own metaphorical archive, that is, to feed the process of their memory-based narratives and thus contribute to the LFG that is the mise-en-scène of Lancio's collective memory. There could be different reasons why, but all fans did at some point stop buying and reading Lancio, until their recent "rediscovery" via LFGs. As P.F. writes via Facebook Messenger: "I read them and bought them since the early 80s, then I rediscovered them here a few years ago, a dive into my youth."[49] And in the words of M.I.: "It was the seventies and I did not miss reading even one issue. . . . I loved and I love Gasparri especially paired with Michela and I adored Lucky Martins. . . . I read them until Franco's accident in 1980 then I had a sort of rejection for what happened and I abandoned them . . . until by surfing the web I stumbled upon these photoromances groups and magically the passion exploded again. Thanks to the girlfriends in the group who post them I discovered and read photoromances from the 80s and until Lancio closed."[50]

LFGs members do not necessarily *see* themselves as rogue archivists and do not consider the value of the repertoire of their metaphorical archives. Rather, they show a strong attachment to printed issues and doubt that digital copies can substitute for the actual objects. This behavior creates an interesting situation in which the rogue archive of LFGs serves the commercial purpose to build private collections. Quite interestingly, a unique but still relevant episode that happened in one LFG shows the contradictions inherent in this situation. In a post, A.M. lamented that among members the cost of issues should be lower than in other platforms such as eBay; his plead did not receive any positive responses but rather angry comments regarding the fairness of transactions happening on the group's page. A.M. then posted a brief message in which he apologized if he offended anyone, and the episode stopped there. However, the event revealed the possibility that in fact not all users believe that the LFGs are only for the sake of keeping the "family" alive. In fact, I believe that A.M.'s suggestion was so bitterly received not only because it was supposedly based on false premises, but also (and perhaps, above all), because it refocused the attention on the commercial nature of the group itself and of the "family" bond as well.

To put it another way, the conflict between the archive and the collector cracks the fantasy of a digital space of free transactions. Indeed, members are willing to share and, while attached to their own collections, happy to blend into a community of other fans, and hopeful they can make a difference as individuals. A very interesting post about the opening of a "museum of the photoromance" serves to trigger a discussion about collecting and the desire to "make history." F.F. writes in "Noi lettori":

I have supported it for years
A museum of the photoromance is needed
To establish a museum of the photoromance is essential
I wonder what will happen to my 2000 photoromances when I will die
I would donate them to the museum
And you *lancetti* who shield your *foto* [sic] like relics, do you ask yourself what will be of them after your departure?
Let's collect signatures and ask the Ministry of Cultural Heritage for the only museum of the photoromance in the world
Where, in addition to looking at the virtual history of the photoromance since its origins, one can also read them on the premises
Do you agree?[51]

As opposed to De Kosnik's argument about the fact that rogue archives replace state- or capitalist-controlled ones, F.F. hopes for an institutional space to preserve and make public the treasures of private collectors like herself. Her naïveté is disarming: F.F. longs for rather than suspects government control, and believes that the objects in her possession would only be valued if managed by public agencies (despite the fact that not only photoromances, but also their readers have been historically despised; as if the repertoire of fanship and the archive would be of any interest to the government, also allegedly willing to pay in order to handle private collections). Responses to F.F.'s post reveal how Lancio fans are not necessarily similar but in fact have differences from each other. According to R.Q.C, private collections should all be digitized since paper copies can deteriorate; F.F. instead argues that the government should take over where the capitalists failed: "il ministero deve tutelare" (the Ministry must protect), since Lancio lost its patrimony because of bankruptcy. And fans must take over for Lancio by providing the objects (i.e. the photoromances) that enable the repertoire of fandom. Writes F.F.: "We make the museum with our donations / To safeguard and protect them / They could be patrimony of humanity / They traversed a century / From one generation to another is the global culture of photoromances."[52] J.Z. is more skeptical about the government's interest mostly because of the lack of resources, and while she wonders about copyrights, she also sustains the family myth: "siamo noi soltanto che facciamo vivere il ricordo della lancio" (it's only us who keep the memory of lancio alive").

Here, it is important to point out that publishers obviously encouraged collecting issues, to maintain a loyal readership. In the case of Lancio, the practice of keeping past issues shapes a reader's identity, from the industry's point of view, because of the added social value that a large collection can give to a true female fan. More specifically, as stated by Katiuscia in her response to a fan's letter, a girl should welcome the idea of creating a space for herself where she can store and read Lancio magazines, a place she can decorate according to her own taste. Katiuscia writes: "All of us girls want a spot where we can withdraw into ourselves, happily alone to read our favorite magazines, to listen to music and dream about love. If you can fix your attic with little money and a bit of fantasy, you will solve two problems at the same time: how to escape family drama and how to organize your Lancio-library."[53] A consumer-oriented "room of one's own," to paraphrase Virginia Woolf, both a literal and figurative place for female fans within a patriarchal society, co-opted by a publisher that, rather than looking down at their readers' naïveté, had learned to exploit their purchasing power.

The room of one's own now virtually recreated on the web is always open to new members. It is perhaps in this opening up and sharing with other users that the historical origins of predetermined self-expression can change their course (from the path projected by Katiuscia, for example). Especially with respect to the past, actual familial bonds (linking fans to their mothers, aunts, sisters, and girlfriends) refashion the industrial project of loyal consumership into a shared memory of past experiences that exits the space of commercial transactions. In the words of P.A., for example, printed copies of Lancio issues are only important to her insofar as they speak to the tradition of saving, protecting, and handing them down for others to enjoy. She writes: "Since I can remember, I remember my aunt and my mother and their girlfriends with photoromances in their hands, and I began reading them before I was able to read."[54] Similar to Giet's conclusions on the readership of *Nous Deux*, which I mentioned in the introduction to this book, P.A. describes how buy and borrowing issues "can realize connections between generations."[55] Contrary to Albinati's account of her sister's conflicted relation to their mother, with regard to cultural consumption, lancette can recognize the positive outcomes of reading photoromances. The point is that the myth of the Lancio "family" does not necessarily mean that sentimental bonds are not "real" in the context of the Lancio fandom. The exposed economic basis of fans' relations to the industry and to other fans deconstructs the idea of a Lancio family above and beyond the market. At the same time, expressions of genuine affection persist in the space of business transactions, particularly when connected to a shared tradition of feminine fanship. Always both individual and social, lancette's participation in LFGs intertwines the repertoire with the archive, thus blurring the distinction between capitalist and affective economies, between individual gain and collective individuation.

EPILOGUE: LIKE AN EARTHQUAKE

In their preface to the Italian translation of Jenkins's *Convergence Culture*, in 2007, the collective of writers from Bologna known as Wu Ming stated, "In the best of all possible worlds, the publication of this book would shake the debate on Internet and new communication technologies in Italy like an earthquake."[1] Wu Ming's prediction did not come true, although evidence that media convergence and transmedia storytelling are fundamentally influencing Italian culture via a global perspective has attracted some scholarly attention in the age of digital media. Among the few studies originating from Italy to consider Jenkins's perspective, Giuliana Benvenuti's analysis of what she calls "the brand Gomorrah" sheds light on the structures of media franchise in Italy as "a meta-text potentially infinite and open to creativity."[2] From the international bestselling book *Gomorrah* (2006) to Sky TV's *Gomorrah: La Serie* (Gomorrah: The Series, 2014–) (available globally through Netflix), the stories of Italian organized crime across national borders (from the outskirts of Naples to Honduras) build a narrative world that is branded with the name Roberto Saviano, author of the literary text and creator of the series, as well as screenwriter for a movie drawn from his book (*Gomorrah*, dir. Matteo Garrone, 2008) and coauthor with Mario Gelardi of a theatrical production (*Gomorrah*, 2007). Further, Benvenuti cites as another example Wu Ming novelists, who experiment with "the strategies of active engagement of audiences from below, employed in cultural productions by big corporations."[3] According to Benvenuti, what Wu Ming members understand is that production and reception are now more than ever structurally synergistic, with regard to media objects that not only develop across platforms, but also exploit practices of participatory culture.

With this book, I demonstrated that the paradigm of convergence is not only relevant to the study of new technologies and contemporary Italian media culture, but also to its history, beginning with the changes in the media system that occurred in the immediate postwar period and throughout the following decades, culminating with the capillary spread of celebrity culture in the 1970s. By exploring the industry of the photoromance, we can expand our understanding of how different media industries function(ed) and are related to each other (not only at the economic level but also at the cultural and social levels). In particular, the illustrated magazine that works "in much the same way as the Internet in the contemporary media landscape" is a specific vehicle for film stardom, in the fifties, and then later for music and television celebrity.[4] Furthermore, we discover that the persistent "glocal" aspect of today's media franchises, like Gomorrah (representing a local reality while appealing to global audiences), is also not new. Born from the hybridization of comics, film, and photography, on the foundation of the tendency of Italian cultural industries to privilege imports, photoromances made in Italy not only were successfully exported to communities of the Italian diaspora, across the Alps and the Atlantic, but also translated and reproduced in many more countries through franchises, or appropriated and reinvented by other national publishers. At the dawn of convergence, Italian photoromances appealed to a growing audience of female fans, contributing locally to literacy and globally to the spread of consumer culture and, at the same time, of modern gender discourses.

In this respect, the case of the photoromance functions in this book as a prism through which to understand how shifting strategies in media industries reflect and are reflected in the flux of changing social structures, gender roles and hierarchies, economic demands, and political power relations. In particular, the rise of female fanship and fandom, riding the wave of consumer culture, determined the success of magazines like *Bolero Film*, cleverly exploited by publishers like Mondadori and, at the same time, by advertising companies. While thriving economically, the culture of the photoromance spread moral panic and provoked reactions of contempt among the established political class and the intelligentsia. Also in this sense, the new (for the time) media product was very much a frontrunner. Today, convergence "seems to pervade any media strategy for attracting audiences and business opportunities, thus also penetrating into academic research and curricula."[5] In Italy, however, the practices of convergence today face as much resistance from the cultural elites as they did in the past. According to Wu Ming, "The problem is that the Italian debate on pop culture, ninety times over a hundred, concerns the trash with which TV poisons us, as if the 'popular' were necessarily that, while qualitative distinctions exist and so do historical evolutions. Otherwise, we would think that *Sandokan*, *Star Trek*, *Lost*, TG4 News, and *The Babe and the Nerd* are all on the same level."[6] In fact, this book argues that the issue lies precisely in the hierarchical perspective with which Italian criticism, including that of Wu Ming, has approached mass culture and, more specifically, has dismissed the active role of audiences and the relevance of habits of consumption and fandom. While in their own work Wu Ming members appear to understand precisely the importance of how reader/users access, consume, and appropriate cultural products, by making a distinction between *Sandokan* and *Lost*, they reiterate an understanding of the "quality" of texts as inherent to their structures and interpretations (and their own interpretation, as a matter of fact); meanwhile, the very act of reading still has no value per se and neither does the collective experience of fandom. On the contrary, I claim that the cultural, social and political relevance of the photoromance resides in the economy of production and reception within which both parties at play (makers and users) negotiate both representation and participation.

Wu Ming's critical judgment on the products with which "TV poisons us" ultimately aims to distinguish between technology and its uses, in order to argue for a positive account of new technologies and their potential for political participation. At the same time, the collective falls prey to the same attitude that demeaned photoromances and melodramas vis-à-vis art cinema and, in the seventies, other types of comics. This attitude, as I explain throughout the book, is also implicitly or explicitly gendered: the hierarchization of genres (melodrama, romance) is associated with the femininity of their readers/viewers with the purpose (or effect) of devaluing both. In the context of postwar Europe, the cult of the (male) film *auteur* and the binary opposition between art and commercial cinema define the cultural backdrop against which the irrational and morally unrestrained female fan of photoromances joins those of weepies and pulp romances. Represented in films, these fans respond to unspoken anxieties of an industry and an intellectual class that are fundamentally patriarchal. With the purpose of deconstructing this position, my analyses show that the longing for proximity (to the text, to the star, to the celebrity) and the wish of appropriation (against the moral rights of the authors and the economic rights of the industries) by which critics debased fans, are rather powerful tools of self-recognition and collective identification. My netnographic study of the Lancio fandom in contemporary digital platforms particularly addresses this shift in perspective, thus dismantling conceptions of the female fan that, in the words of Mary Ann Doane, "can only be seen as reinforcing her submission."[7] Lancette (female Lancio fans, as noted earlier) create meaning and context by sharing, discussing, and archiving both products (images of celebrities, digital copies of photoromances) and their own experiences of consumption. At the boundaries of legality, members of Facebook groups engage with and expand the narrative world of photoromances to the point that they cease to see themselves as simply consumers, but rather become part of the one and only "Lancio family."

"At long last, we can read and watch television at the same time." The ironic comment comes from American journalist Alan Kriegsman, whose 1979 article in the *Washington Post* I quoted at the very beginning of this book. Here at its end, going back to that article we can understand the underpinning critique of value that hierarchizes the products of mass culture to the detriment of Italian imports in the United States. Also, we can trace a tradition in which the same statement is gendered to label not only the products (romances), but also their readers (women) within a scale that places them both at the very bottom (soon it will be soap operas' turn). At the same time, Kriegsman points out a demand that is far from extreme or unusual and to which the advent of the Italian photoromance in the United States appears as the perfect response, predicting what is in store for the future: multitasking users and multi-platform product franchises. In this continuum that links the past of the photoromance to the present of the Internet, *The Photoromance* had the goal of reversing the critical judgment of Kriegsman and others to discover the array of innovations brought forward by the Italian industries and the space for participation not only assigned to but also conquered by readers and viewers.

In a 2019 interview, photoromance maker Francesca Giombini confessed to me: "There is still so much to do!"[8] Giombini has been looking for years for a publisher that would sponsor her work, aside from the market logic of weekly magazines. Burdened by a long tradition of mockery in the press and the dismissal of scholarship, the photoromance may have a future beyond its past. And the future might be brighter if, across national borders, more scholars were to expand, build out, and drill down into the story I have told in this book.

Notes

INTRODUCTION

1. Translation: Mafalda: "Hi Susanita, what are you reading?" Susanita: "Photoromances." M: "But S.; you can't fill your head with such stupidities!" M: "Important things are happening in the world, things that will soon change humanity's destiny." S: "Don't remind me of that, you fool! Why do you think I read photoromances?"

2. In Italian, see Giuseppe Gargiulo, *Cultura popolare e cultura di massa nel fotoromanzo "rosa"* (Messina: G. D'Anna, 1977); Valentino Cecchetti, *Generi della letteratura popolare: feuilletton, fascicoli, fotoromanzi in Italia dal 1870 ad oggi* (Latina: Tunuè, 2011), 343; Ermanno Detti, *Le carte rosa: storia del fotoromanzo e della narrativa popolare* (Firenze: La Nuova Italia, 1990); Giuseppe Sergio, *Liala dal romanzo al fotoromanzo: le scelte linguistiche, lo stile, i temi* (Milano: Mimesi, 2012). In Latin American Studies, see, among others: Cornelia Butler Flora and Jan L. Flora, "The Fotonovela as a Tool for Class and Cultural Domination," *Latin American Perspectives* 5, no. 1 (1978): 134–150; Roberto D. Flores, *Fotonovela argentina: heredera del melodrama* (Buenos Aires: Asociación Argentina de Editores de Revistas, 1995); and Angeluccia Bernardes Habert, *Fotonovela e industria cultural* (Buenos Aires: Petropolis, 1974), 7. As I will discuss later, a recent surge of interest in the photoromance sustains a new, constructive reading of the medium and its social and cultural relevance; see Anna Bravo, *Il fotoromanzo* (Bologna: Il Mulino, 2011); Silvana Turzio, *Il fotoromanzo: Metamorfosi delle storie lacrimevoli* (Milan: Meltemi, 2019); Jan Baetens, *The Film Photonovel: A Cultural History of Forgotten Adaptations* (Austin: University of Texas Press, 2019) and "Between Adaptation, Intermediality, and Cultural Series: The Example of the Photonovel," *Artnodes* 18 (2016): 47–55; Sylvette Giet, *"Nous Deux" 1947–1997: apprendre la langue du coeur* (Paris: Peeters, 1997); Isabelle Antonutti, *Cino Del Duca: De "Tarzan" à "Nous Deux": itinéraire d'un patron de presse* (Rennes: PU Rennes: 2013); Carlos Roberto de Souza, "The Law of the Heart: Genealogy, Narrative and Audience of a Minor Genre: the Argentinean Fotonovela," dissertation (University of Santa Barbara, 2009).

3. The representation of the female reader as helpless victim is also applicable to most scholarship; for example, see: Evelyne Sullerot, *La presse féminine* (Paris: Armand Colin, [1963] 1966); Serge Saint-Michel, *Le roman-photo* (Paris: Larousse, 1979); and Detti, *Le carte rosa*.

4. For example, it is well known that film stars Gina Lollobrigida and Sophia Loren began their careers as photoromance actresses in *Sogno*. See Roberto Baldazzini, *Sofia Loren: rapita dal cinema: i fotoromanzi di Sofia Lazzaro (1950–1952)* (Roma: Struwwelpeter, 2010). Neither of them, however, have openly talked about that experience.

5. Jan Baetens, "The Photo-Novel: A Minor Medium?," *NECSUS: European Journal of Media Studies* 1, no. 1 (2012): 1–12.

6. Titled "A True Life Photoromance: Kiss" and "Photoromance: Darling," these American magazines are in fact Italian imports, produced by the Roman publisher Lancio and printed in the United States by Omnium Publishing Corporation (New York). Flora and Flora, "The Fotonovela as a Tool for Class and Cultural Domination."

7. The first issue was published March 1, 1947, by Novissima, a small Roman publisher associated with Rizzoli. *Sogno*'s creator was Giorgio Canus de Fonseca.

8. *BF* was directed by Luciano Pedrocchi and the first issue was published on November 30, 1947. The first issue of *Grand Hotel* was sold on June 29, 1946.

9. Cecchetti, *Generi della letteratura popolare*; Bravo, *Il fotoromanzo,* chap. 1, Kindle.

10. David Forgacs, "An Oral Renarration of a Photoromance," in *Orality and Literacy in Modern Italian Culture,* ed. Michael Caesar and Marina Spunta (Oxford: Legenda, 2006), 67–76; Emma Barron, *Popular High Culture in Italian Media, 1950–1970: Mona Lisa Covergirl* (New York: Palgrave Macmillan, 2018), 253.

11. Barron, *Popular High Culture in Italian Media*, 254.

12. Milly Buonanno, *Naturale come sei: indagine sulla stampa femminile in Italia* (Rimini: Guaraldi Editore, 1975), 45–46.

13. Bravo, *Il fotoromanzo*, chap. 3, Kindle.

14. See for example: Thierry Crépin, Christophe Chavdia, and Thierry Groensteen, *On tue à chaque page! La loi de 1949 sur les publications destinées à la jeunesse* (Paris: Editions du Temps Musée de la bande dessinée, 1999); Paula Rabinowitz, *American Pulp: How Paperbacks Brought Modernism to Main Street* (Princeton: Princeton University Press, 2014); Isabelle Antonutti, "La phobie des lectures du people," in Antonutti, *Cino Del Duca*, 115–122.

15. For a summary of these positions, see also Michele Mattelart's report to UNESCO, *Women and the Cultural Industries* (UNESCO, 1981).

16. See also *L'amorosa menzogna* (Lies of Love, written and dir. Michelangelo Antonioni, 1949), a compassionate but top-down account of this readership; and the neorealist film *Riso Amaro* (Bitter Rice, dir. Giuseppe De Santis, 1949), whose female protagonist is an avid reader of photoromances as well as a fan of American imported cultural practices such as dancing the boogie-woogie and chewing gum. *Lies of Love* is available online at https://www.youtube.com/watch?v=1oMv4uIVNIs. I will discuss *Bitter Rice* and its protagonist, played by Silvana Mangano, in chapter 2.

17. Baetens, "The Photo-Novel," 6.

18. Ezio Colombo, "Il film della settimana: Lo sceicco bianco," *Hollywood* 8, no. 369 (1952): 22.

19. "[N]on per nulla [i fotoromanzi] appassionano soprattutto le donne, c'è sempre un bisogno di abbandono tipicamente femminile." Unless otherwise noted, all translations are mine.

20. Giorgio Capua, "Fumetti terzo tempo," *Hollywood*, January 12, 1952, 16.

21. Ibid., 16.

22. Giorgio Capua, "I fumetti impegnano cinema e Parlamento nell'esame di un male del secolo" (photoromances engage cinema and the Parliament in the analysis of an evil of the century), *Hollywood*, March 1, 1952.

23. *Cinema nuovo: rassegna quindicinale* 11, no. 160 (1962): 420. The photoromance was published in *Super Star*, no. 83 (August 1, 1961).

24. "Immagino la sua intransigenza nei confronti di questo tipo di letteratura popolare, e la condivido. Ma non le pare che, nell'ambito di un complesso d'interessi per il cinema che vadano al di là di quelli strettamente estetici per collegarsi a quelli sociologici e politici, potrebbe essere utile esaminarne le sue caratteristiche e la natura dell'influenza che essa esercita sui suoi lettori? Mi sembra in fondo lamentevole il fatto che racconti polizieschi e fantascientifici, fumetti e fotoromanzi abbiano tanti lettori sprovveduti e che quasi nessun critico d'altra parte li prenda in considerazione per studiarne l'azione—e il modo d'azione—sul pubblico."

25. "Film che solo da una reale indipendenza dalle attuali strutture economiche troppo vincolanti, possono trarre quel grado di libertà e di ispirazione da riuscire a influenzare in profondità il proprio tempo, la cultura del proprio tempo, anziché subire i peggiori miti."

26. See Theodor Adorno and Max Horkheimer, "The Culture Industry: Enlightenment as Mass Deception," in *Dialectic of Enlightenment*, trans. Edmund Jephcott (Stanford: Stanford University Press, 2002), 94–136.

27. For a discussion of this issue, see Wu Ming, preface to *Cultura Convergente* by Henry Jenkins (Milan, Apogeo Editore, 2007), https://www.wumingfoundation.com/italiano/outtakes/culturaconvergente.htm. According to Wu Ming, in Italy, popular culture means folk and pre-industrial.

28. The title of the original script, collected at the Cesare Zavattini Archives in Reggio Emilia, was "Maria e Corrado" (1961). Documents related to this story appeared in one of the exhibitions at the international photography festival "Fotografia Europea" held in Reggio Emilia, titled "Fotoromanzo e poi . . ." (Photoromance and Then . . .), April–July, 2018, https://www.fotografiaeuropea.it/blog/2018/nessunacolpafotoromanzo-un-racconto-fotografico-per-instagram-2/.

29. "La maggioranza può identificarsi [nei fotoromanzi], trovare i propri sentimenti, il che significa purtroppo che si tratta di problemi di persone non molto evolute."

30. "La letteratura è un fenomeno di casta," says Zavattini, "ma non si tratta di far scendere la letteratura, di volgarizzare, ma di porre il letterato nella consapevolezza della destinazione del suo prodotto e porsi in una prospettiva diversa che rinnova il linguaggio."

31. This is a quote from the voice-over commentary of the documentary film *La vita a fumetti* (Life in Comics, dir. Giuseppe Ferrara, 1964), collected at RAI Teche (Italian Public Radio and Television Archives).

32. "Il fotoromanzo ha una precisa funzione mitica, è la proiezione del livello ego verso il superego, una proiezione che controllatamente avviene nei termini che la borghesia appunto indica: accrescimento di benessere, matrimonio fra uguali, competitività, e, poi, a livello affettivo: sentimenti eterni, rapporti paternalistici familiari, concezione servile della donna nell'interno della casa." Quintavalle, preface to *Nero a strisce: La reazione a fumetti* by Luigi Allegri, Adelmina Bonazzi, and Arnaldo Conversi (Parma: Istituto di storia dell'arte, 1971), 12–13. *Nero a strisce* (Black Strips) is a catalogue of an exhibition that Quintavalle curated with a group of students, which aimed at criticizing this particular "tool" (strumento) of mass culture. For a similar reading, with respect to fotonovelas, see Flora and Flora, "The Fotonovela as a Tool for Class and Cultural Domination."

33. Umberto Eco, *Apocalypse Postponed* (Bloomington: Indiana University Press, 1994); Luigi Compagnone, "Femminismo," *Corriere della Sera*, March 3, 1974, 3.

34. "Per questo genere di fumetto, non può non parlarsi di fascism." Allegri, Bonazzi, and Conversi, *Nero a strisce,* 14.

35. Evelyn Sullerot, "I fotoromanzi," in *La paralettura: il melodramma, il romanzo popolare, il fotoromanzo, il romanzo politziesco, il fumetto*, ed. Michele Rak (Naples: Liguori, 1977), 100. Data about Latin American countries is taken from de Souza, "The Law of the Heart." Serge Saint-Michel provides information about photoromances in African countries in *Le roman-photo*, 166–168.

36. Founded in 1928 with his brothers. In addition, he expanded his business by creating French versions of the youth magazines (for example, *Hurrah!*).

37. Giet, *"Nous Deux" 1947–1997*, 16. Like *Grand Hotel*, *Nous Deux* initially published only drawn-romances. Its first photoromance came out on August 9, 1950. The French magazine was also as successful as *Grand Hotel*: 700,000 copies sold in 1948, and more than one million through in the fifties.

38. Edizioni Universo, owned by Cino Del Duca's brothers in Italy, Domenico and Alceo, had a franchise in Brazil, since 1946 (*Grande Hotel*), where the first photoromance appeared in 1951. In Argentina, *Rapsodia* had acquired copyrights of *Grand Hotel's* materials and regularly published its stories in translation since 1958. Among others, *Rapsodia* featured *Grand Hotel's* big productions based on literary classics and casting famous film and theater actors, such as Vittorio Gassman and Anna Maria Ferrero starring in *Romeo and Juliet*.

39. Eugenia Scarzanella, "Entre Dos Exilios: Cesare Civita, un editor italiano en Buenos Aires, desde la Guerra Mundial hasta la dictaduara militar (1941–1976)," *Revista de Indias* 64, no. 245 (2009): 67.

40. Eugenia Scarzanella, *Abril: da Peron a Videla: un editore italiano a Buenos Aires* (Nova Delphi: Rome, 2013).

41. De Souza, 119. As I mentioned, *Tormento* is the title of a well-known Italian melodrama directed by Matarazzo in 1950, also starring, like *Catene*, Amedeo Nazzari and Yvonne Sanson.

42. These photoromances were labeled as produced by "Bolero Film-Surameris."

43. Scarzanella, "Entre Dos Exilios," 74.

44. Baetens, "The Photo-Novel," 1.

45. Enrico Decleva, *Arnoldo Mondadori* (Turin: UTET, 2007), 348–394.

46. Giet, *"Nous Deux" 1947–1997"*; and Antonutti, *Cino Del Duca*. In addition, an article on the Spanish photoromance analyzes the magazines from the point of view of photography: Juan Miguel Sanchez Vigil and Maria Oliverta Zaldua, "La fotografia en las fotonovelas españolas," *Documentacion de la Ciencias de la Informacion* 35 (2012): 31–51.

47. Saint-Michel, *Le roman-photo*, 168: "Les sortilèges du monde aseptise et anhistorique du roman-photo s'exercent plus facilement sur les mal-nantis que sur les autres" (The spells of the sterilized and ahistorical world of the photoromance rubbed off more easily on the unprivileged than on other).

48. Sullerot, *La presse féminine*.

49. Mattelart, *Women and the Cultural Industries*, 24.

50. Similarly, speaking of other "paraletteratura" (comics, dime novels, etc.) or "letteratura di consumo" (pulp fiction), Umberto Eco and Vittorio Spinazzola agree that readers may be aware of the "fantasies" at play, and yet, would enjoy them to their satisfaction. See Vittorio Spinazzola, *Il successo letterario* (Milan: Unicopli, 1985); Umberto Eco, *Il superuomo di massa* (Milan: Bompiani, 1978).

51. Janice A. Radway, "Women Read Romance: The Interaction of Text and Context," *Feminist Studies* 9, no. 1 (1983): 55. See also by Radway, *Reading the Romance: Women, Patriarchy, and Popular Literature* (Chapel Hill: University of North Carolina Press, 1983) and Sally Stain, "The Graphic Ordering of Desire: Modernization of a Middle-Class Women's Magazine 1914–1939," *Heresies* 5, no. 2 (1985): 7–16.

52. Radway, "Women Read Romance," 72.

53. Joost van Loon, "Ethnography: A Critical Turn in Cultural Studies," in *Handbook of Ethnography*, ed. Paul Atkinson, Amanda Coffey, Sara Delamont, John Lofland, and Lyn Lofland (Lonon: Sage, 2001), 275.

54. Buonanno, the research group of Maria Teresa Anelli, and to a certain extent Bravo have made some use of these approaches. See Maria Teresa Anelli, Paola Gabbrielli, Marta Morgavi, and Roberto Piperno, *Fotoromanzo, fascino e pregiudizio: storia, documenti e immagini di un grande fenomeno popolare: 1946–1978* (Rome: Savelli, 1979); Buonanno, *Naturale come sei*; and Bravo, *Il fotoromanzo*.

55. Stuart Hall, "Encoding, Decoding," in *The Cultural Studies Reader*, ed. Simon During (London: Routledge, 2007), 90–103.

56. Henry Jenkins, "Fandom, Negotiation, and Participatory Culture," in *A Companion to Media Fandom and Fan Studies*, ed. Paul Booth (Hoboken, NJ: John Wiley and Sons, 2018), 16.

57. Giet, *"Nous Deux" 1947–1997*, 159.

58. Alan M. Kriegsman, "TV Soap Operas in Magazine Format," *Washington Post*, January 21, 1979, https://www.washingtonpost.com/archive/lifestyle/1979/01/21/tv-soap-operas-in-magazine-format/03577f06-3b96-4eab-93d6-df5f5d49cbf5/?utm_term=.1150df32392c.

59. Henry Jenkins, *Convergence Culture* (New York: New York University Press, 2006).

60. Matthew Freeman, "Branding Consumerism: Cross-Media Characters and Story-Worlds at the Turn of the 20th Century," *International Journal of Cultural Studies* 18, no. 6 (2014): 630. See also Paolo Bertetti, Matthew Freeman, and Carlos A. Scolari, *Transmedia Archaeology: Storytelling in the Borderlines of Science Fiction, Comics and Pulp Magazines* (New York: Palgrave Macmillan, 2014).

61. Freeman, "Branding Consumerism," 632.

62. Urs Meyer, "From Intermediality to Transmediality: Cross-Media Transfer in Contemporary German Literature," in *Transmediality and Transculturality*, ed. Nadja Gernalzick and Gabriele Pisarz-Ramirez (Heidelberg: Universitaetsverlag Winter, 2013), 27–38.

63. For example, Rizzoli expanded into cinema with both a production company (Novella Film, whose first film was *La Signora di tutti* [Everybody's Lady, dir. Max Ophuls, 1934], with Isa Miranda) and a distribution outlet, Cineriz. According to Antonutti, Del Duca's expansion into the film production business was due to his experience in Italy, where he was in contact with Angelo Rizzoli. Isabelle Antonutti, "Producteurs de films," in Antonutti, *Cino Del Duca*, 127–130.

64. Scott McCloud, *Understanding Comics* (New York: Harper Perennial, 1994), 63.

65. The expression is used in several instances, particularly in a popular series named *Cineromanzo per Tutti* that stated in the titles that the magazine was a "versione fotoromanzata" (photoromanced version) of a film.

66. Raffaele De Berti, "Il nuovo periodico. Rotocalchi tra fotogiornalismo, cronaca e costume," in *Forme e modelli del rotocalco italiano tra fascismo e guerra*, ed. Raffaele De Berti and Irene Piazzoni (Milan: Cisalpino-Monduzzi, 2009), 5; Baetens, *The Film Photonovel*, 14–16.

67. Among other titles, *Il grido* (dir. Michelangelo Antonioni, 1957) and *La strada* (dir. Federico Fellini, 1954). Other examples will be discussed in chapter 2.

68. I will discuss this question in chapter 3.

69. Mondadori Foundation Archive (Milan), Sezione Arnoldo Mondadori, Fascicolo Pedrocchi Luciano, Letter from Pedrocchi to Mondadori ("Illustre Presidente"), June 26, 1964. "Il disco della Cinquetti che la sua Casa discografica ha stampato. Le vendite procedono assai brillantemente malgrado la spesa sia di ben 2000 lire. Una operazione consolante perche dimostra che tra i lettori del settimanale c'è chi ha buone possibilita d'acquisto."

70. Adaptations of Jane Austen's novel by the same title (1813) and Octave Feuillet's novel, *Le roman d'un jeune home pauvre* (1867).

71. Sanremo is the name of a small town in Italy that has hosted since 1951 the most important music contest in Italy. Notably, between 1953 and 1971, each song was performed twice by two different artists, one Italian and one international guest singer.

72. I will study this fandom in chapter 6.

73. See Angela McRobbie, *The Aftermath of Feminism: Gender, Culture, and Social Change* (London: Sage, 2008).

74. In their words, "If one would observe the culture industry through an Adornian lens, the photo novel necessarily would come out as utterly silly and alienating." See Jan Baetens, Carmen Van den Bergh, and Bart Van Den Bossche, "How to Write a Photo Novel. Ennio Jacobelli's *Istruzioni pratiche per la realizzazione del fotoromanzo* (1956)," *Authorship* 6, no. 1 (2017): 3.

75. Jenkins, *Convergence Culture*, 14.

76. Free-to-air television network of Mediaset, Canale Cinque, founded by Silvio Berlusconi, started broadcasting in 1974.

77. See Mario Lombardi and Fabrizio Pignatel, *La stampa periodica in Italia: Mezzo secolo di riviste illustrate* (Rome: Editori Riuniti, 1985).

78. Mondadori sells *Bolero Film* to Staff Studio in 1984, but Lancio series are still popular at that time, and so are its celebrities such as Franco Gasparri, Claudia Rivelli, and Franco Dani.

79. Olivier Driessens, "The Celebritization of Society and Culture: Understanding the Structural Dynamics of Celebrity Culture," *International Journal of Cultural Studies* 16, no. 16 (2013): 641–657.

80. Liliana Madeo, "A fumetti il controllo delle nascite" (Birth Control in Comics), *La Stampa*, January 30, 1974, 7.

81. Jenkins, *Convergence Culture*, 20.

82. In the words of Jenkins, "part fan and part academic." See "Who The &%&# is Henry Jenkins?," in *Confessions of an Aca-Fan*, http://henryjenkins.org/aboutmehtml.

1 CHASING THE AUDIENCE

1. The first is an expression used by photoromance director Dante Guardamagna in a letter to Ulrike Schimming of June 18, 1996. See Ulrike Schimming, *Fotoromane: Analyse Eines Massenmediums* (Frankfurt am Main: Peter Lang, 2002), 224. Guardamagna worked from 1947 to 1959 as director at *Bolero Film* and *Le grandi firme (Signature Works)*, both published by Mondadori, then as director of production at Rizzoli. "A complete illustrated soap opera" is printed on the cover, above the title, in many issues of *Darling*, the U.S. edition of Lancio, printed by Omnium Publishing Corporation. "A movie that you can take home with you" was also printed on the label that appeared in each cover of *Darling* and of *Kiss,* another Lancio publication in the United States.

2. For example, directors Damiano Damiani and Mario Landi, who later became production manager at Rizzoli, screenwriter Dante Guardamagna, and writer Luciana Peverelli.

3. See the results of the 1962 Doxa survey about Mondadori periodicals discussed later in this chapter: *I lettori di otto periodici italiani: Epoca, Grazia, Arianna, Confidenze, Bolero Film, Storia illustrata, il giallo Mondadori, Topolino: studio statistico sulle caratteristiche demografiche, economiche, sociali e culturali* (Milan: Mondadori, 1963).

4. Giet, *"Nous deux" 1947–1997*, 107–108. For a study on the political relevance of generational bonds among readers, see also chapter 6 in this book.

5. Fausto Colombo, *La cultura sottile: Media e industria culturale in Italia dall'Ottocento agli anni Novanta* (Milan: Bompiani 1998), 28. "Il destinatario con cui si dialoga davvero è l'investitore pubblicitario."

6. Freeman, "Branding Consumerism," 642.

7. Ibid. I will discuss the figure of Bongiorno in more detail later in this chapter.

8. "Un moderno carattere imprenditoriale e di massa." See Claudia Patuzzi, *Mondadori* (Naples: Liguori Editore, 1978), 11. See also David Forgacs and Stephen Gundle, *Mass Culture and Italian Society from Fascism to the Cold War* (Bloomington: Indiana University Press, 2007), 99.

9. Forgacs and Gundle, *Mass Culture and Italian Society*, 99.

10. An important figure in the regime, the industrialist Senator Borletti, was president of Mondadori from 1923 to 1939 and sustained the company with both financial and political capital. At the same time, Emil Ludwig, a Jewish Democratic author published with Mondadori, including his book *I colloqui con Mussolini* (interview with Mussolini), despite Mussolini's veto. See Patuzzi, *Mondadori*, 25 and 34.

11. Angelo Ventrone, "Tra propaganda e passione: 'Grand Hotel' e l'Italia degli anni '50," *Rivista di Storia Contemporanea* 17, no. 4 (1988): 603–631.

12. Ibid., 604.

13. From two photoromances, sixteen pages, and a limited number of pages dedicated to gossips and news about the film world, to forty pages and four photoromances in 1957, and fifty-six pages and five photoromances in 1963.

14. See Henry Jenkins, *Textual Poachers: Television Fans and Participatory Culture* (New York: Routledge, [1992] 2013).

15. Written and directed by Damiano Damiani, executive producer Enzo Tabacchi, story by Albert Georges, script by G. Martina.

16. According to the radio commentator, "Sconosciuto amore" was "Una nuova appassionata canzone ispirata dal fotoromanzo di Bolero Film: ascoltatela alla radio, domenica 21 agosto, alle ore 14, 10 sulle stazioni della rete rossa" (A new passionate song inspired by the photoromance in *BF*: listen to it on the radio, Sunday, August 21, at 2:10 p.m. on Red Channel stations). "Beguine" was a kind of dance and music from the island of Martinique.

17. Michael Nicholas Salvatore Bongiorno (1924-2009), known as Mike Bongiorno, was born in New York City but moved to Turin, Italy when he was very young.

18. "Oh my God, did you see him? It was Mike Bongiorno! . . . You should have asked [for] his autograph, *signora* Tina," says an extra in the photoromance "È successo a Milano" (It Happened in Milan), when she sees the television host outside a bar. See "È successo a Milano," with Mike Bongiorno, Gabriele Tinti, and Nadia Marlowa, by Licia Trevisan and Aldo Aldi, *BF*, no. 855 (1963), episode no. 9.

19. See, for example, "Terra ingrata," in which Bongiorno plays himself and acts as an intermediary between a woman, her estranged husband who has left her in Italy to become a gangster in the United States, and an American friend of his, who is genuinely in love with the woman (first episode published in *BF*, no. 648 [1959]).

20. Umberto Eco, *Diario minimo* (Milan: Mondadori, [1963] 1975).

21. "Un esempio vivente e trionfante della mediocrità."

22. "Un amante ideale, sottomesso e fragile, dolce e cortese."

23. *BF*, no. 926–927 (1965): 56. "Rievoca in questo fotoromanzo un episodio della sua vita: quando, ricercato dalla polizia tedesca, trovò rifugio tra le mura di una villa abitata da una giovane donna e potè così salvarsi la vita."

24. "[A] cancellare il passato e a dare una speranza d'avvenire."

25. Baetens, "Between Adaptation, Intermediality and Cultural Series," 49.

26. Carolina Invernizio was an Italian author of feuilletons in the late 1800s and Liala (aka Amalia Liana Negretti Odescalchi) was a romance writer, especially popular in the 1930s and 1940s. See Lucia Cardone, *Con lo schermo nel cuore: Grand Hotel e il cinema* (Roma: ETS, 2004).

27. Literally "banditry," banditismo is a social phenomenon peculiar to Southern Italy, particularly in the Sicily, Calabria, and Sardinia regions, connecting organized crime with political and social issues.

28. Peter Brooks, *The Melodramatic Imagination: Balzac, Henry James, Melodrama and the Mode of Excess* (New Haven: Yale University Press, [1976] 1995).

29. Schimming, "Briefe von Dante Guardamagna (Brief 1: June 6, 1996)," *Fotoromane*, 222–223.

30. Schimming, "Briefe von Dante Guardamagna (Brief 2: June 18, 1996)," *Fotoromane*, 226. "L'idea era che i lettori ricevessero da noi un film stampato."

31. Schimming, "Briefe von Dante Guardamagna (Brief 1)," 223.

32. Forgacs and Gundle, *Mass Culture and Italian Society*, 110.

33. For an introduction to the Italian *sceneggiato* and its relation to literary classics, see Milly Buonanno, *Italian TV Drama and Beyond: Stories from the Soil, Stories from the Sea* (Chicago: Intellect, 2012), 11–26.

34. Schimming, "Briefe von Dante Guardamagna (Brief 1)," 223. "I fotoromanzi se non piacevano ai lettori dovevano essere tagliati, ma se piacevano (la tiratura dei settimanali lo stabiliva . . .) non dovevano finire MAI. O almeno durare più a lungo."

35. Schimming, "Briefe von Dante Guardamagna (Brief 2)," 228. "Si poteva gonfiare la puntata, con ingrandimenti che portavano la tipica pagina di sei/otto foto o anche tre e perfino passando da puntate di quattro pagine (tavole) a puntate di tre."

36. "Realizzata sulla base di un assoluto rigore scientifico, l'indagine vuole essere un aggiornato mezzo tecnico capace di consentire una precisa, chiara e approfondita valutazione dei periodici Mondadori dal punto di vista pubblicitario."

37. Readers in the family who are older than sixteen are only 72.3 percent women. 48.9 percent of women who read *BF* calls themselves "casalinghe" (housewives) and see themselves as belonging to the middle (37.6 percent) or lower-middle (38.1) bracket of economic status. Noticeably, 70.3 percent of BF readers are located in the North, with only 15 percent in the center and 10.1 percent in the South, mostly in Lombardia (29.7 percent), and in cities of more than one-hundred-thousand people (36.6 percent). Expanding readership in southern regions was definitely one of the main talking points of Pedrocchi, writing to Arnoldo Mondadori in 1965 about necessary changes to be made on *BF*. See Pedrocchi's letter to Mondadori cited later in this chapter, and collected at the Mondadori Archives, Sezione Arnoldo Mondadori, Fascicolo Pedrocchi Luciano. Given the fact that purchasing power was lower in southern regions, these numbers do not say much about the actual number of readers, since the same issue could be shared among many. In fact, 66 percent of buyers lend their copies to other readers. Therefore, while women who buy *BF* generally hold primary (74.2 percent) or middle school degrees (19.5 percent), it is also possible that buyers were in charge of reading to others.

38. "Costituiscono un mercato che può assorbire alcuni o tutti gli elettrodomestici considerati. Tenendo conto di queste percentuali e nello stesso tempo del reddito si possono progettare in modo razionale campagne dirette a vendere determinati beni, come primo acquisto o per rinnovo."

39. "Buon cammino che le famiglie stanno percorrendo sulla via della elevazione socio-economica."

40. Pedrocchi to "Illustre Presidente," letter of June 26, 1964, Mondadori Archives (Milan), Sezione Arnoldo Mondadori, Fascicolo Pedrocchi Luciano. "Una operazione consolante perché dimostra che tra i lettori del settimanale c'è chi ha buone possibilità d'acquisto."

41. See Pedrocchi to Mondadori, letter of June 15, 1965 and of July 12, 1965; Pedrocchi to Gianfranco Cantini, "velina" (inter-office communication) of December 13, 1965. All materials discussed in this chapter are collected at Mondadori Foundation (Milan), Arnoldo Mondadori Archive, Folder Pedrocchi Luciano.

42. This survey is included with Pedrocchi's inter-office communication to Cantini, December 13, 1965.

43. The survey addresses readers formally. These are the questions in Italian: "Quale dei fotoromanzi attualmente piace di più? Le piacciono i fotoromanzi polizieschi e di avventure moderne? Lei ritiene che Bolero Film sia migliorato con l'inserimento di un fotoromanzo a colori? Gradirebbe che Bolero Film pubblicasse un fotoromanzo in costume? Fra i personaggi maschili che appaiono quale le piace di più? E fra i personaggi femminili? Le interessano i testi delle canzoni? Le interessa il programma delle trasmissioni radio e tv? Lei acquista altre riviste? Lavora? È uno studente? È celibe o nubile?"

44. In the Pedrocchi inter-office communication to Cantini from December 13, 1965, Pedrocchi complains about Tom Dollar's failure to increase sales and asks to further advance the project of expanding the market to central and Southern Italy.

45. See "Nuovo agente segreto da fotoromanzo" (A New Secret Agent, Photoromance Style), *Corriere della Sera*, February 8, 1967, 13.

46. "Non è possibile continuare a considerare l'Italia un paese di condizione medioevale, con una piccola percentuale intellettuale e il resto di stato brado. Lo prova Bolero che ha perduto copie dopo aver promesso (e non mantenuto) mari e monti col passaggio a 70 lire 72 pagine (per 4 numeri), lo prova *Confidenze* con le sue indiscriminate avventure direzionali. I giornali popolari sono i più difficili da fare perché parlano a un pubblico che ricorda quello che gli viene promesso, che ha le sue pretese, un pubblico per niente abitudinario, quindi molto facile ad abbandonarti."

47. "Per fortuna disubbedendo a lei e al dr. Senn, io non ho parlato di carta nuova al mio lettore. Un sesto senso, o meglio l'esperienza che mi sto facendo mi hanno salvato da una figuraccia. Oggi tutta l'editoria ne riderebbe."

48. Luciano Pedrocchi, "L'angolo del direttore Fotoromanzi e . . . referendum," *BF*, no. 1410 (1974). "Per certa stampa il popolo italiano è da considerarsi fatto di mentecatti, di individui pronti a modificare le proprie scelte politiche persino secondo i desideri del noto comico milanese [Walter Chiari]. . . . Gli amici lettori sanno che non è vero. Capisco le loro lettere indignate per l'odiosa calunnia e capisco anche i giudizi severi sulla credibilità di certa stampa."

49. Written from the point of view of a fictional female character, Ottavia, *Le lettere d'Ottavia* (Ottavia's Letter) was published by installments in the leftist film journal *Cinema Nuovo* between February and November 1956. See Luigi Malerba, *Le lettere d'Ottavia* (Milan: Archinto, 2004).

50. *BF,* nos. 107, 111, and 116 (1949).

51. Graeme Turner, *Understanding Celebrity* (London: Sage, 2013).

52. Forgacs and Gundle, *Mass Culture and Italian Society*, 111. Unfortunately, Forgacs and Gundle do not include the original Italian in their citation.

53. Castrocaro Terme is a town in the province of Forlì.

54. Singers placing first and second at Castrocaro were given the opportunity to participate in Sanremo the following spring.

55. To get a sense of the numbers of participants, Castrocaro received 3,000 applications in 1962 and 4,000 in 1963.

56. *BF,* no. 926/927 (1963): 21. "Quando questi ragazzi hanno ritagliato da Bolero film la scheda di iscrizione al Concorso erano degli sconosciuti. Oggi i loro nomi figurano nel cast della più grande manifestazione canora del mondo."

57. "Ha molto di un romanzo popolare e strappalacrima." Produced by Compagnia Italiana Attualità Cinematografiche (CIAC), October 1964, *Istituto Luce Archives*, https://patrimonio.archivioluce.com/luce-web/detail/IL5000058164/2/castrocaro-finale-voci-nuove.html?startPage=0&jsonVal={%22jsonVal%22:{%22query%22:[%22castrocaro%22],%22fieldDate%22:%22dataNormal%22,%22_perPage%22:20}}. Newsreels were a main source of information in Italy, before televised news programming started in 1954, and were shown in movie theaters, before featured presentations, until the early 1960s. The most popular among Italian newsreels, *La settimana Incom* featured several episodes about photoromances. See "La settimana Incom (1946–1965)," *Istituto Luce Archives*, https://www.archivioluce.com/la-settimana-incom/.

58. "La prima notorietà che domani, grazie a Castrocaro e a Bolero Film, può diventare la fama e perché no, anche il conto in banca."

59. From 1957 to 1975, advertisement on Italian TV was exclusively shown as part of a program called *Carosello*, from which the term *musicarello originated.*

60. *Nessuno mi può giudicare*, written by Luciano Beretta, Miki Del Prete, Daniele Pace, and Mario Panzeri, produced by CGD.

61. "Caterina," *BF,* no. 926 (1965), episode 19, 12–13. "È un capolavoro d'intrapredenza e di civetteria" and "si tiene sulla sua e lo snobba."

62. "Motivetti leziosi e insulsi," "più vere," "con più grinta," and "che mi divertono di più." "Caterina," *BF,* no. 926 (1965), episode 19.

63. "Il lavoro è lavoro e va preso sul serio sempre. Io non li posso vedere invece quando si mettono a fare i divi, quando si danno delle arie da padreterno. Ci sono tante persone piu importanti di loro!"

64. See also the following photoromances published in *BF*: "La ragazza di Sanremo" (The Girl of Sanremo) by Licia Trevisan and Aldo Aldi, with Johnny Dorelli and Nives Zegna; "È nata una donna" (A Woman Is Born), by Licia Trevisan and Aldo Aldi from a story by Luigi Pedrocchi, with Alberto Lupo and Franca Badeschi, featuring singers Giorgio Consolini, Anna D'amico, Wilma De Angelis, Natalino Otto, Narciso Parigi, Mario Petre, Flo Sandon; "Giostra di amori" (Wheel of Love Affairs) starring, according to an ad, "quattro assi della canzone italiana" (four stars of Italian music): Nilla Pizzi, Marisa Del Frate, Nunzio Gallo, and Johnny Dorelli.

65. Sandra Falero, *Digital Participatory Culture and the TV Audience: Everyone's a Critic* (New York: Palgrave, 2016), 29 and 30.

66. Maurizio Cesari, *La censura in Italia oggi (1944–1980)* (Naples: Liguori, 1982).

67. Dagmar Herzog, *Sexuality in Europe: A Twentieth Century History* (Cambridge: Cambridge University Press, 2011), 133.

68. McRobbie, *The Aftermath of Feminism,* chap. 1.

69. Hilary Radner, *Neo-Feminist Cinema: Girly Films, Chick Flicks and Consumer Culture* (New York: Routledge, 2013), 6.

70. Ibid., 7.

71. "Il progetto commerciale e quello educativo sono mirabilmente fusi." Buonanno, *Naturale come sei*, 28.

72. "Chi sono? Il solito onore," *BF*, no. 855 (1963): 4. "Un amico un po' più saggio ed esperto."

73. Scarzanella also notices the contrast between traditional advice and modern behaviors promoted in *Idilio* (Idyll), but doesn't analyze it in detail. See Scarzanella, "Entre Dos Exilios," 74.

74. "Il tuo compagno non il tuo padrone," *BF*, no. 858 (1963), 3. "[La donna] è un essere libero e complesso come lo sei tu [uomo], non un oggetto fatto per i tuoi capricci," *BF*, no. 857 (1963): 3.

75. "Chi sono? Il solito onore," 4.

76. Art. 587 of the Italian penal code, repealed in 1981.

77. The film was also inspired by Giovanni Arpino's novel *Un delitto d'onore*, published by Mondadori in 1960.

78. See Maggie Günsberg's study on masculinity in Italian-style comedies in *Italian Film: Gender and Genre* (New York: Palgrave, 2005), 60–96.

79. "Nei vostri capelli un richiamo che dice . . . amami."

80. *BF* begins its transformation in 1966, no. 1018, when its name changes to *Bolero Film Teletutto*, no. 1018. By October 1967, it becomes *Bolero Teletutto* but noticeably by first covering the word "Film" on the front page (no. 1068, October 22, 1967) and then leaving "Film" off entirely in the following issue (no. 1069, October 29, 1967).

81. "Del resto, stai pur certa che in Germania avrà fatto anche lui la sua parte. E allora? Ai signori uomini è concesso tutto: possono fare i loro comodacci e le povere donne se ne devono stare sottomesse ad aspettare che si decidano a fare il loro dovere!" *Bolero Teletutto* 22, no. 1080 (1968): 15.

82. "La frigida per errore," *BF,* no. 980; "La frigida vera," no. 981; "La ragazza duemila," no. 982; "La zitella per convinzione," no. 983; "L'incontentabile," no. 984 (all published in March 1966).

83. "Salvaguardare la felicità della vostra vita coniugale." "Sistema Combinato C.D.I.," *BF,* no. 980 (1966): 46. I will further discuss the importance of this ad, in relation to the Italian planned parenthood movement, in chapter 5.

2 MORE THAN ROMANCES

1. *Grease* (Los Angeles: Fotonovel Publications, 1978). Emphasis is mine. Other titles are *Hair* (1978), *Ice Castles* (1978)*, Heaven Can Wait* (1978), *Invasion of the Body Snatchers* (1979), *Americathon* (1979), and *The Champ* (1979).

2. Henry Allen, "Look! It's the Fotonovel!," *Washington Post*, September 28, 1978. See also David Stnrk, "Movie + Book = Hit," *New York Times*, November 24, 1978, 2.

3. "La valle del destino," *I grandi fotoromanzi d'amore*, no. 1 (November 1952).

4. Among these relatively unknown titles, only *Il mondo le condanna* (The World Condemns Them, dir. Gianni Franciolini, 1953), produced by Lux Film, features well-known film stars: Alida Valli and Amedeo Nazzari.

5. The genre soon caught on in Spain as well. For example, Mandolina's *Cine Ensueño* published several cineromances in weekly installments, including Fellini's *Las Noches de Cabiria* (1959).

6. Baetens, *The Film Photonovel,* 15. Regarding new forms, a good example is Chris Marker's *La Jetée: ciné-roman*, published by Zone Books in 1992. On film novelization, particularly in the early twentieth century, see also the collection of essays edited by Alice Auteliano and Valentina Re, *Il racconto del film: la novellizzazione, dal catalogo al trailer: XII convegno internazionale di studi sul cinema (*Narrating the Film: Novelization, from the Catalogue to the Trailer: XII International Film Studies Conference) (Udine, Italy: Forum, 2006).

7. De Berti, "Il nuovo periodico," 5.

8. Baetens, *The Film Photonovel*, 22.

9. De Berti, "Leggere il film."

10. Gianni Amelio, "Non voglio perderti," in *Lo schermo di carta: Storia e storie dei cineromanzi*, ed. Emiliano Morreale (Turin: Il Castoro, 2007), 14. "[N]on c'era il cinema, figuriamoci un'edicola di giornali."

11. Leonardo Quaresima, "La voce dello spettatore," *Bianco e nero* 64, no. 548 (2004): 30.

12. "Non esiste poi distinzione tra cinema alto e basso, tra piccola produzione e grande casa." Giuliana Muscio, "Tutto fa cinema: La stampa popolare del secondo dopoguerra," in *Dietro lo schermo: Ragionamenti sui modi di produzione cinematografica in Italy*, ed. Vito Zagarrio (Venice: Marsilio, 1988), 109.

13. De Berti, "Leggere il film," 20.

14. In fact, De Berti only looks in depth at film novelization before World War II, and Muscio at the cinenovella, rather than the cineromance properly.

15. Muscio, "Tutto fa cinema," 106. "Ciò che si stimola non è semplicemente il consume di un film, ma un desiderio di cinema, di divi, di storie e di immagini."

16. Ventrone, "Tra propaganda e passione"; Franco Fossati, "Dal fotoromanzo alle telenovelas," in *Dal feuilleton al fumetto*, ed. Carlo Bordoni and Franco Fossati (Rome: Editori Riuniti, 1985), 123–136.

17. Henry Jenkins, "Transmedia Storytelling," *MIT Technology Review*, January 15, 2003, https://www.technologyreview.com/s/401760/transmedia-storytelling/.

18. For a discussion on "postfeminist" culture in the context of photoromances, see chapter 1.

19. Allen, "Look! It's the Fotonovel!"

20. See Cardone, "*Catene amare*: un cineromanzo tra film e teatro," *Bianco e Nero* 45, no. 1 (2004), 76. "[I] film nel diventare cineromanzi assumono il rosa cupo del feuilleton, perché ne ereditano lo stesso pubblico appassionato e, a suo modo, esigente." Cardone has developed this idea in other essays; see "Cinema da sfogliare: *Perdonami!* (Mario Costa, 1953) dal film al cineromanzo," *Polittico*, no. 3 (2004): 197–207; and "Il 'discorso amoroso' dallo schermo alla carta: la rappresentazione delle passioni nei cineromanzi degli anni Cinquanta," in Auteliano and Re, *Il racconto del film*, 241–247.

21. In this chapter, and throughout the book, I use the quotation marks to indicate the title of a cineromance, instead of italics, as for the title of a film. "Catene amare," *I vostri film romanzo-Grande serie* 46, no. 2 (August 25, 1955). The verb "to photoromance" is used in the magazines themselves, to talk about the relationship between cineromances and films.

22. *Cpt*, no. 7 (1954), 2. *Le infedeli/The Unfaithfuls* stars Gina Lollobrigida, Marina Vlady, and Anna Maria Ferrero.

23. *Bitter Rice* (dir. Giuseppe De Santis, 1949); *Little World of Don Camillo* (dir. Julien Duvivier, 1952); *Bread, Love and Dreams* (dir. Luigi Comencini, 1953).

24. "Amore proibito," *Cineromanzo per tutti,* no. 10 (November 13, 1954). *The Bandit* was released in 1946 and starred Anna Magnani and Amedeo Nazzari.

25. As a side note, but a relevant one, cineromances, both in their Italian and French versions, are useful tools to film scholars who are interested in understanding not only cinema cultures of the period, but also film archaeology. For example, while Vittorio Cottafavi's *In amore si pecca in due* (In Love, You Sin Together) is not available at any archive, one can "read" it in *Hebdo Roman*, the French version of Victory's *I grandi fotoromanzi d'amore*.

26. Pauline Small, *Sophia Loren: Moulding the Star* (Bristol: Intellect Books, 2009), 22. For another example of this type, see also Paola Bonifazio, "Unlikely Partners: Salvo d'Angelo, David O. Selznick, and Zavattini's 'Stazione Termini,'" *The Italianist-Film Issue* 39, no. 2 (2019): 231–241.

27. Tullio Kezich and Alessandra Levantesi, *Dino: De Laurentiis, la vita e i film* (Milan: Feltrinelli, 2009), 99.

28. Among others: "Notorious: L'amante perduta" ([Notorious: The Lost Lover] from *Notorious*, dir. Alfred Hitchcock, 1946), "Un posto al sole" (from *A Place in the Sun*, dir. George Stevens, 1951), "Fronte del porto" (from *On the Waterfront*, dir. Kazan, 1954), "Guerra e pace" (from *War and Peace*, dir. King Vidor, 1956).

29. The publication of "Ulisse" is advertised in "Amore proibito" as an exclusive "preview." "Amore proibito," *Cineromanzo per tutti*, no. 10 (October 13, 1954): 2.

30. *Mambo,* directed by Robert Rossen and produced by De Laurentiis for Lux Film, starring Mangano and Vittorio Gassman. The film was first screened in Italy on September 18, 1954. "Mambo," *Cg,* no. 4 (January 1955).

31. "Anna," *Cpt,* no. 1 (May 1954): 2; *Anna* (dir. Alberto Lattuada, produced by Lux, 1951).

32. Captions are in the original. "Come esistono DIVI DI SUCCESSO, come esistono REGISTI DI SUC-CESSO, così esistono case di produzione, il cui successo è sicuro perché garantito dalla esperienza e dall'eccellenza dei prodotti. In Italia è questo [image] il marchio che contraddistingue i film di successo PONTI-DE LAURENTIIS." Capital letters are in the original text.

33. Small's analysis of Loren's relationship to her husband and producer Carlo Ponti is an exception. *The Lady without Camelias* (dir. Michelangelo Antonioni, 1953) tells the story of an Italian film starlet played by Lucia Bosè, who struggles to make a career on her own, away from her producer husband, who discovered her.

34. "Come si diventa divi," "Bottega delle idee," and "Il quaderno della massaia."

35. Réka Buckley, "Marriage, Motherhood, and the Italian Film Stars of the 1950s," in *Women in Italy, 1945–1960: An Interdisciplinary Study*, ed. Penelope Morris (New York: Palgrave Macmillan, 2006), 47.

36. Marcia Landy, *Stardom Italian Style* (Bloomington: Indiana University Press, 2008), 110. On the beauty contest "Miss Italy" and the role it play(ed) in Italian culture and the career of many Italian actresses, see Emondo Berselli, ed., *Miss Italia 1939–2009: Storia, protagoniste, vincitrici* (Milan: Mondadori Electa, 2009).

37. Mary P. Wood, "From Bust to Boom: Women and Representations of Prosperity in Italian Cinema of the Late 1940s and 1950s," in *Women in Italy, 1945–1960: An Interdisciplinary Study*, ed. Penelope Morris (New York: Palgrave Macmillan, 2006), 51–63.

38. Stephen Gundle, *Bellissima: Feminine Beauty and the Idea of Italy* (New Haven: Yale University Press, 2007).

39. "È molto triste affermarlo ma l'industria cinematografica italiana tende oggi sopra tutto a mettere in risalto gambe e seni vistosi, opulenti."

40. "Lo scandalo delle curve," *Cinema Nuovo* 2, no. 6 (1952): 133. "Le nostre attrici, eccetto qualcuna e in taluni film (la Magnani a esempio) sono piu belle che brave."

41. "Il problema degli attori in Italia. Vogliamo andare a scuola," *Cinema Nuovo* 2, no. 13 (1953): 364–366.

42. Anna Garofalo, "Inflazione delle curve," *Cinema Nuovo* 5, no. 74 (1956): 24. She writes: "La bellezza quando non è accompagnata da intelligenza educazione, senso della misura, può diventare più un castigo di dio che un dono."

43. The name of Jennifer Jones is in the contract signed by De Sica and collected at the Harry Ransom Center of the University of Texas at Austin (HRC), David O. Selznick Collection, Production Files 1950–1952, Box 753, Folder 6. In another set of documents titled "Comments on Jennifer Jones," De Sica's statement about the actress includes the following comment: "Gina Lollobrigida [and] Silvana Mangano are beauti-ful . . . but with them the emphasis is on the legs and busts." See HRC, Publicity Files 1953–53, Box 708,

Folder 10 (unknown date), documents from Arthur P. Jacobs about Jennifer Jones. I thank Vanessa Fanelli for the reference.

44. *Cinema Nuovo* 4, no. 71 (November 25, 1955): 369.

45. "Sensualità: Your Press Book" (New York: I. F. E., 1954), 2–3. *Sensualità* (dir. Clemente Fracassi, 1952), with Eleonora Rossi Drago and Marcello Mastroianni, produced by Ponti-De Laurentiis Cinematografica.

46. *What's My Line?*, August 19, 1956, YouTube, https://www.youtube.com/watch?v=4Pjv9egt-Ok. The episode features Arlene Francis, Robert Q. Lewis, Dorothy Kilgallen, and Bennett Cerf.

47. Mangano actually answers no to the question and noticeably a YouTube viewer (named "tricky dick") posts that "Actually she had the measurements, as shown in Bitter Rice. She just didn't make a show of it."

48. Edgar Morin, *The Stars* (Minneapolis: University of Minnesota Press, 2005), 21.

49. In the Hollywood context, for example, Jane Gaines shows that 1940s American fan magazines reflect the introduction of the Hays Code by turning stars into models of conduct, rejecting the excessive and sexy images of the 1920s and 1930s. Jane Gaines, "War Women and Lipstick: Fan Mags in the Forties," *Heresies* 5, no. 18 (1985): 42–47.

50. Luisa Cicognetti and Lorenza Servetti, "On Her Side: Female Images in Italian Cinema and the Popular Press, 1945–1955," *Historical Journal of Film, Radio and Television* 16, no. 4 (1966): 555.

51. Ibid., 555.

52. Ibid., 559. I do wonder whether Cicognetti and Servetti are simply unaware of the business of cineromances.

53. Lucia Cardone, "Pellicole e film di carta: Un nuovo protagonismo femminile," *Cinema e storia* 5, no. 1 (2016): 191–202.

54. Ibid., 202.

55. Buckley, "Marriage, Motherhood, and the Italian Film Stars of the 1950s."

56. Vittorio Spinazzola argued that Lollobrigida similarly used motherhood for publicity purposes. He claimed that "Lollobrigida's popularity benefitted from the advertisement campaign that accompanied her maternity status" ("La popolarità della Lollobrigida si è giovata della vistosa campagna pubblicitaria che ha accompagnato la maternità"). See Spinazzola, "Belle e materne," *Cinema Nuovo* 6, no. 112 (1957): 93.

57. See Giuseppe Rosso, "Lo Star-Sistem e gli attori occasionali," *Cinema* 2, no. 24 (1949): 201–202.

58. "Corriere di Cinelandia," in "Riso Amaro," *Cg*, no. 2 (November 1954): 63. All six films interpreted by Mangano appear as cineromances in Lanterna Magica's publications: "Bitter Rice," "Ulysses," and "Mambo" in *Cg*; "Lure of the Sila," "Outlaw Girl," and "Anna" in *CpT*; with the exception of "Bitter Rice" and "Il lupo della Sila," all cineromances were published around the same time as films are available in the theaters.

59. Daniela Treveri Gennari, "'If You Have Seen It, You Cannot Forget!' Film Consumption and Memories of Cinema-Going in 1950s Rome," *Historical Journal of Film, Radio and Television* 35, no. 1 (2015): 53–74.

60. *L'oro di Napoli* (*The Gold of Naples*, dir. Vittorio De Sica), produced by Ponti-De Laurentiis Cinematografica, 1954.

61. See Joyce Aschenbrenner, *Katherine Dunham: Dancing a Life* (Urbana: University of Illinois Press, 2002).

62. Giovanni Cimmino and Stefano Masi, *Silvana Mangano: Il teorema della bellezza* (Rome: Gremese Editore, 1994), 37. In their view, costume designers had an important role in remaking Mangano's image.

63. Richard Dyer, *Heavenly Bodies: Films Stars and Societies* (New York: Routledge, [1989] 2010). Pauline Small translates "maggiorate fisiche" as "physically well-endowed stars" and "shapely stars." See Small, *Sophia Loren*, 36.

64. Caught while she reads *Grand Hotel*, Silvana likes to dance the boogie-woogie and chew gum, dreams about expensive jewelry, and pursues a handsome and dangerous man named Walter (played by Vittorio Gassman). Her chase ends when Walter violently attacks and rapes her (although the sexual violence is not shown on the screen); after the rape, Silvana decides to help Walter rob her fellow workers and then, when she is done, she jumps from a tower and dies, buried with pity by the same coworkers.

65. "Un articolo di Silvana Mangano: i miei tre contratti" (An Article by Silvana Mangano: My Three Contracts) *Hollywood*, no. 239 (April 15, 1950): 13. *Lure of the Sila* (dir. Duilio Coletti) was released December 27, 1949, and *Outlaw Girl* (dir. Mario Camerini) was released December 6, 1950.

66. Daria Argentieri, "Silvana (suo malgrado) Mangano" (Silvana [despite herself] Mangano), *Hollywood*, no. 278 (1951): 6. "Attrice suo malgrado, celebre suo malgrado, ammirata suo malgrado."

67. "J'ai la vocation d'une mere de famille, et non celle d'une vedette." In the words of *Hollywood* reporter Luigi Lucchesi, "Le attrici sono soprattutto donne" (Actresses are first and foremost women). Luigi Lucchesi, "Dolce la torta e amare le dive" (Sweet the Cake, Bitter the Stars), *Hollywood*, no. 379 (1952): 3.

68. And as the title of a 1949 *Hollywood* article suggests, it may have also been a publicity stunt: "Every [female] star asks the same question: will I go on?" writes actress Lianella Carrell in her ironic account of Italian actresses' conflicting relationships to stardom. Lianella Carrell, "In tutte la stessa domanda: continuerò?," *Hollywood*, no. 193 (May 28, 1949): 5. Carrell is known for her secondary role as Antonio Ricci's wife in *Bicycles Thieves* but did not really have a successful career in the film industry.

69. Giorgio Gaglieri, "La lunga strada di Silvana Mangano da 'Riso amaro' al convento" (Silvana Mangano's Long Road from 'Bitter Rice' to the Convent), *Hollywood*, no. 327 (1951). "Non era con la bellezza che ella voleva convincere critica e pubblico, ma con l'intelligenza e la perfetta aderenza al personaggio."

70. "Silvana Mangano darà la completa misura delle sue capacità drammatiche ed una nuova immagine della sua femminilità a tutti coloro che la ricordano sensuale e perversa in *Riso amaro*."

71. Eligio Gualdoni, "La miss e il cavallo di Troia" (The Miss and the Trojan Horse), *Hollywood*, no. 357 (1952): 3.

72. "Le due successive interpretazioni ci hanno mostrato una Mangano sostanzialmente mutata: non più una bellezza procace e sfrontata la sua, ma casta, tranquilla, riposante."

73. See also Italo Dragosei, "Il trionfo dell'attore: l'inflazione dei concorsi di bellezza favorisce l'orientamento della produzione verso gli attori professionisti" (The Triumph of the Actor: The Oversaturation of Beauty Contests Leads Film Producers to Invests in Professional Actors), *Cinema Nuovo*, no. 364 (1952): 22; I. S., "Buone speranze per le reginette di bellezza: giovani che sognate di esser baciati in fronte dalla fortuna, tenete d'occhio le paghe dei 'generici'!," *Cinema Nuovo*, no. 352 (1952): 22.

74. The film was directed by Michael Ritt and produced by De Laurentiis.

75. *Idolos del Cine*, no. 87 (1959), 2. "Pero Silvana no vaciló, al dia siguiente compareció en lose studios de Cinecittà y se puso en manos del peluquero." *Jovanka e le altre* (Five Branded Women, dir. Martin Ritt, 1960), produced by Dino De Laurentiis Cinematografica and Paramount Pictures.

76. "Caso raro per un'attrice, [Silvana Mangano] darà vita a due personaggi che si presentano assolutamente diversi: come Penelope dovrà fare risaltare le virtù, la dolcezza di una sposa fedele e come Circe sarà invece la maga che incanta gli uomini con il suo conturbante fascino sensuale, con le sue arti sovrumane."

77. Rosalind Gill, "From Sexual Objectification to Sexual Subjectification: The Resexualisation of Women's Bodies in the Media," *Feminist Media Studies* 3, no. 1 (2003): 100–106.

78. Jane Desmond, *Meaning in Motion: New Cultural Studies in Dance* (Durham, NC: Duke University Press, 1997), 37.

79. Mary Russo, *The Female Grotesque: Risk, Excess and Modernity* (New York: Routledge, 1994), 53–54.

80. "Esuberanza giovanile" and "una voluttuosa sfida alla miseria che opprime la sua fresca giovinezza."

81. "Il suo volto è rigato di lacrime, lacrime di pentimento, lacrime di dolore; suprema offerta al Dio di pietà che tanto perdona."

82. The case of "Bitter Rice" is not unique. For example, "Lure of the Sila" expands the film's plot to reinterpret Mangano's character, Rosaria, a peasant woman who seduces an older man, Don Rocco Barra, and his son. She does so only to avenge the deaths of her brother and mother, which were caused by the rich and greedy Don Rocco. Rosaria is blamed for her "civetteria," she is labeled an insidious seductress who makes both men lose their minds; the captions highlight her intention to vindicate her family, but also condemn her for her actions. The cineromance eliminates any possible interpretation of Rosaria's motives in a political way; rather, it is once again a moral tale in which Rosaria learns from the experience and repents.

83. "Giace a terra, immota e i suoi occhi aperti guardano ancora verso il cielo come per chiedere aiuto e pietà."

84. Paolo Di Valmarana, "Mambo," *Cinema Nuovo* 11, no. 33 (1954): 262–265.

85. "Preemptive Review" ("recensione preventiva"), signed by Annibale Scicluna, November 12, 1953, Central State Archives, Rome (ACS), Ministero del turismo e dello spettacolo. Direzione generale spettacolo. Archivio cinema. Lungometraggi. Fascicoli per opera (Concessione certificato di nazionalità), CF1845 *busta* (folder) 97. The Italian Law Decree ratified in 1947 (Legge Cappa, n. 379) created a committee to evaluate proposals requesting government funds and to control their national and foreign distribution. I will talk more about this committee and its relevance to the business of cineromances in chapter 3.

86. "Toni aveva ragione. Inutile cercare la propria realtà, negli altri, al di fuori di sè stessi. Nulla si conquista con un colpo di fortuna e a Giovanna resta solo cio che le è costato fatica e sofferenza. E, soprattutto, l'amore per la propria arte." The image on this page is not included in the film, and was probably used for publicity purposes.

87. Advertisements for her company and their shows can be found in *Cinefoto romanzo gigante*. According to Dorotea Fischer-Hornung, Caribbean dances, Afro-American culture, and the techniques of what Katherine Dunham calls "Negro dance" can all be found in *Mambo*. See Dorotea Fischer-Hornung, "The Body Possessed: Katherine Dunham Dance Technique in *Mambo*," in *EmBODYing Liberation: The Black*

Body in American Dance, ed. Dorothea Fischer-Hornung and Alison D. Goeller (Hamburg: Verlag, 2001), 91–112.

88. Fischer-Hornung, "The Body Possessed," 98.

89. Figure 8 is a still photo from the dance, used as the closing image of the cineromance.

90. Glauco Viazzi, "La Dunham vuole dirigere" (Dunham wants to direct), *Cinema* 3, no. 35 (1950): 184.

91. In fact, there are no indications to my knowledge that Hollywood majors were aware of or profited from the business. As I explain in chapter 3, my claim is that cineromances were indeed considered only as products of publicity and thus they fell within the limits of approved exploitation in co-production or distribution agreements.

3 PIRATES OF THE FILM INDUSTRY

1. "Come facevano ad avere i permessi per fare queste cose?" A DVD of the film, *Sfogliare il film* [Browsing a Film], directed by Lorenzo d'Amico de Carvalho, is included in the exhibition's catalogue: Emiliano Morreale, ed., *Lo schermo di carta* (Turin: Il Castoro, 2007). See also Silvio Alovisio, ed., *Cineromanzi: la collezione del Museo Nazionale del Cinema* (Turin: Museo Nazionale del Cinema, 2007).

2. The National Museum Collection consists mostly of pre-World War II magazines.

3. "E come sapevamo? Credi che ci davano qualcosa per tirare fuori 'ste cose Allora non chiedevano e facevano."

4. Dino De Laurentiis and Carlo Ponti of Ponti-De Laurentiis Cinematografica produced *Le infedeli*, starring Gina Lollobrigida and Anna Maria Ferreri, among others.

5. "Quindi non so, se poi potevano. Probabilmente si, perchè poi ci facevano firmare sia me che a Steno, a tutti i cinematografari d'allora, dei contratti in cui cedavamo i diritti per un numero infinito di anni indeterminato e poi soprattutto per qualsiasi altro sfruttamento." By "cinematografari," Monicelli means *directors*.

6. See Baetens, Van den Bergh, and Van Den Bossche, "How to Write a Photo Novel."

7. Quaresima, "La voce dello spettatore," 31.

8. "Un fenomeno economicamente rilevante" and "talvolta in violazione di terzi." Mario Fabiani, "Cineromanzi a fumetti e diritti del produttore cinematografico" (Cineromances in Comics and the Rights of the Film Producer), *Rassegna di diritto cinematografico* 5, no. 3–4 (1956): 66.

9. The entire text of the lda is available online at the website of SIAE (Società Italiana degli Autori ed Editori-Italian Society of Authors and Editors). See SIAE, accessed June 21, 2019, https://www.siae.it/it/diritto-dautore.

10. "La giurisprudenza, colmando la lacuna riguardante la valutazione comparativa degli autori dell'opera cinematografica previsti all'art. 44, ha assecondato gli indirizzi della critica cinematografica, riconoscendo una titolarita quasi esclusiva al regista in funzione del suo ruolo predominante, mentre in dottrina hanno raccolto piu consensi le teorie che pur riconoscendo la preminenza al direttore artistico del film sugli altri collaboratori, non arrivano a definirlo come autore unico." See Lorenzo Gangarossa, *Guida alla tutela*

dell'opera cinematografica (Milan: Nyberg, 2005), 107. For a case in favor of the director's claim of authorship, see Court of Appeals, Paris, *Soc. Des erablissements Gaumont and Syndicat des producteurs des films v. Pierre Blanchard, Arthur Honneger, Bernard Zimmer and Association des auteurs de film*, June 14, 1950. The verdict is quoted in Gabriele Poli, "L'attore e il regista cinematografico sono lavoratori subordinati?" (Are the Actor and the Film Director Subordinate Employees?), *Rassegna del diritto cinematografico* 5, no. 5 (1956): 116.

11. Amedeo Giannini, *Il diritto dello spettacolo: cinematografia, teatro, radiodiffusione, televisione, fonogramme, l'artista-interprete* (Rome: Jandi Sapi, 1959).

12. These words are used in the report on a lawsuit, *Pratolini v. soc. Lanterna Magica*, July 16, 1955, published in *Rassegna di diritto cinematografico* 5, no. 6 (November–December 1956): 167–169. The hearing took place in Rome, on February 2, 1956.

13. On the idea of directors as film "authors," see Alexandre Astruc, "The Birth of a New Avant-Garde: La Caméra-Stylo," in *The New Wave: Critical Lanmarks*, ed. Peter Graham (London: BFI, 2009), 17–23; André Bazin, "On the *politiques des auteurs*," in *Cahiers du Cinéma: The 1950s: Neo-Realism, Hollywood, New Wave*, ed. Jim Hillier (Cambridge, MA: Harvard University Press, 1985), 248–259. Astruc's essay is translated from "Naissance d'une nouvelle avant-garde: la caméra-stylo," published in *L'Écran Français* on March 30, 1948. In the 1950s and 1960s, Italian directors also frequently wrote about themselves as authors; see Roberto Rossellini, *Il mio metodo*, ed. Adriano Aprà (Roma: Marsilio, 2006).

14. Gangarossa, *Guida alla tutela dell'opera cinematografica*, 6.

15. Art. 44 and 45 of Law n. 633, "Legge sul diritto d'autore" (April 22, 1941). See Ugo Capitani, *Il film nel diritto d'autore* (Rome: Edizioni Italiane, 1943), 345. For a discussion of the role of producers as "authors" of a film, see Pauline Small, "Producer *and* Director? Or 'Authorship' in 1950s Italian Cinema," in *Beyond the Bottom Line: The Producer in Film and Television Studies*, ed. Andrew Spicer, Anthony T. McKenna, and Christopher Meir (London: Bloomsbury, 2014), 109–123.

16. See Poli, "L'attore e il regista cinematografico sono lavoratori subordinati?," 116. Poli bases his statement that the director is concurrent but not exclusive owner of the final cut on case no. 170 of 1938 (*Genina v. Società Romana Film*) and of March 31, 1941 (*Antamoro v. Soc.art.rom.cine*), both held in Rome.

17. Luigi Sordelli, *L'opera dell'ingegno: interpretazione, riproduzione meccanica, e diffusione sonora* (Milan: Giuffrè, 1954), 233.

18. Vittorio Sgroi, "La tutela dell'immagine dell'attore cinematografico nell'elaborazione del film sotto forma di fotoromanzo," *Rivista di Diritto Industriale*, no. 5 (1956): 237. "Gli attori non creano, ma eseguono."

19. Ibid., 237.

20. "La sua [Rutili's] partecipazione a fumetti potrebbe arrestare il suo cammino verso la piena notorietà."

21. "Questo però non vale in questo caso perche il fumetto è strettamente collegato al film." Sgroi, "La tutela dell'immagine dell'attore cinematografico," 241.

22. "L'attore cinematografico non può quindi invocare un diritto alla riservatezza a somiglianza di qualsiasi privato." Ibid., 244.

23. "La madre della Ferida vince una causa per 2 fotoromanzi," *Corriere d'informazione*, February 28–March 1, 1962. Ferida was extremely popular under Fascism and she was killed in unclear circumstances right after the end of the war, in 1945, together with her partner Osvaldo Valenti (also a film star).

24. Originally published by installments in the literary magazine *Botteghe Oscure* in 1949, Pratolini's novel was published in Italy by Vallecchi (Florence) in 1952, and then translated and published in English by Pocket Books (New York) in 1954 under the title *The Girls of Sanfrediano (Took Their Love Seriously)*.

25. "Pratolini c. soc. Lanterna Magica nonchè Lux Film—Atto di citazione 16-7-1955," *Rassegna di diritto cinematografico* 5, no. 6 (1956), 167–169. The hearing took place in Rome on February 2, 1956. For information and discussion of this case, see also Gangarossa, *Guida alla tutela dell'opera cinematografica*, 344; Fabiani, "Cineromanzi a fumetti e diritti del produttore cinematografico," 66–67; Morreale, ed., *Lo schermo di carta*, 14.

26. "Soggetto liberamente tratto dall'omonimo racconto di Vasco Pratolini—Edizioni Vallecchi."

27. "Un'opera di carattere creativo, autonoma e distinta da quella cinematografica." Unless otherwise noted, quotes from the lawsuit debate and verdict are taken from "Pratolini c. soc. Lanterna Magica," *Rassegna di diritto cinematografico*, 167.

28. "Un'opera originaria, con ogni possibilità di sfruttamento."

29. "Non era stato tratto dal racconto del Pratolini, ma dal film della Lux, la quale aveva autorizzato la pubblicazione, come mezzo di pubblicità per il film medesimo."

30. "Il pubblicare un fotoromanzo di contenuto analogo a quello del film, utilizzando i fotogrammi e i dialoghi dell'opera cinematografica, rientra tra le facoltà di utilizzazione economica del film e costituisce una forma, per così dire, naturale, di sfruttamento del film stesso." In *Browsing the Film*, one of the actresses in *The Girls of San Frediano*, Giovanna Ralli says that she probably knew that they could use her image for commercial purposes, but that release of copyright was normally included in her film contract.

31. "È consuetudine costante dei produttori cinematografici di fare diffondere fotoromanzi, ricavati utilizzando i fotogrammi e i dialoghi del film, senza chiedere autorizzazione all'autore dell'opera letteraria dalla quale il soggetto cinematografico è tratto."

32. Other newspapers published the results of this sentence, including *La Nazione* (Firenze) (June 7, 1956) and *Corriere della sera* (June 8, 1956). These and other relevant clippings can be found at the Central State Archives, Rome (ACS), Ministero del turismo e dello spettacolo. Direzione generale spettacolo. Archivio cinema. Lungometraggi. Fascicoli per opera (Concessione certificato di nazionalità), CF 2025, *folder* 114.

33. Trib. Di Roma, March 2–April 15, 1956, in *Diritto d'autore* (1956), 282, cit. in Gangarossa, *Guida alla tutela dell'opera cinematografica*, 344–345. "La legge sul diritto d'autore non prevede, tra le opere protette, il fotoromanzo. . . . Ora, il cineromanzo, la cui diffusione, specie in Italia, risale ad epoca recente, pur non mirando ai fini dell'arte e indirizzandosi ad un determinato ceto sociale, [il fotoromanzo] costituisce tuttavia una creazione della fantasia ed ha una forma di rappresentazione tutta propria. Esso risulta, infatti, dalla combinazione di elementi fotografici e letterari e rappresenta un contenuto di fatti mediante la successione di fotografie, riproducenti i personaggi e gli ambienti della vicenda o favola, collegate tra loro da un elemento letterario e vivificato attraverso la riproduzione, in forma scritta, dei dialoghi tra i personaggi rappresentati. Per gli elementi di cui si compone e per la sua particolare forma di rappresentazione, il

fotoromanzo si distingue nettamente dalle opere letterarie e dalle opere cinematografiche e costituisce senza dubbio una categoria di opera a se stante. . . . Ciò posto, appare evidente l'infondatezza delle tesi secondo cui il fotoromanzo non costituirebbe altro che una forma di rappresentazione dell'opera cine-matografica. Questa, invero, ha come forma di rappresentazione sua propria solo quella della proiezione sullo schermo e non anche quella della pubblicazione, che è propria, invece, delle opere letterarie e, come si è visto, anche del fotoromanzo."

34. "Pratolini c. soc. Lanterna Magica," *Rassegna di diritto cinematografico*, 169. "Molte persone, specie nella categoria sociale alla quale il fotoromanzo si rivolge, avendo la possibilità di scegliere tra l'opera originale e il fotoromanzo, darebbe evidentemente la preferenza a quest'ultimo, con indubbio pregiudizio dell'autore dell'opera originale."

35. "Lavorano e amano, dolci e chiassose, tenere e ardenti, sfrontate e fedeli."

36. "Vento di primavera!" "Portano la primavera con i loro sogni d'amore—Le ragazze di Sanfrediano."

37. "Poveri ragazzi vittime della loro avvenenza."

38. ACS, CF 2025, folder 114, film review, *L'Unità*, March 11, 1955.

39. Pauline Small translates the "commissione di revisione cinematografica" as "Censorship Office." I prefer to use "Film Revision Committee" to indicate that, in the government's view, there was no censorship in Democratic Italy. See Small, "Producer *and* Director?," 114.

40. ACS, CF 2025, folder 114, May 22, 1954. The signatories are Panfilo Gentile, Francesco Carnelutti, Emilio Cecchi, Vincenzo Cardarelli, and Silvio d'Amico.

41. Eitel Monaco to Annibale Scicluna (Direzione Generale dello Spettacolo), *Report of the Film Revision Committee*, ACS, CF 2025, folder 114, August 2, 1954. Some of these words are in Tuscan dialect such as "bischero" (stupid), "becco" (literally "mutton," meaning idiot), and "bucona" (whore).

42. "La fine vedrà Bob sposato e alle prese con i problemi seri della famiglia." A copy of the nulla-osta is available online, thanks to the "Progetto di ricerca sulla censura cinematografica in Italia-Italia Taglia," sponsored by the Ministry of Heritage and Culture (MiBAC) in collaboration with the Cineteca di Bolo-gna: http://www.italiataglia.it. The date of the first theatrical release of *Le ragazze di San Frediano* is stated in a document collected at the ACS, CF 2025, folder 114.

43. For example, at a crucial parliamentary discussion in the context of the debate on governmental control of citizens' behaviors via protective law against publications that were deemed "scandalous, immoral, pornographic, criminal," DC deputy Alessandro Gerini listed *Grand Hotel*, together with soft porn magazines such as *Coquette* and *Scandalo*, among those magazines that needed to be prohibited. Gerini's recommendation, however, was not approved by the Parliament. See Vittorio Frajese, *La censura in italia: dall'Inquisizione alla polizia* (Bari: Laterza, 2014), 39.

44. See Abigail Derecho, "Archontic Literature: A Definition, a History, and Several Theories of Fan Fiction," *Fan Fiction and Fan Communities in the Age of the Internet: New Essays*, ed. Karen Hellekson and Kristina Busse (Jefferson, NC: McFarland & Co., 2006), 61–78.

45. "Come sfondo, appena intravisto attraverso i portali di vetro, l'arrivo di un capo di stato con la scorta d'onore dei corazzieri." The "corazzieri" are a special corps of the Italian army. De Sica to Scicluna, ACS,

Ministero del turismo e dello spettacolo. Direzione generale spettacolo. Archivio cinema. Lungometraggi. Fascicoli per opera (Concessione certificato di nazionalità), CF 1196, folder 31, February 19, 1953.

46. "Il film s'ispira a dei criteri decorosi ed estetici e che l'uso fugace che sarà fatto di tale ripresa non potrà in maniera alcuna intaccare la giusta fierezza e la somma dignità del Corpo dei Corazzieri."

47. For a discussion on Montgomery Clift's performance as Giovanni, and of the nephew as a surrogate husband, see Sam Gaglio, "Indiscretion of an Italian Lover: Montgomery Clift, Masculinity and Melodrama," *The Italianist* 39, no. 2 (2019): 242–250.

48. "Bella mora, è geloso il fidanzato vero? Pensare che invece dello schiaffo ti darei tanto volentieri un bel bacetto!"

49. See Dylan Levy, "Atoning for an Indiscretion," *The Italianist* 39, no. 2 (2019): 251–266.

50. Today, the MiBAC (Ministero per i Beni e le Attività Culturali [Ministry of Cultural Heritage and Activities]) has this role.

51. This law was followed by another three, which both further opened the market to foreign import and attempted to sustain national production by means of financial incentives: 1947 Legge Cappa, 1949 Legge Andreotti, and 1956 Legge Corona.

52. "L'acquiescenza alle direttive governative." Lorenzo Quaglietti, *Storia economica-politica del cinema italiano, 1945–1980* (Roma: Editori Riuniti, 1980).

53. Ibid., 91. "Le recenti dichiarazioni ed iniziative dell'attuale sottosegretario alla presidenza del Consiglio dei ministri stanno per chiudere sotto una lapide la già spenta libertà di espressione."

54. About the production history of *Senso*, including the dispute with the Ministry of Defense and Visconti's comments on the issue, see Franco Vigni, "Buon costume e pubblica morale," in *Storia del cinema italiano*, vol. 9, ed. Sandro Bernardi (Rome: Marsilio, 2004), 65–74; Pietro Cavallo, *Viva l'Italia: storia, cinema e identità nazionale (1932–1962)* (Naples: Liguori, 2009), 352–363; *Cinema*'s special issue on *Senso*, no. 136 (1954); and the documents collected at the Italia Taglia project website, http://www.italiataglia.it/search/dettaglio_opera.

55. Film Revision Committee Report, signed On. Luigi Oscar Scalfaro, October 30, 1954, http://www.italiataglia.it/search/dettaglio_opera.

56. Ibid.. "Livia è ancora a letto, dopo consumato il convegno amoroso, Franz le sta vicino. La bacia sulla spalla. Livia si pettina con la spazzola i capelli, sempre stando a letto. (Eliminare tutta la scena)."

57. See Ernesto Laura, *Alida Valli* (Rome: Gremese Editore, 1979).

58. Wilma Montesi was twenty-one years old when she was found dead on the beach of Torvaianica, near Rome, in 1953. The mystery surrounding her death (considered an accident by the police and a murder by journalists) provoked a scandal, involving allegations of drug and sex orgies. The case later became symbolic of the age of *paparazzi* (photo-reporters) in Italy and was alluded to in films such as Federico Fellini's *La dolce vita* (1960). See Karen Pinkus, *The Montesi Scandal: The Death of Wilma Montesi and the Birth of the Paparazzi in Fellini's Rome* (Chicago: University of Chicago Press, 2003).

59. Film Revision Committee Report, October 30, 1954. The line reads: "Who do you think you are? You have such a high opinion of yourself that you cannot sit at the table with a prostitute? What is the difference between the two of you? I will tell you. She is young, she is beautiful, and men are ready to pay for her, while you are ready to . . . (reel 13, page 4)." ("Mi dici chi ti credi di essere? . . . Hai una tale opinione di te stessa che non puoi stare a tavola accanto a una sgualdrina? . . . Ma che differenza c'è tra voi due? . . . Te lo dico io . . . Lei è giovane . . . è bella . . . e gli uomini sono disposti a pagare per lei . . . mentre tu sei disposta. . . . [rullo 13 pag. 4])."

60. "Che differenza c'è tra voi due? Ve lo dico io. Tu sei giovane e bella . . . e tu sei vecchia. Gli uomini per lei pagano e tu, per un'ora d'amore, hai dovuto pagarmi."

61. *Cahiers du Cinéma*, no. 93 (March 1959), cited in Cavallo, *Viva l'Italia*, 355.

62. "Non vede nemmeno quelle mani protese e quei visi ghignanti."

63. See Cardone, "*Catene amare*, 76. "I film nel diventare cineromanzi assumono il rosa cupo del feuilleton, perché ne ereditano lo stesso pubblico appassionato e, a suo modo, esigente."

4   COLD WAR PHOTOROMANCES

This chapter is derived, in part, from an article published in *Italian Studies* on September 4, 2017, https://www .tandfonline.com/doi/abs/10.1080/00751634.2017.1370790?journalCode=yits20.

1. The name of the company is also sometimes spelled "SamPaolo." "Non commettere atti impuri," San Paolo Film, n.d., Istituto Luce Archives, https://patrimonio.archivioluce.com/luce-web/detail/IL3000095981/1/ vi-non-commettere-atti-impuri.html.

2. "Attenti dunque a non farsi sorprendere dalla fantasia, invochiamo la Madonna perchè ci liberi dalle suggestioni della mente."

3. "Dobbiamo evitare le letture e le compagnie cattive, i peccati di pensiero sono come tante spine che configgiamo nel capo di Gesù."

4. For this reason, while "Non commettere atti impuri" has no date, we can argue that it was released after 1945 and most likely (given its style), in the 1950s.

5. Chris Rojek, *Celebrity* (London: Reaktion Books, 2001), chapter 2: "Celebrity and Religion," Kindle.

6. Ibid., chapter 1: "Celebrity and Celetoids," Kindle.

7. Stephen Gundle, *Between Hollywood and Moscow: The Italian Communists and the Challenge of Mass Culture, 1943–1991* (Durham, NC: Duke University Press, 2000), 97.

8. Cecchetti, *Generi della letteratura popolare*, 352.

9. Sandro Bellassai, *La morale comunista* (Rome: Carocci, 2000), 119.

10. Ibid.

11. Mario Marazziti, "Cultura di massa e valori cattolici: il modello di 'Famiglia Cristiana,'" in *Pio XII*, ed. Andrea Riccardi (Bari: Laterza, 1985), 310.

12. Ibid., 315.

13. Stephen Gundle, "Cultura di massa e modernizzazione: 'Vie nuove' e 'Famiglia cristiana' dalla Guerra fredda alla società dei consume," in *Nemici per la pelle: sogno americano e mito sovietico nell'Italia contemporanea,* ed. Pier Paolo D'Attorre (Milan: Franco Angeli, 1991), 236.

14. Quoted on several occasions, the actual source of Saladino's article on *Quaderni dell'attivista* is never cited in its entirety. A long excerpt from the article is included in Giovanna Calvenzi's presentation at the conference "Scene da fotoromanzo: storia, forme, modi di un genere popolare," organized by the Museum of Contemporary Photography in Milan on January 14, 2012. Many thanks to Calvenzi for providing me with a copy of the script.

15. "Se alla Conferenza nazionale della Gioventù comunista qualche delegata avrà Gran Hotel nella borsa, . . . non ci si deve scandalizzare: anche per questa via le ragazze vanno verso la democrazia."

16. "Solo l'aspirazione a qualche cosa di migliore del presente, cioè ad una vita più bella e gioiosa, meno difficile e meno faticosa, più pacifica e civile, senza le gravi preoccupazioni della disoccupazione e del salario insufficiente, della casa stretta e insalubre, del domani malsicuro." Cited in Bravo, *Il fotoromanzo,* chap. 4, Kindle.

17. In his article on the educational use of comics in the postwar period, Juri Meda mentions the debate within the Communist Party, and particularly the discussion between Nilde Jotti and Gianni Rodari. Here, I want to argue that not only did the PCI utilize the photoromance to educate women, but it also engaged with the entertaining function and exploited the emotional appeal of the media. See Juri Meda, "'Cose da grandi': identità collettive e valori civili nei fumetti italiani del secondo dopoguerra (1945–1955)," *Annali di storia dell'educazione e delle istituzioni scolastiche,* no. 9 (2002): 285–335.

18. I refer to the previously quoted presentation by Calvenzi at the Museum of Contemporary Photography in Milan (2012). Gundle mentions the experiment but does not provide the title of the same fotoromanzo in *Between Hollywood and Moscow,* 97.

19. Information about dates and publishers are based on the Istituto Gramsci's catalogue. In his book, Gundle says that "The Great Hope" and "Stronger than Destiny" were published in Bologna in 1956. See Gundle, *Between Hollywood and Moscow,* 97.

20. Saint-Michel, *Le roman-photo,* 168.

21. Sullerot, *La presse féminine,* 117.

22. "Dalla storia di Giovanna e di Carlo appare la vera, reale condizione umana, di centinaia di migliaia di famiglie italiane che sono state divise dalla politica migratoria seguita dai governi avvicendatisi finora alla direzione del paese. . . . Occorre dunque negare il voto alla D.C. e a tutti gli altri partiti governativi responsabili dell'emigrazione in massa e della divisione di centinaia di migliaia di famiglie italiane." "Heart of Emigrants," 15.

23. "Una compensazione profonda a livello affettivo." Sullerot, "I fotoromanzi," 113.

24. See, for example, *La terra trema* (*The Earth Tremble,* 1948) and *Rocco e i suoi Fratelli* (*Rocco and His Brothers,* 1960), both directed by Luchino Visconti.

25. "Io in questo giorno voglio la promessa che non mi lascerai mai. . . . Deve essere anche per noi la festa dei sentimenti."

26. In fact, Maria takes the "psicotecnico" test with Franco at the beginning of the photoromance, but then refuses the job and there are no other female workers in the story.

27. Baetens, "The Photo-Novel," 2.

28. Created in the 1930s by publisher San Paolo, *Famiglia Cristiana* initially targeted only women and later fashioned itself as an appropriate reading for the entire family. See Stefania Portaccio, "La donna nella stampa popolare cattolica: Famiglia Cristiana, 1931–1945," *Italia Contemporanea* 1, no. 143 (1981): 45–68.

29. I must thank Mr. Giorgio Chiappello, who kindly provided me with such information on the basis of his extensive collection of *Famiglia Cristiana*'s issues from the 1950s and 1960s.

30. These are Saint Alessio, Saint Thomas Moore, Saint Anthony from Padua, and Saint Sebastian. Saint Alessio, Saint Sebastian, and Saint Anthony were all missionaries, and they also lived in poverty. Saint Sebastian and Saint Thomas Moore are considered martyrs. Saint Sebastian and Saint Anthony were also extremely popular among Italian Catholics. Saint Alessio is the only one who was initially married, but eventually left his family to live in absolute poverty and solitude (his story of marriage and hermitage seems quite similar to Saint Rita's).

31. Marazziti, "Cultura di massa e valori cattolici," 319.

32. "Ideali accessibili ai comuni fedeli nella vita quotidiana." Ibid.

33. Niahm Cullen, "Morals, Modern Identities and the Catholic Woman: Fashion in Famiglia Cristiana, 1954–68," *Journal of Modern Italian Studies* 18, no. 1 (2013): 35.

34. "Le virtù dell'anima femminile. . . . Il marito bestiale sarà apostrofato dal sacerdote, ma le buone madri, spose fedeli, debbono continuare a offrire con fede al Signore il quotidiano martirio."

35. Story by Sara Fuzier, written and directed by Eduardo Falletti, photographed by Adolfo Guerrieri.

36. Cullen, "Morals, Modern Identities and the Catholic Woman," 39.

37. Story by Sara Fuzier, written and directed by Eduardo Falletti, photographed by Adolfo Guerrieri. Maria Goretti's story was also made into a film, *Cielo sulla palude* (dir. Augusto Genina, 1949) and, more recently, into a film for television produced by RAI Fiction and Lux Vide, a media firm associated with the religious congregation of "Passionisti" (dir. Giulio Base, 2003).

38. Fuzier du Cayla is also author of other novels, including a romance, *Aspettar l'amore: romanzo* (Waiting for Love: A Novel, 1958).

39. "Non temete coloro che uccidono il corpo: essi non possono uccidere l'anima; temete piuttosto colui che può mandare l'anima in perdizione e il corpo all'inferno."

40. "Si presenta con tutti i caratteri della 'sub-cultura' cattolico-popolare, principalmente interessata non all'informazione o alla politica, ma alla 'formazione,' nel senso dichiarato di una continuazione chiara e articolata della predicazione domenicale." Marazziti, "Cultura di massa e valori cattolici," 307.

41. Forgacs and Gundle, *Mass Culture and Italian Society*, 256.

42. "Da qualche tempo il ragazzo si abbandona perdutamente a letture insane."

43. "Letture che lo esaltano e lo lasciano stravolto. Mentre un pensiero torbido, fisso come un chiodo, da qualche tempo non lo abbandona più."

44. "La fanciulla in quel momento sta passando e non sospetta che occhi impuri la scrutano da una finestra."

45. "Subito . . . senza aspettare più . . . Adesso! Eccola che viene."

46. "Dopo quel rifiuto di Assunta, la vita alle ferriere diventa impossibile."

47. "Il suo visetto triste parla chiaramente di tutte le sofferenze, di tutte le paure, di tutte le privazioni alle quali *la sua famiglia è sottoposta da sempre*." Emphasis is mine.

48. Marazziti, "Cultura di massa e valori cattolici," 310.

49. "Avvisare il lettore, sin dall'inizio, che seguirà le vicende amorose, apparentemente gaie, di due giovani già segnati da un destino tragico, favorisce l'accettazione dello choc finale, lo pone sotto il segno della necessità, lo svuota di ogni potere provocatorio; e inoltre aiuta il lettore a pregustare pagina per pagina, il risvolto atteso." Eco, *Il superuomo di massa*, 25–26.

50. Baetens, "The Photo-Novel," 2.

51. One exception was Silvana Pampanini, who appeared in the Christmas issue of 1960.

52. Marazziti, "Cultura di massa e valori cattolici," 314.

53. See Paola Bonifazio, *Schooling in Modernity: The Politics of Sponsored Films in Postwar Italy* (Toronto: University of Toronto Press, 2014).

5 BIRTH CONTROL IN COMICS

This chapter is derived, in part, from an article published in *gender/sexuality/italy* on August 18, 2018, https://www.gendersexualityitaly.com/3-the-secret-pill-aied-fotoromanzi-and-sexual-education-in-1970s-italy/.

1. Umberto Eco, "Divertendosi si educano alla libertà," *Corriere della Sera*, March 23, 1976, 12. "Saper leggere criticamente questi nuovi miti, scoprire qual è l'insegnamento nascosto sotto le forme del divertimento è un modo di fare la scuola preparandosi alla vita."

2. Compagnone, "Femminismo," 2. "[N]on 'dà da leggere' ma da guardare, quindi elude il linguaggio, quindi abitua a non pensare."

3. Luigi Compagnone, "Fotoromanzo e politica" (Photoromance and Politics), *Corriere della Sera*, March 31, 1974, 2. "[I]l lettore di fotoromanzi è un soggetto passivo perchè privato del linguaggio."

4. See Anelli, et al., *Fotoromanzo, fascino e pregiudizio*, which talks about such experiments. See also Bravo, *Il fotoromanzo,* chap. 5, Kindle. Bravo mentions specifically the case of AIED's photoromances but does not delve into any detailed analysis of their rhetorical strategies, sponsorship, and the American contribution to the campaign.

5. "Italy: The New Domestic Landscape," Press Release n. 45 (The Museum of Modern Art, New York, 1972), 1 (1–5).

6. Daniel Weaks and Eliza Sola, *The Photonovel: A Tool for Development* (Washington, DC: Action, Peace Corps, 1976).

7. Ibid., 12.

8. Compagnone, "Fotoromanzo e politica," 2.

9. According to Dagmar Herzog, only one in ten Italian women was using oral contraceptives in 1969; in 1975, Lucia Purisol claimed that only 5 percent of Italian women used the pill. See Herzog, *Sexuality in Europe*, 137; and Lucia Purisol, "Paola Pitagora a fumetti insegna a usare la pillola" (Paola Pitagora Teaches How to Use the Pill in Comics), *Corriere della Sera*, January 30, 1975, 5. Official numbers of illegal abortions are obviously unavailable; however, Maria Luisa Zardini De Marchi affirmed in her study conducted in the Roman housing projects that, on average, the 588 women she assisted were thirty-one years old, had been married for ten years and pregnant every two years, and had had two abortions for every three living children. See Lucia Sollazzo, "Inumane Vite," *La Stampa*, October 4, 1969, 17.

10. Complete copies of the AIED photoromance are available online; see "I fotoromanzi di De Marchi sul controllo delle nascite," Rientro dolce, accessed June 25, 2019, http://www.rientrodolce.org/index .php?option=com_content&task=view&id=250&Itemid=0.

11. See also Elisabetta Remondi, "Tre fotoromanzi AIED. Noi Giovani. La trappola, Il segreto," *Genesis* 3, no. 1 (2004): 201–219. Remondi argues in this essay that De Marchi's use of "motivational psychology" was original, and does not acknowledge a long tradition of motivational films for educational and training purposes, both in the United States and in Europe.

12. Madeo, "A fumetti il controllo delle nascite," 7.

13. Ibid. Madeo also writes that the photoromances will be included in "alcune riviste di fumetti" (some comics magazines) but she does not say which, and I did not find any evidence that indeed the AIED photoromances were published in magazines for sale.

14. See Franco Marchiaro, "Alessandria fa l'esame di educazione sessuale" (Alessandria Takes a Test in Sexual Education), *Corriere di Alessandria e Asti*, January 23, 1976, 1. In addition to the opining of a "consultorio," the article announces the release of a film in theaters. About the focus group in a factory see Silvano Villani, "La classe operaia vuole gli anticoncezionali" (The Working Class Wants Contraceptives), *Corriere della Sera*, November 11, 1976, 7. The public polling company in charge of distributing the survey and analyzing the results was Demoskopea, whose President Giampaolo Fabris also coauthored with Rowena Davis an important study on the sexual behaviors of Italians. See Giampaolo Fabris and Rowena Davis, *Il mito del sesso: Rapporto sul comportamento sessuale degli italiani* (Milan: Mondadori, 1978).

15. Madeo, "A fumetti il controllo delle nascite," 7. See also Lamberto Furso, "Perchè non è più reato dopo 40 anni la propaganda degli anticoncezionali," *La Stampa*, March 18, 1971, 8. De Marchi was secretary of the AIED Roman branch since February 28, 1954 and became national secretary of the association in 1961. He had a degree in literature, and was a United States Information Services officer, director of *Mondo Occidentale*, and editor of *Globo* and *Umanità*.

16. Gianfranco Porta, *Amore e libertà: Storia dell'AIED* (Rome-Bari: Laterza, 2013), 3. See also Doone Williams and Greer Williams, *Every Child a Wanted Child: Clarence James Gamble and His Work in the Birth Control Movement*, ed. Emily P. Flint (Boston: Harvard University Press for Francis A. Countway Library of Medicine, 1978), 375. "Le normative fondanti del natalismo fascista" and "un reato contro l'integrità e la sanità della stirpe."

17. Elena Petricola, "Dal discorso sulle donne al discorso delle donne. Birth control, contraccezione e depenalizzazione dell'aborto tra ambienti laici e movimenti delle donne" (From the Discourse on Women to the Discourse of Women. Birth Control, Contraception, and Decriminalization of Abortion in Secular Groups and Women's Movements), *Quaderni di storia contemporanea*, no. 48 (2010), http://www.isral.it/web/pubblicazioni/qsc_48_07_petricola.pdf.

18. Cited in Porta, *Amore e libertà*, 4. "Chiunque pubblicamente incita a pratiche contro la procreazione e fa propaganda a favore di esse è punito con la reclusione fino a un anno e con la multa fino a lire quattrocentomila."

19. See newsreel no. 417, "Notizie Cinematografiche" (1975), published on the Internet portal of the Senato della Repubblica and created in collaboration with Archivio Istituto Luce, titled "Dibattito a Roma su 'La contraccezione e il lavoro della donna' organizzato dall'IRIDE (Istituto per le ricerche e le iniziative demografiche) in collaborazione con l'AIED. Presiede Luigi De Marchi, intervengono giornaliste e deputati" (Debate in Rome on 'Contraception and Woman's Work' Organized by IRIDE in Collaboration with AIED: Chaired by Luigi De Marchi with Presentations by Journalists and Deputies), http://senato.archivioluce.it/senato-luce/scheda/video/IL5000046833/2/Dibattito-a-Roma-su-La-contraccezione-e-il-lavoro-della-donna-organizzato-dallIRIDE-Istituto-per-le-ricerche-e-le-iniziative-demografiche-in-collaborazione-con-lAIED-Pres.html. "Occorre un'opera d'informazione fatta in profondità, cominciando dal punto che la maternità consapevole non ha niente a che fare con il libero amore."

20. The text of this proposal can be found in Giovanni Berlinguer, Giorgio Bini, and Antonio Faggioli, *Sesso e società* (Roma, Editori Riuniti, 1976), 333–350. It was presented to the Parliament on March 13, 1975, by the following deputies: Giorgio Bini, Adriana Fabbri Seroni, Carmen Casapieri Quagliotti, Giuseppe Chiarante, Cecilia Chiovini, Renato Finelli, Gabriele Gannantoni, Adriana Lodi Faustini Fustini, Giuseppa Mendola, Alessandro Natta, Maria Agostina Pellegatta, Gino Picciotto, Marino Raicich, Giulio Tedeschi, Alessandro Tessari, Rosala Vagli, and Nazzareno Vitali.

21. Herzog, *Sexuality in Europe*, 133.

22. See for example, "Nascite controllate con l'aiuto dei fumetti" (Birth Control Thanks to Comics), *Corriere della Sera*, January 29, 1974, 11.

23. Aida Ribero, "Lui mi nasconde la pillola nel cassetto" (He Hides My Pill in a Drawer), *La Stampa*, July 30, 1974, 10. "Storicamente la sessualità si è sempre retta su un equilibrio nevrotico, come peccato con conseguente senso di colpa per cui superare il quale si tende all'espiazione. Sinora non si è fatto altro che presentare queste espiazioni sotto forma scientifica."

24. These are the words used by De Marchi in an interview with Guido Credazzi, titled "Solo un figlio per famiglia altrimenti l'Italia scoppia" (Only One Child per Couple or Italy Will Explode). *Corriere dell'informazione*, January 18, 1978, 2. "Una forma di rivolta nei confronti della civiltà dei loro padre."

25. "Una volta, la gente faceva poco amore e molti figli. Noi giovani, invece, vogliamo pochi figli e molto amore!!"

26. Ugo Fornari, "Il segreto" (Rome: Iride, 1975).

27. Ibid. "Quella almeno non fa tante storie e non ha mille paure."

28. Ibid. "Il segreto della [loro] nuova felicità" and "gustare per la prima volta il piacere supremo . . ."

29. Fabris and Davis, *Il mito del sesso*, 203, quoted in Fiammetta Balestracci, "The Influence of American Sexual Studies on the 'Sexual Revolution' of Italian Women," in *Children by Choice? Changing Values, Reproduction, and Family Planning in the 20th Century*, ed. Ann-Katrin Gembries, Theresia Theuke, and Isabel Heinemann (Munich: De Grutyer Oldenbourg, 2017), 148.

30. Balestracci, "The Influence of American Sexual Studies on the 'Sexual Revolution' of Italian Women," 158.

31. Herzog, *Sexuality in Europe*, 145.

32. See also the film *Le italiane e l'amore* (Italian Women and Love, dir. Marco Ferreri et al., 1961), based on Gabriella Parca's collection of letters from women readers of *photoromances*, *Le italiane si confessano* ([1959] 1966); and Luigi Comencini's television series *Gli italiani e l'amore* (1978).

33. Purisol, "Paola Pitagora a fumetti insegna a usare la pillola," 5. "I settimanali femminili hanno cercato di sopperire alla mancanza totale di educazione sessuale con inchieste, servizi e con inserti 'vietati ai minori.'"

34. Balestracci, "The influence of American Sexual Studies on the 'Sexual Revolution' of Italian Women," 146.

35. Eleonora Bertolotto et al., "Ma sì, parliamo di sesso" (Yes, Let's Talk about Sex), *La Stampa*, January 29, 1974, 3.

36. "I fotoromanzi come la pillola," *La Stampa*, January 29, 1974, 3.

37. *Bolero Film* no. 980 (1966): 46.

38. "FIGLI, SI (ma al momento desiderato)" and "tutti, e solo, i figli desiderati, al tempo desiderato." Vittoria Olivetti Berla, "Il problema della popolazione," (The Issue of Population), *La Voce repubblicana*, February 10, 1954; cited in Porta, *Amore e libertà*, 20.

39. This was the term officially used by the AIED and other supporters of the birth control movement until 1971 to avoid legal problems.

40. Porta, *Amore e libertà*, 19. "Un'azione di carattere economico" and "il mezzo che consente all'individuo di essere pienamente libero e cosciente di fronte a se stesso e alla propria discendenza."

41. See Petricola, "Dal discorso sulle donne al discorso delle donne."

42. Credazzi, "Solo un figlio per famiglia altrimenti l'Italia scoppia," 2.

43. "Preti e padroni" want workers "pieni di figli e fitti come formiche per meglio dominar[li] e sfruttar[li]."

44. Virginia Visani, "Il sogno di carta" (A Dream Made of Paper), *Corriere della sera*, September 29, 1975, 5. "Non c'è nudo, non c'è pornografia. In una scena di letto, lei indossa una camicia accollatissima con maniche lunghe e lui una maglietta alla marinara."

45. "Servizi sui problemi della donna e della sua vita intima" (Reports on Women's Issues and Their Intimate Lives), *Grand Hotel*, no. 1470 (1974), 6–7, and no. 1471 (1974), 4–7.

46. "Un centro dove si insegna come fare l'amore senza che la donna resti incinta."

47. "Con franchezza e senza pregiudizi" and "come evitare una gravidanza non voluta."

48. "Servizi sui problemi della donna e della sua vita intima," *Grand Hotel*, no. 1470 (1974), 6. "Il fine del matrimonio non è più soprattutto quello di avere figli, ma è principalmente quello della felicità e della

comunione fra i coniugi. . . . Occorre imparare, però, a non concepire bambini, se non quando lei e lui lo desiderino. Occorre che tutti sappiano come fare per raggiungere questo scopo."

49. Cited in Porta, *Amore e libertà*, 4. Emphasis is mine. "Ridurre [le] nascite di illegittimi, infanticidi, aborti procurati, suicidi di ragazze madri, *prole ereditariamente tarata*."

50. Maria Luisa Zardini De Marchi had a degree in social work, and was employed as a phone operator at the U.S. Embassy.

51. For more information about this relationship, see Williams and Williams, *Every Child a Wanted Child*, in particular, chap. 23, "The De Marchis and the Pope's Children," 372–410. See also Luigi De Marchi and Maria Luisa Zardini, "Bringing Contraception to Italy," in *Courageous Pioneers: Celebrating 50 Years of Pathfinder International and 80 years of Pioneering Work in Family Planning and Reproductive Health around the World*, ed. Linda Suttenfield, Patricia E. Collings, and Daniel E. Pellegrom (Watertown, MA: Pathfinder International, 2007), 37–41

52. De Marchi and Zardini, "Bringing Contraception to Italy," 41. In this respect, Anna Treves is incorrect in saying that AIED did not have any financial sponsors of notice, but only limited financial help from "private individuals" and from Adriano Olivetti. See Anna Treves, *Le nascite e la politica nell'Italia del Novecento* (Milano: LED, 2001), 397.

53. Williams and Williams, *Every Child a Wanted Child*, 395.

54. The IPPF was formed in 1952 as a nonprofit global organization, also functioning as the international branch of the American Planned Parenthood. Gamble initially was associated with the IPPF, before opening his own organization, the Pathfinder Fund in 1958.

55. Treves, *Le nascite e la politica nell'Italia del Novecento*, 402. "Non solo volevano, in qualche modo essi esigevano di essere denunciati; e poi sistematicamente si opponevano alla tendenza della magistratura ad archiviare le denounce."

56. De Marchi and Zardini, "Bringing Contraception to Italy," 41. According to this chapter, the AIED also produced short TV advertisements in the soap opera format.

57. Their work would be published in 1969 in the volume *Inumane Vite*, whose title refers to Pope Paul VI's Encyclical Letter on birth control issued on July 25, 1968. Zardini conducted, with only one other coworker, about forty thousand visits in ten years among 558 couples, who lived in the poorest neighborhood: Tufello, Tiburtino III, Ponte Mammolo, San Basilio, Villa Gordiani, La Rustica, Centocelle, Quarticciolo, and Borghetto Lanuvio. See "Tre testimonianze dal diario di un'assistente dell'AIED" (Three Testimonies from the Diary of an AIED Social Worker) in *ABC* 5, no. 52 (Winter 1965): 36.

58. De Marchi and Zardini, "Bringing Contraception to Italy," 38.

59. Porta, *Amore e libertà*, 117.

60. *I misteri di Roma* (Rome's Mysteries) is a documentary film in several episodes created by Cesare Zavattini, produced by S.P.A. Cinematografica, and directed in 1963 by many filmmakers, including Bernardo Bertolucci, Libero Bizzarri, Ansano Giannarelli, and Lorenza Mazzetti.

61. For a study of the influence of the women's movement in shaping the debate on contraception in Italy in the 1970s, see Petricola, "Dal discorso sulle donne al discorso delle donne."

62. Associazione Educazione Demografica, *Manuale di contraccezione* (Rome: AED, 1975), 8. "Il potere non ha alcun interesse che gli individui si autogestiscano sotto l'aspetto procreativo. La conquista della libertà vanificherebbe il monopolio del rubinetto della fertilità."

63. In particular, the manual criticizes the distribution of the T.A.R.O. cap (foam tablets, a type of vaginal suppository) as dangerous to women because it did not provide accurate protection from unwanted pregnancies. See *Manuale di contraccezione*, 64.

64. Remondi, "Tre fotoromanzi AIED," 201. "L'obiettivo a cui si guardava era una coppia in cui gli individui fossero tenuti insieme non più da un modello di soggezione all'uomo, tipico delle società patriarcali, nè dalla paura della solitudine che caratterizzava tante vite femminili, bensì dallo scambio reciproco di maturità e conoscenze."

65. Fornari, "Il segreto," n.p. "Ora gli altri uomini non mi interessano più, perchè tu mi dai tutto."

66. Herzog, *Sexuality in Europe*, 145.

67. Purisol, "Paola Pitagora a fumetti insegna a usare la pillola," 5.

68. Aida Ribero, "Lui mi nasconde la pillola nel cassetto."

69. De Marchi and Zardini, "Bringing Contraception to Italy," 39.

70. In the words of De Marchi, in his autobiographical book *Il solista*: "la contraccezione o come una valida difesa contro qualche evento temuto, o come valido strumento per la realizzazione di un desiderio profondo" (contraception either as a valid defense against some feared event, or as a valid instrument to realize a profound wish). See Luigi De Marchi, *Il solista* (Rome: Edizioni Interculturali Uno, 2003), 128–129.

71. See for example: Barry Cardwell, *Film and Motivation: The "Why We Fight" Series* (Carlisle Barracks, PA: U.S. Army War College, 1991); Ken Smith, *Mental Hygiene: Classroom Films 1945–1970* (New York: Blast Books 1999); Heide Solbrig, "The Personal Is Political: Voice and Citizenship in Affirmative-Action Videos in the Bell System, 1970–1984," in *Films that Work: Industrial Film and the Productivity of Media*, ed. Vinzenz Hediger and Patrick Vonderau (Amsterdam: Amsterdam University Press, 2009), 259–282; Devin Orgeron, Marsha Gordon, and Dan Streible, *Learning with the Lights Off* (Oxford: Oxford University Press, 2012).

72. Ribero, "Lui mi nasconde la pillola nel cassetto," 10.

73. Purisol, "Paola Pitagora a fumetti insegna a usare la pillola," 5.

74. "Interpreti volontari non retribuiti" and "motivi sociali."

75. "Ho assicurato la mia collaborazione all'iniziativa dell'AIED, inoltre perchè mi sembra che i lavoratori possano meglio lottare se non sono angosciati da una famiglia troppo numerosa."

76. *In ginocchio da te* (On My Knees for You, dir. Ettore Maria Fizzarotti, 1964), also starring Laura Efrikian, Morandi's wife.

77. Achille Ciccaglione, "Innamoratissimi a Capri Paola Gassman e Ugo Pagliai" (Paola Gassman and Ugo Pagliai, Madly in Love in Capri), *Corriere della sera*, July 21, 1973, 4.

78. Milena Cardarelli, "Dimentica Lisa non Paola" (He Forgets Lisa, not Paola), *Corriere della sera*, October 22, 1976, 3.

79. "Una cosa civile." In Carlo Brusati, "Alle femministe piacciono molto gli uomini: Intervista provocatoria con la provocante Paola Pitagora" (Feminists Like Men Very Much: A Challenging Interview with Provocative Paola Pitagora), *Corriere della Sera*, July 29, 1975, 3.

80. "Più libera e consapevole." Ibid.

81. Directed by Ruggero Miti. "Morandi porta sulla scena la vita di Jacopone" (Morandi Brings Jacopone's Life to the Stage), *Corriere della Sera*, September 18, 1973, 13. Pitagora later denied the affair, making the news once again when suing Morandi's wife, Laura Efrikian, for slander a few years later. See "Paola Pitagora querela l'ex-moglie di Morandi" (Paola Pitagora sues Morandi's ex-wife), September 29, 1979, 17.

82. "C'è ancora l'ombra della Pitagora . . . fra Morandi e Laura." Morandi and his wife had at the same time appeared in a propaganda short film in favor of legalizing divorce (voting "no" at the 1974 Referendum): "Gianni Morandi spot elettorale referendum sul divorzio 1974." YouTube video, 02:42, October 10, 2010, https://www.youtube.com/watch?v=hg4cBFJXOkM.

83. "L'irresistibile conquistatore di ruoli femminili," in "Ugo Pagliai (Casanova) evade" (Ugo Pagliai [Casanova] Escapes), *Corriere della Sera*, August 3, 1972, 9. See also Mimma Quirico, "Un uomo tranquillo con qualche tormento" (A Quiet Man, Sometimes in Agony), *Corriere della Sera*, August 21, 1971, 13.

84. Alfredo Pigna, "Sette ragazze alla conquista del telequiz" (Seven Girls Conquering a Quiz Show), *Corriere della Sera*, April 11–12, 1957, 9.

85. Giuliano Gramigna, "Ha conquistato i cinque milioni il giovane esperto di 'western'" (The Young Western Expert Won the Five Million Lira Prize), *Corriere della Sera*, April 12, 1957, 9; Alfredo Pigna, "Tra le quinte del telequiz" (Behind the Scenes of the Quiz Show), *Corriere della Sera*, March 29–30, 1957, 9.

86. V.B., "Primo giro di manovella con Valdemarin alla stazione" (Cranking the Handle for the First Time with Valdemarin at the Train Station), *Corriere della Sera*, April 13, 1957, 6.

87. Driessens, "The Celebritization of Society and Culture," 644.

88. Ibid., 645.

6 REVENGE OF THE FANS

1. "Perchè aspettare ore in strada una star della televisione per un autografo non è solo stupido, molto peggio . . . è una *cosa da cameriere*." Edoardo Albinati, *La scuola cattolica* (Milan: Rizzoli, 2016), Kindle. Emphasis is mine.

2. "L'attore che interpretava in tv il personaggio di Sandokan."

3. "50% degli italiani stavano leggendo i [nostri] fotoromanzi [negli anni settanta]. Però nessuno ha il coraggio di confessarlo—stupidamente." Ulrike Schimming, *Fotoromanze: Analyse Eines Massenmediums* (Frankfurt Am Main: Peter Lang, 2002), 237.

4. De Souza, "The Law of the Heart," 255.

5. The first photoromance in color was "5 ragazzi in cerca di sogni," with Franco Gasparri, Claudia Rivelli, Katiuscia, Kirk Morris, Heros Zamara, *Kolossal*, no. 1 (1974).

6. 4,403 members, accessed December 27, 2019, https://www.facebook.com/groups/36043182938/.

7. The post about the survey reached 29, 539 people and received 849 engagements, including 773 post clicks and 76 reactions (likes, comments, shares).

8. Robert Kozinets, *Netnography: Doing Ethnographic Research Online* (Sage: London, 2009), 60.

9. See Kevin Roberts, *Lovemarks: The Future beyond Brands* (New York: powerHouse Books, 2004).

10. There are some differences between series, in particular, *Kolossal* and *Sogno* are closer to *Bolero Film* in their content, since the issues includes several columns in addition to photoromances. *Idilio* (Idyll), *The Adventures of Lucky Martin*, and *The Adventures Jack Douglas*, instead, mostly consist of one story and a few pages with the celebrity's columns, some news or a short romance. As I previously mentioned, these series were extremely popular in South America, particularly in Brazil and also in Argentina, at least until the dictatorship (1976).

11. "[L]a Lancio non recluta i suoi interpreti in questo modo. Lo riteniamo quanto meno una presa in giro e noi per i lettori e le lettrici abbiamo un rispetto . . . sacrale."

12. *Kolossal*, no. 58 (September 1979): 86.

13. "La Lancio intuisce i vostri desideri e cerca di assecondarli, quando non riesce addirittura a prevenirli."

14. See Katiuscia as Genny in *The Adventures of Lucky Martin*, who claims to adore Franco Gasparri.

15. Kozinets, *Netnography*, 60.

16. Ibid., 72.

17. "Persone che purtroppo non conosco personalmente, ma che mi sono state vicine in tanti momenti."

18. Jenkins, *Textual Poachers*, 23.

19. Ibid.

20. Bravo, *Il fotoromanzo*, chap. 4, Kindle.

21. See Anelli, et al., *Fotoromanzo: fascino e pregiudizio*.

22. Bravo, *Il fotoromanzo*, chap. 4, Kindle.

23. E.V. also writes that her parents trashed her Lancio collection once she moved out of their house. Others regret having lost their collections since now the issues have become much more valuable via e-commerce.

24. "Che tenerezza se ripenso a questa bimbetta che partiva il pomeriggio per il chiosco a comprare i fotoromanzi! L'edicolante era un po' scettico, ma alla fine me li teneva anche da parte fino a quando non avevo tutti i soldi per comprarli. E all'epoca le uscite erano veramente tante! Per fortuna qualcuno me lo regalava anche la mia amata zia E. Negli anni non mi sono lasciata scappare un'uscita e avevo una collezione che dovevo sempre cercare di nascondere perché altrimenti finiva nella spazzatura."

25. She writes that her parents did not consider them appropriate for a young person.

26. In fact, there were a few instances in which I noticed that gender binaries are not always appropriate to describe the world of Lancio fandom, despite the fact that its celebrity system and the narratives appear to be structured exclusively according to heteronormative rules (romances are always based on man-woman

relationships, male and female celebrities are defined in the narratives and publicity according to traditional heterosexual standards of masculinity/femininity, etc.).

27. My comments are mostly about LFGs even though there are a few other blog posts that I found on the topic. However, LFGs are still the most relevant place to draw data about fans.

28. "Noi ci chiamiamo in qualche modo una famiglia Lancio e abbiamo un rapporto abbastanza stretto con tutti quanti. C'è la possibilità di avere un contatto continuo con tutti. E quindi, si travasa anche questa sensazione, questo rapporto col pubblico." Schimming, *Fotoromane*, 230.

29. "Un gesto di sincero affetto"; "per salvaguardare un patrimonio di esperienza e di popolarità"; "oltre il semplice aspetto economic."

30. "Commovente"; "rispettosa e intelligente"; "di altri tempi."

31. C. Lee Harrington and Denise D. Bielby, *Soap Fans: Pursuing Pleasure and Making Meaning in Everyday Life* (Philadelphia: Temple University Press, 1995), 10.

32. "Purtroppo ad un certo punto arrivavi in edicola e sconsolato l'edicolante ti dava i pochi pezzi che era riuscito a trovare e tenerti da parte fino a quando io ne persi le tracce. Niente. Non arrivava più nemmeno una pagina. Un lutto per me. Poi nel 2013 ho aperto il mio profilo fb [sic] e con mio grande stupore ho trovato diversi gruppi di appassionati Lancio. Per fortuna mi sono iscritta a questo. Credo che *la vera* Lancio ora sia qui grazie alle amministratrici e ai tanti componenti del gruppo, in particolare a coloro che con tanto impegno e tanta passione pubblicano qui tantissime storie che in questo modo non moriranno mai." Emphasis is mine.

33. "Le occasioni di dialogo tra *noi* e voi si sono moltiplicate e con esse anche le possibilità offerte alle lettrici e ai lettori di . . . venirci e trovare, sia pure a livello virtuale." Emphasis in the original.

34. To educate readers on the use of the web, a special box on the page is dedicated to instruct those who may be new to surfing.

35. "La Lancio, ed io ne sono un piccolo puzzle, non appartiene a nessuno in particolare ma è di tutte/i coloro che l'hanno amata." "Noi lettori dei fotoromanzi . . . Lancio!!!" June 6, 2018 post; 92 comments. In this and all other posts and communication, fans attribute to the company the feminine gender.

36. Out of sixty-three respondents, thirty-two are between age forty and fifty-nine.

37. In the words of survey respondents to the question why do you read photoromances today: "ricordare quei periodi dove si sognava con loro [i divi]" (to remember when we used to dream with [celebrities]); "perchè ricordano la gioventù" (because they remind me of my youth); "sfogliare, ricordare, immaginare" (to browse, remember, imagine).

38. "I fotoromanzi degli anni 60–70 erano la cosa più bella che c'era noi ragazze che sognavamo a leggerli . . . ci sono stati amori tragedie morti incidenti ma loro ci facevano sognare lo stesso io sono cresciuta con loro mi hanno conquistata con le loro storie." There is no punctuation in the original.

39. "Avevo 13 anni, facevo la terza media e non li conoscevo. Me ne parlò un'amica delle elementari che abitava vicino a casa mia. Lei aveva un gruppo di amiche della sua classe che adoravano Franco Gasparri e dei genitori di mentalità aperta (anche se era la generazione pre-68) che le compravano i fotoromanzi, così me li passava lei. Invece i miei genitori li consideravano roba per cameriere, e quindi figuriamoci se me li

avrebbero comprati. A dire la verità, Franco Gasparri piaceva anche a me. Per non essere 'diversa' facevo finta di interessarmi alle storie, ma sinceramente mi sembrava tutto finto, a cominciare dalla faccia di certi attori (per esempio non sopportavo Katiuscia con l'espressione finta imbronciata, trovavo ridicolo il modo in cui veniva rappresentato lo schiaffo in faccia, ecc.)."

40. Rojek, *Celebrity*, chap. 1, Kindle.

41. Mary Ann Doane, *The Desire to Desire: The Woman's Film of the 1940s* (Bloomington: Indiana University Press, 1987), 16.

42. "Il lieto fine sminuisce i capolavori, salvo qualche rara eccezione."

43. "Io più bruttina di un rospo, sognavo di diventare una donna bellissima come Claudia (e infatti sono identica!)."

44. Jenkins, *Convergence Culture*, 63.

45. These two terms are first theorized, in relation to fandom, by Diana Taylor in *The Archive and the Repertoire: Performing Cultural Memory in the Americas* (Durham, NC: Duke University Press, 2003).

46. Abigail De Kosnik, introduction to *Rogue Archives: Digital Cultural Memory and Media Fandom* (Cambridge, MA: MIT Press, 2016), Kindle.

47. Ibid.

48. Ibid.; reference to Achille Mbembe, "The Power of the Archive and Its Limits," in *Refiguring the Archive*, ed. Carolyn Hamilton et al. (Capetown: Clyson Printers, 2002), 20.

49. "Li ho letti e comprati sino ai primi anni 80, poi li ho riscoperti qui qualche anno fa, un tuffo nella mia gioventù."

50. "Erano gli anni 70 e non ne persi nemmeno uno da leggere . . . . amavo e amo Gasparri specialmente in coppia con Michela e adoravo i Lucky Martin . . . . li ho letti fino all'incidente di Franco nell'80 poi ho avuto come un rifiuto per ciò che era accaduto e li ho abbandonati . . . . fino a quando navigando sul web mi sono imbattuta nei gruppi di fotoromanzi e come per magia è riscoppiata la passione. Grazie alle amiche del gruppo che li postano ho scoperto e letto i fotoromanzi dall'80 fino a quando la Lancio ha chiuso."

51. I am reproducing here the same structure of the post as it was published on the digital interface. The original reads: "Sono anni che lo sostengo / Serve un museo del fotoromanzo / Fondare il museo del fotoromanzo è fondamentale / Mi chiedo cosa ne sarà dei miei 2000 fotoromanzi quando io morirò / Li donerei al museo / E voi lancetti che custodite come reliquie i vostri foto vi chiedete cosa sarà di loro dopo la vostra dipartita? / Raccogliamo le firme e chiediamo al ministero dei beni culturali l'unico museo al mondo del fotoromanzo / Dove oltre che vedere virtualmente la storia con le origini del fotoromanzo si possono anche leggere in sede / Siete d'accordo?"

52. "Il museo lo facciamo donando i nostri fotoromanzi Per tutelarli e proteggerli Potrebbero essere patrimonio dell'umanità Hanno percorso un secolo Da una generazione all'altra c'è la cultura mondiale nei fotoromanzi."

53. "Tutte vorremmo un buco dove rinchiuderci in beata solitudine a leggere i nostri giornali preferiti, ad ascoltare i dischi e a sognare l'amore. Se tu con pochissima spesa e un po' di fantasia sistemerai la tua soffitta,

avrai risolto un doppio problema: evasione dalle rotture familiari e organizzazione della tua 'Lancio'-biblioteca.' Katiuscia ironically closes her letter suggesting that the library would store "I tuoi amici . . . ossia i tuoi fotoromanzi . . . ossia noi. Katia in scatola . . . chissa se starò comoda?!? (Your friends . . . that is, your photoromances . . . that is, us. Katia in a box . . . I wonder, would I be comfortable?!?)"

54. "Da che ho memoria mi ricordo di mia zia e mia mamma e le loro amiche con in mano i fotoromanzi, e ho iniziato a leggerli prima di saper leggere."

55. Giet, *"Nous deux" 1947–1997*, 108. "Permet de materializer le lien entre ces generations."

EPILOGUE

1. Wu Ming, preface to *Cultura Convergente* by Henry Jenkins. "Nel migliore dei mondi possibili, la pubblicazione di questo libro scuoterebbe come un terremoto il dibattito italiano su Internet e le nuove tecnologie di comunicazione."

2. Giuliana Benvenuti, *Il brand Gomorra: dal romanzo alla serie TV* (Bologna: Il Mulino, 2018), chap. 4, ebook. "Un metatesto potenzialmente infinito e aperto alla creativita." See also Luca Barra and Massimo Scaglioni, "Il ruolo della televisione nel sostegno al cinema italiano," in *Il cinema di Stato: Finanziamento pubblico ed economia simbolica nel cinema italiano contemporaneo*, ed. Marco Cucco and Giacomo Manzoli (Bologna: Il Mulino, 2017). Kindle.

3. Benvenuti, *Il brand Gomorra*, chap. 4. "Un utilizzo dal basso delle strategie di coinvolgimento attivo del pubblico messe in atto dalle grandi case produttrici di beni culturale."

4. Freeman, "Branding Consumerism," 632.

5. Domingo Sanchez-Mesa et al., "Transmedia (Storytelling?): A Polyphonic Critical Review," *Artnodes*, no. 18 (2016): 8–17.

6. "Il problema è che il dibattito italiano sulla cultura pop novanta volte su cento riguarda la spazzatura che ci propina la televisione, come se il 'popular' fosse per forza quello, mentre esistono distinzioni qualitative ed evoluzioni storiche altrimenti dovremmo pensare che *Sandokan*, *Star Trek*, *Lost*, il TG4 e *La pupa e il secchione* sono tutti allo stesso livello."

7. Doane, *The Desire to Desire*, 16.

8. Paola Bonifazio and Francesca Giombini, "Fare Fotoromanzi: Un'intervista con Francesca Giombini," *gender/sexuality/italy* 6 (2019), 184.

Bibliography

Abruzzese, Alberto. "Fotoromanzo." In *Letteratura Italiana, Storia e Geografia*, vol. 1, ed. Alberto Asor Rosa. Turin: Einaudi, 1989.

Adorno, Theodor, and Max Horkheimer. "The Culture Industry: Enlightenment as Mass Deception." In *Dialectic of Enlightenment: Philosophical Fragments*, trans. Edmund Jephcott, 94–136. Stanford: Stanford University Press, 2002.

Albinati, Edoardo. La scuola Cattolica. Milan: Rizzoli, 2016. Kindle.

Allegri, Luigi, Adelmina Bonazzi, and Arnaldo Conversi. *Nero a strisce: La reazione a fumetti*. Parma: Istituto di storia dell'arte, 1971.

Alovisio, Silvio, ed. *Cineromanzi: la collezione del Museo Nazionale del Cinema*. Turin: Museo Nazionale del Cinema, 2007.

Amelio, Gianni. "Non voglio perderti." In *Lo schermo di carta: Storia e storie dei cineromanzi*, ed. Emiliano Morreale, 13–16. Turin: Il Castoro, 2007.

Anelli, Maria Teresa, Paola Gabbrielli, Marta Morgavi, and Roberto Piperno. *Fotoromanzo: fascino e pregiudizio: storia, documenti e immagini di un grande fenomeno popolare: (1946–1978)*. Rome: Savelli, 1979.

Antonutti, Isabelle, *Cino Del Duca: De "Tarzan" à "Nous Deux": itinéraire d'un patron de presse*. Rennes: PU Rennes: 2013.

Aschenbrenner, Joyce. *Katherine Dunham: Dancing a Life*. Urbana: University of Illinois Press, 2002.

Associazione Educazione Demografica, *Manuale di contraccezione*. Rome: AED, 1975.

Astruc, Alexandre. "The Birth of a New Avant-Garde: La Caméra-Stylo." In *The New Wave: Critical Lanmarks*, ed. Peter Graham, 17–23. London: BFI, 2009.

Auteliano, Alice, and Valentina Re. *Il racconto del film: la novellizzazione, dal catalogo al trailer: XII convegno internazionale di studi sul cinema*. Udine, Italy: Forum, 2006.

Baetens, Jan. "Between Adaptation, Intermediality, and Cultural Series: The Example of the Photonovel," *Artnodes* 18 (2016): 47–55.

Baetens, Jan. *The Film Photonovel: A Cultural History of Forgotten Adaptations.* Austin: University of Texas Press, 2019.

Baetens, Jan. "The Photo-Novel: A Minor Medium?" *NECSUS: European Journal of Media Studies* 1, no. 1 (2012): 1–3. https://necsus-ejms.org/the-photo-novel-a-minor-medium-by-jan-baetens/.

Baetens, Jan, Carmen Van den Bergh, and Bart Van Den Bossche. "How to Write a Photo Novel. Ennio Jacobelli's *Istruzioni pratiche per la realizzazione del fotoromanzo* (1956)." *Authorship* 6, no.1 (2017): 1–16.

Baldazzini, Roberto. *Sofia Loren: rapita dal cinema: i fotoromanzi di Sofia Lazzaro (1950–1952).* Roma: Struwwelpeter, 2010.

Balestracci, Fiammetta. "The Influence of American Sexual Studies on the 'Sexual Revolution' of Italian Women." In *Children by Choice? Changing Values, Reproduction, and Family Planning in the 20th Century,* ed. Ann-Katrin Gembries, Theresia Theuke, and Isabel Heinemann, 145–162. Munich: De Grutyer Oldenbourg, 2017.

Barra, Luca, and Massimo Scaglioni. "Il ruolo della televisione nel sostegno al cinema italiano." In *Il cinema di Stato: Finanziamento pubblico ed economia simbolica nel cinema italiano contemporaneo,* ed. Marco Cucco and Giacomo Manzoli. Bologna: Il Mulino, 2017. Kindle.

Barron, Emma. *Popular High Culture in Italian Media, 1950–1970.* New York: Palgrave Macmillan, 2018.

Bazin, André. "On the *politiques des auteurs.*" In *Cahiers du Cinéma: The 1950s: Neo-Realism, Hollywood, New Wave,* ed. Jim Hillier, 248–259. Cambridge, MA: Harvard University Press, 1985.

Bellassai, Sandro. *La morale comunista.* Rome: Carocci, 2000.

Benvenuti, Giuliana. *Il brand Gomorra: dal romanzo alla serie TV.* Bologna: Il Mulino, 2018. ebook.

Berlinguer, Giovanni, Giorgio Bini, and Antonio Faggioli. *Sesso e società.* Roma, Editori Riuniti, 1976.

Berselli, Emondo, ed. *Miss Italia 1939–2009: Storia, protagoniste, vincitrici.* Milan: Mondadori Electa, 2009.

Bertetti, Paolo, Matthew Freeman, and Carlos A. Scolari. *Transmedia Archaeology: Storytelling in the Borderlines of Science Fiction, Comics and Pulp Magazines.* New York: Palgrave Macmillan, 2014.

Bonifazio, Paola. *Schooling in Modernity: The Politics of Sponsored Films in Postwar Italy.* Toronto: University of Toronto Press, 2014.

Bonifazio, Paola. "Unlikely Partners: Salvo d'Angelo, David O. Selznick, and Zavattini's 'Stazione Termini.'" *The Italianist-Film Issue* 39, no. 2 (2019): 231–241.

Bonifazio, Paola, and Francesca Giombini. "Fare Fotoromanzi: Un'intervista con Francesca Giombini," *gender/sexuality/italy* 6 (2019): 179–185.

Bravo, Anna. *Il fotoromanzo.* Bologna: Il Mulino, 2011. Kindle.

Brooks, Peter. *The Melodramatic Imagination: Balzac, Henry James, Melodrama and the Mode of Excess.* New Haven: Yale University Press, [1976] 1995.

Buckley, Réka. "Marriage, Motherhood, and the Italian Film Stars of the 1950s." In *Women in Italy, 1945–1960: An Interdisciplinary Study,* ed. Penelope Morris, 35–49. New York: Palgrave Macmillan, 2006.

Buonanno, Milly. *Italian TV Drama and Beyond: Stories from the Soil, Stories from the Sea.* Chicago: Intellect, 2012.

Buonanno, Milly. *Naturale come sei: indagine sulla stampa femminile in Italia*. Rimini: Guaraldi Editore, 1975.

Butler Flora, Cornelia. "Fotonovelas: Message Creation and Reception." *Journal of Popular Culture* 14, no. 3 (1980): 524–534.

Butler Flora, Cornelia, and Jan L. Flora. "The Fotonovela as a Tool for Class and Cultural Domination." *Latin American Perspectives* 5, no. 1 (1978): 134–150.

Capitani, Ugo. *Il film nel diritto d'autore*. Rome: Edizioni Italiane, 1943.

Cardone, Lucia. "*Catene amare*: un cineromanzo tra film e teatro." *Bianco e Nero* 45, no. 1 (2004): 71–77.

Cardone, Lucia. "Cinema da sfogliare: *Perdonami!* (Mario Costa, 1953) dal film al cineromanzo." *Polittico*, no. 3 (2004): 197–207.

Cardone, Lucia. *Con lo schermo nel cuore: Grand Hotel e il cinema*. Roma: ETS, 2004.

Cardone, Lucia. "Il 'discorso amoroso' dallo schermo alla carta: la rappresentazione delle passioni nei cineromanzi degli anni Cinquanta." In Il racconto del film la novellizzazione, dal catalogo al trailer: XII convegno internazionale di studi sul cinema, ed. Alice Auteliano and Valentina Re, 241–247. Udine, Italy: Forum, 2006.

Cardone, Lucia. "Pellicole e film di carta: Un nuovo protagonismo femminile." *Cinema e storia* 5, no. 1 (2016): 191–202.

Cardwell, Barry. *Film and Motivation: The "Why We Fight" Series*. Carlisle Barracks, PA: U.S. Army War College, 1991.

Carr, Allan, Brontè Woodard, and Michael Newman. *Grease*. Los Angeles: Fotonovel Publications, 1978.

Carrillo, Loretta, and T. A. Lyson. "The Fotonovela as a Cultural Bridge for Hispanic Women in the United States." *Journal of Popular Culture* 17, no. 3 (Winter 1983): 59–64.

Cavallo, Pietro. *Viva l'Italia: storia, cinema e identità nazionale (1932–1962)*. Naples: Liguori, 2009.

Cecchetti, Valentino. *Generi della letteratura popolare: feuilletton, fascicoli, fotoromanzi in Italia dal 1870 ad oggi*. Latina: Tunuè, 2011.

Cesari, Maurizio. *La censura in Italia oggi (1944–1980)*. Naples: Liguori, 1982.

Cicognetti, Luisa, and Lorenza Servetti. "On Her Side: Female Images in Italian Cinema and the Popular Press, 1945–1955." *Historical Journal of Film, Radio and Television* 16, no. 4 (1966): 555–563.

Cimmino, Giovanni, and Stefano Masi, *Silvana Mangano: Il teorema della bellezza*. Rome: Gremese Editore, 1994.

Colombo, Fausto. *La cultura sottile: Media e industria culturale in Italia dall'Ottocento agli anni Novanta*. Milan: Bompiani, 1998.

Crépin, Thierry, Christophe Chavdia, and Thierry Groensteen, *On tue à chaque page! La loi de 1949 sur les publications destinées à la jeunesse*. Paris: Editions du Temps Musée de la bande dessinée, 1999.

Cullen, Niahm. "Morals, Modern Identities and the Catholic Woman: Fashion in Famiglia Cristiana, 1954–68." *Journal of Modern Italian Studies* 18, no. 1 (2013): 33–52.

De Berti, Raffaele. "Il nuovo periodico. Rotocalchi tra fotogiornalismo, cronaca e costume." In *Forme e modelli del rotocalco italiano tra fascismo e guerra*, ed. Raffaele De Berti and Irene Piazzoni, 3–64. Milan: Cisalpino-Monduzzi, 2009.

De Berti, Raffaele. "Leggere il film." *Bianco e nero* 44, no. 548 (2004): 19–25.

Decleva, Enrico. *Arnoldo Mondadori*. Turin: UTET, 2007.

De Kosnik, Abigail. *Rogue Archives: Digital Cultural Memory and Media Fandom*. Cambridge, MA: MIT Press, 2016.

De Marchi, Luigi. *Il solista*. Rome: Edizioni Interculturali Uno, 2003.

De Marchi, Luigi, and Maria Luisa Zardini, "Bringing Contraception to Italy." In *Courageous Pioneers: Celebrating 50 Years of Pathfinder International and 80 years of Pioneering Work in Family Planning and Reproductive Health around the World*, ed. Linda Suttenfield, Patricia E. Collings, and Daniel E. Pellegrom, 37–41. Watertown, MA: Pathfinder International, 2007.

Derecho, Abigail. "Archontic Literature: A Definition, a History, and Several Theories of Fan Fiction." In *Fan Fiction and Fan Communities in the Age of Internet: New Essays*, ed. Karen Hellekson and Kristina Busse, 61–78. London: McFarland and Co., 2006.

De Souza, Carlos Roberto. "The Law of the Heart: Genealogy, Narrative and Audience of a Minor Genre: The Argentinean Fotonovela." Dissertation. University of Santa Barbara, 2009.

Desmond, Jane. *Meaning in Motion: New Cultural Studies in Dance*. Durham, NC: Duke University Press, 1997.

Detti, Ermanno. *Le carte rosa: storia del fotoromanzo e della narrativa popolare*. Firenze: La Nuova Italia, 1990.

Doane, Mary Ann. *The Desire to Desire: The Woman's Film of the 1940s*. Bloomington: Indiana University Press, 1987.

Driessens, Olivier. "The Celebritization of Society and Culture: Understanding the Structural Dynamics of Celebrity Culture." *International Journal of Cultural Studies* 16, no. 16 (2013): 641–657.

Dyer, Richard. *Heavenly Bodies: Films Stars and Societies*. New York: Routledge, [1989] 2010.

Eco, Umberto. *Apocalittici ed integrati comunicazioni di massa e teorie della cultura di massa*. Milan: Bompiani, 1964. Trans. *Apocalypse Postponed*. Bloomington: Indiana University Press, 1994.

Eco, Umberto. *Diario minimo*. Milan: Mondadori, [1963] 1975.

Eco, Umberto. *Il superuomo di massa*. Milan: Bompiani, 1978.

Fabiani, Mario. "Cineromanzi a fumetti e diritti del produttore cinematografico." *Rassegna di diritto cinematografico* 5, no. 3–4 (1956): 66–67.

Fabris, Giampaolo, and Rowena Davis, *Il mito del sesso: Rapporto sul comportamento sessuale degli italiani*. Milan: Mondadori, 1978.

Falero, Sandra. *Digital Participatory Culture and the TV Audience: Everyone's a Critic*. New York: Palgrave, 2016.

Fischer-Hornung, Dorotea. "The Body Possessed: Katherine Dunham Dance Technique in *Mambo*." In *EmBODYing Liberation: The Black Body in American Dance*, ed. Dorothea Fischer-Hornung and Alison D. Goeller, 91–112. Hamburg: LIT Verlag, 2001.

Flores, Roberto D. *Fotonovela argentina: heredera del melodrama.* Buenos Aires: Asociación Argentina de Editores de Revistas, 1995.

Forgacs, David. "An Oral Renarration of a Photoromance." In *Orality and Literacy in Modern Italian Culture*, ed. Michael Caesar and Marina Spunta, 67–76. Oxford: Legenda, 2006.

Forgacs, David, and Stephen Gundle. *Mass Culture and Italian Society from Fascism to the Cold War.* Bloomington: Indiana University Press, 2007.

Fossati, Franco. "Dal fotoromanzo alle telenovelas." In *Dal feuilleton al fumetto*, ed. Carlo Bordoni and Franco Fossati, 123–136. Rome: Editori Riuniti, 1985.

Frajese, Vittorio. *La censura in italia: dall'Inquisizione alla polizia.* Bari: Laterza, 2014.

Freeman, Matthew. "Branding Consumerism: Cross-Media Characters and Story-Worlds at the Turn of the 20th Century." *International Journal of Cultural Studies* 18, no. 6 (2014): 629–644.

Gaglio, Sam. "Indiscretion of an Italian Lover: Montgomery Clift, Masculinity and Melodrama." *The Italianist* 39, no. 2 (2019): 242–250.

Gaines, Jane. "War Women and Lipstick: Fan Mags in the Forties." *Heresies* 5, no. 18 (1985): 42–47.

Gangarossa, Lorenzo. *Guida alla tutela dell'opera cinematografica.* Milan: Nyberg, 2005.

Gargiulo, Giuseppe. *Cultura popolare e cultura di massa nel fotoromanzo "rosa."* Messina: G. D'Anna, 1977.

Gernalzick, Nadja, and Gabriele Pisarz-Ramirez, eds. *Transmediality and Transculturality.* Universitaetsverlag Winter: Heidelberg (Germany), 2013.

Giannini, Amedeo. *Il diritto dello spettacolo: cinematografia, teatro, radiodiffusione, televisione, fonogramme, l'artista-interprete.* Rome: Jandi Sapi, 1959.

Giet, Sylvette. *"Nous Deux" 1947–1997: apprendre la langue du coeur.* Paris: Peeters, 1997.

Gill, Rosalind. "From Sexual Objectification to Sexual Subjectification: The Resexualisation of Women's Bodies in the Media." *Feminist Media Studies* 3, no. 1 (2003): 100–106. https://mronline.org/2009/05/23/from-sexual-objectification-to-sexual-subjectification-the-resexualisation-of-womens-bodies-in-the-media/.

Gundle, Stephen. *Bellissima: Feminine Beauty and the Idea of Italy.* New Haven: Yale University Press, 2007.

Gundle, Stephen. *Between Hollywood and Moscow: The Italian Communists and the Challenge of Mass Culture, 1943–1991.* Durham, NC: Duke University Press, 2000.

Gundle, Stephen. "Cultura di massa e modernizzazione: 'Vie nuove' e 'Famiglia cristiana' dalla Guerra fredda alla società dei consume." In *Nemici per la pelle: sogno americano e mito sovietico nell'Italia contemporanea*, ed. Pier Paolo D'Attorre, 236–268. Milan: Franco Angeli, 1991.

Günsberg, Maggie. *Italian Film: Gender and Genre.* New York: Palgrave, 2005.

Habert, Angeluccia Bernardes. *Fotonovela e industria cultural.* Buenos Aires: Petropolis, 1974.

Hall, Stuart. "Encoding, Decoding." In *The Cultural Studies Reader*, ed. Simon During, 90–103. London: Routledge, 2007.

Harrington, C. Lee, and Denise D. Bielby. *Soap Fans: Pursuing Pleasure and Making Meaning in Everyday Life.* Philadelphia: Temple University Press, 1995.

Hediger, Vinzenz, and Patrick Vonderau. *Films That Work: Industrial Film and the Productivity of Media*. Amsterdam: Amsterdam University Press, 2009.

Herzog, Dagmar. *Sexuality in Europe: A Twentieth Century History*. Cambridge: Cambridge University Press, 2011.

Istituto Doxa. *I lettori di otto periodici italiani: Epoca, Grazia, Arianna, Confidenze, Bolero Film, Storia illustrate, il giallo Mondadori, Topolino: studio statistico sulle caratteristiche demografiche, economiche, sociali e culturali*. Milan: Mondadori, 1963.

Jacobelli, Ennio. *Istruzioni pratiche per la realizzazione del fotoromanzo*. Roma: Ed. Politecnica Italiana, 1956.

Jenkins, Henry. *Convergence Culture*. New York: New York University Press, 2006.

Jenkins, Henry. "Fandom, Negotiation, and Participatory Culture." In *A Companion to Media Fandom and Fan Studies*, ed. Paul Booth, 11–26. Hoboken, NJ: John Wiley and Sons, 2018.

Jenkins, Henry. *Textual Poachers: Television Fans and Participatory Culture*. New York: Routledge, [1992] 2013.

Kezich, Tullio, and Alessandra Levantesi. *Dino: De Laurentiis, la vita e i film*. Milan: Feltrinelli, 2009.

Kozinets, Robert. *Netnography: Doing Ethnographic Research Online*. Sage: London, 2009.

Landy, Marcia. *Stardom Italian Style*. Bloomington: Indiana University Press, 2008.

Laura, Ernesto. *Alida Valli*. Rome: Gremese Editore, 1979.

Levy, Dylan. "Atoning for an Indiscretion." *Italianist* 39, no. 2 (2019): 251–266.

Lombardi, Mario, and Fabrizio Pignatel. *La stampa periodica in Italia: Mezzo secolo di riviste illustrate*. Rome: Editori Riuniti, 1985.

Malerba, Luigi. *Le lettere d'Ottavia*. Milan: Archinto, 2004.

Marazziti, Mario. "Cultura di massa e valori cattolici: il modello di 'Famiglia Cristiana.'" In *Pio XII*, ed. Andrea Riccardi, 307–334. Bari: Laterza, 1985.

Mattelart, Michele. *Women and the Cultural Industries*. UNESCO, 1981.

Mbembe, Achille. "The Power of the Archive and Its Limits." In Refiguring the Archive, ed. Carolyn Hamilton, Verne Harris, Michèle Pickover, Graeme Reid, Razia Saleh, and Jane Taylor, 19–27. Capetown: Clyson Printers, 2002.

McCloud, Scott. *Understanding Comics*. New York: Harper Perennial, 1994.

McRobbie, Angela. *The Aftermath of Feminism: Gender, Culture, and Social Change*. London: Sage, 2008.

Meda, Juri. "'Cose da grandi': identità collettive e valori civili nei fumetti italiani del secondo dopoguerra (1945–1955)." *Annali di storia dell'educazione e delle istituzioni scolastiche*, no. 9 (2002): 285–335.

Meyer, Urs. "From Intermediality to Transmediality: Cross-Media Transfer in Contemporary German Literature." In *Transmediality and Transculturality*, ed. Nadja Gernalzick and Gabriele Pisarz-Ramirez, 27–38. Heidelberg: Universitaetsverlag Winter, 2013.

Morin, Edgar. *The Stars*. Minneapolis: University of Minnesota Press, 2005.

Morreale, Emiliano, ed. *Lo schermo di carta: Storia e storie dei cineromanzi*.Turin: Il Castoro, 2007.

Muscio, Giuliana. "Tutto fa cinema: La stampa popolare del secondo dopoguerra." In *Dietro lo schermo: Ragionamenti sui modi di produzione cinematografica in Italy*, ed. Vito Zagarrio, 105–115. Venice: Marsilio, 1988.

Orgeron, Devin, Marsha Gordon, and Dan Streible. *Learning with the Lights Off*. Oxford: Oxford University Press, 2012.

Parca, Gabriella. *Le italiane si confessano*. Milan: Feltrinelli, [1959] 1966.

Patuzzi, Claudia. *Mondadori*. Naples: Liguori Editore, 1978.

Petricola, Elena. "Dal discorso sulle donne al discorso delle donne. Birth control, contraccezione e depenalizzazione dell'aborto tra ambienti laici e movimenti delle donne." *Quaderni di storia contemporanea*, no. 48 (2010). http://www.isral.it/web/pubblicazioni/qsc_48_07_petricola.pdf.

Pinkus, Karen. *The Montesi Scandal: The Death of Wilma Montesi and the Birth of the Paparazzi in Fellini's Rome*. Chicago: University of Chicago Press, 2003.

Poli, Gabriele. "L'attore e il regista cinematografico sono lavoratori subordinati?" *Rassegna del diritto cinematografico* 5, no. 5 (1956): 115–116.

Porta, Gianfranco. *Amore e libertà: Storia dell'AIED*. Bari: Laterza, 2013.

Portaccio, Stefania. "La donna nella stampa popolare cattolica: Famiglia Cristiana, 1931–1945." *Italia Contemporanea* 1, no. 143 (1981): 45–68.

Pratolini, Vasco. *Le ragazze di Sanfrediano*. Florence: Vallecchi, 1952. Trans. *The Girls of Sanfrediano (Took Their Love Seriously)*. New York: Pocket Books, 1954.

Quaglietti, Lorenzo. *Storia economica-politica del cinema italiano, 1945–1980*. Roma: Editori Riuniti, 1980.

Quaresima, Leonardo. "La voce dello spettatore." *Bianco e nero* 64, no. 548 (2004): 29–33.

Rabinowitz, Paula. *American Pulp: How Paperbacks Brought Modernism to Main Street*. Princeton: Princeton University Press, 2014.

Radner, Hilary. *Neo-Feminist Cinema: Girly Films, Chick Flicks and Consumer Culture*. New York: Routledge, 2013.

Radway, Janice A. *Reading the Romance: Women, Patriarchy, and Popular Literature*. Chapel Hill: University of North Carolina Press, 1983.

Radway, Janice A. "Women Read Romance: The Interaction of Text and Context," *Feminist Studies* 9, no. 1 (1983): 53–78.

Remondi, Elisabetta. "Tre fotoromanzi AIED. Noi Giovani. La trappola, Il segreto." *Genesis* 3, no. 1 (2004): 201–219.

Roberts, Kevin. *Lovemarks: The Future beyond Brands*. New York: powerHouse Books, 2004.

Rojek, Chris. *Celebrity*. London: Reaktion Books, 2001. Kindle.

Rossellini, Roberto. *Il mio metodo*, ed. Adriano Aprà. Roma: Marsilio, 2006.

Russo, Mary. *The Female Grotesque: Risk, Excess and Modernity*. New York: Routledge, 1994.

Sainati, Augusto. *La settimana Incom: Cinegiornali e informazione negli anni '50*. Turin: Lindau, 2001.

Saint-Michel, Serge. *Le roman-photo*. Paris: Larousse, 1979.

Sanchez-Mesa, Domingo, Espen Aarseth, Robert Pratten, and Carlos A. Scolari. "Transmedia (Storytelling?): A Polyphonic Critical Review." *Artnodes*, no. 18 (2016): 8–17.

Scarzanella, Eugenia. *Abril: da Peron a Videla: un editore italiano a Buenos Aires*. Rome: Nova Delphi, 2013.

Schimming, Ulrike. *Fotoromane: Analyse Eines Massenmediums*. Frankfurt am Main: Peter Lang, 2002.

Sergio, Giuseppe. *Liala dal romanzo al fotoromanzo: le scelte linguistiche, lo stile, i temi*. Milano: Mimesis, 2012.

Sgroi, Vittorio. "La tutela dell'immagine dell'attore cinematografico nell'elaborazione del film sotto forma di fotoromanzo." *Rivista di Diritto Industriale*, no. 5 (1956): 232–245.

Small, Pauline. "Producer and Director? Or 'Authorship' in 1950s Italian Cinema." In Beyond the Bottom Line: The Producer in Film and Television Studies, ed. Andrew Spicer, Anthony T. McKenna, and Christopher Meir, 109–123. London: Bloomsbury, 2014.

Small, Pauline. *Sophia Loren: Moulding the Star*. Bristol: Intellect Books, 2009.

Smith, Ken. *Mental Hygiene: Classroom Films 1945–1970*. New York: Blast Books, 1999.

Solbrig, Heide. "The Personal Is Political: Voice and Citizenship in Affimative-Action Videos in the Bell System, 1970–1984." In *Films that Work: Industrial Film and the Productivity of Media*, ed. Vinzenz Hediger and Patrick Vonderau, 259–282. Amsterdam: Amsterdam University Press, 2009.

Sordelli, Luigi. *L'opera dell'ingegno: interpretazione, riproduzione meccanica, e diffusione Sonora*. Milan: Giuffrè, 1954.

Spinazzola, Vittorio. *Il successo letterario*. Milan: Unicopli, 1985.

Stain, Sally. "The Graphic Ordering of Desire: Modernization of a Middle-Class Women's Magazine 1914–1939." *Heresies* 5, no. 2 (1985): 7–16.

Sullerot, Evelyne. "I fotoromanzi." In *La paralettura: il melodramma, il romanzo popolare, il fotoromanzo, il romanzo politziesco, il fumetto*, ed. Michele Rak, 100–114. Naples: Liguori, 1977.

Sullerot, Evelyne. *La presse féminine*. Paris: Armand Colin, [1963] 1966.

Suttenfield, Linda, Patricia E. Collings, and Daniel E. Pellegrom, eds. *Courageous Pioneers: Celebrating 50 Years of Pathfinder International and 80 years of Pioneering Work in Family Planning and Reproductive Health around the World*. Watertown, MA: Pathfinder International, 2007.

Taylor, Diana. *The Archive and the Repertoire: Performing Cultural Memory in the Americas*. Durham, NC: Duke University Press, 2003.

Treveri Gennari, Daniela. "'If You Have Seen It, You Cannot Forget!' Film Consumption and Memories of Cinema-Going in 1950s Rome." *Historical Journal of Film, Radio and Television* 35, no. 1 (2015): 53–74.

Treves, Anna. *Le nascite e la politica nell'Italia del Novecento*. Milano: LED, 2001.

Turner, Graeme. *Understanding Celebrity*. London: Sage, 2013.

Turzio, Silvana. *Il fotoromanzo: Metamorfosi delle storie lacrimevoli*. Milan: Meltemi, 2019.

Van Loon, Joost. "Ethnography: A Critical Turn in Cultural Studies." In *Handbook of Ethnography*, ed. Paul Atkinson, Amanda Coffey, Sara Delamont, John Lofland, and Lyn Lofland, 273–284. London: Sage, 2001.

Ventrone, Angelo. "Tra propaganda e passione: 'Grand Hotel' e l'Italia degli anni '50," *Rivista di Storia Contemporanea* 17, no. 4 (1988): 603–631.

Vigni, Franco. "Buon costume e pubblica morale." In *Storia del cinema italiano*, vol. 9, ed. Sandro Bernardi, 65–74. Rome: Marsilio, 2004.

Weaks, Daniel, and Eliza Sola. *The Photonovel: A Tool for Development*. Washington, DC: Action, Peace Corps, 1976.

Williams, Doon, and Greer Williams. *Every Child a Wanted Child: Clarence James Gamble and His Work in the Birth Control Movement*, ed. Emily P. Flint. Boston: Harvard University Press for Francis A. Countway Library of Medicine, 1978.

Wood, Mary P. "From Bust to Boom: Women and Representations of Prosperity in Italian Cinema of the Late 1940s and 1950s." In *Women in Italy, 1945–1960: An Interdisciplinary Study*, ed. Penelope Morris, 51–63. New York: Palgrave Macmillan, 2006.

Wu Ming. Preface to *Cultura Convergente* by Henry Jenkins. Milan, Apogeo Editore, 2007. https://www.wumingfoundation.com/italiano/outtakes/culturaconvergente.htm.

Zardini De Marchi, Maria Luisa. *Inumane Vite*. Rome: Sugar, 1969.

MAGAZINES

Photoromances
Bolero Film. Milan: Mondadori, 1947–1966.

Bolero Film Teletutto. Milan: Mondadori, 1966–1967.

Bolero Teletutto. Milan: Mondadori, 1967–1984.

Capricho. Buenos Aires: Editorial Abril, 1952–1982.

Charme. Rome: Lancio, 1961–2011.

Confidenze. Milan: Mondadori, 1951–.

Confidenze di Liala. Milan: Mondadori, 1946–1951.

Grand Hotel. Milan: Edizioni Universo, 1946-.

Idilio. Buenos Aires: Editorial Abril, 1948–1981.

Idilio. Rome: Lancio, 1963–1987.

Kolossal. Rome: Lancio, 1974–2011.

Le avventure di Jacques Douglas. Rome: Lancio, 1965–1980.

Le avventure di Lucky Martin. Rome: Lancio, 1968–1980.

Le grandi firme. Milan: Mondadori, 1948–1954.

Letizia. Rome: Lancio, 1961–2011.

Nocturno. Buenos Aires: Editorial Abril, 1952–1966.

Nous Deux. Paris: Les Editions Mondiales, 1947–.

Rapsodia. Buenos Aires: Columba, 1958–1959.

Sogno. Milan: Rizzoli, 1947–1974; Rome: Lancio, 1974–2011.

Cineromances

Cinefoto Romanzo. Rome: La Torraccia, 1955–1961.

Cine-intimità. Edizioni Mondiali: 1961–1963.

Cineromanzo gigante. Rome: Lanterna Magica. 1954–1957.

Cineromanzo per tutti. Rome: Lanterna Magica. 1954–1957.

Hebdo Roman. Milan: Victory, 1956–1961.

I grandi fotoromanzi d'amore. Milan: Victory, 1952–1957.

I vostri film romanzo. Rome: Ed. I.M.O., 1954–1964.

Les films du coeur. Rome: Franco Bozzesi Editore, 1956–1964.

Mon Film. Paris: Mon Film, 1924–1967.

Index